I0605807

Hitler's Heroes During the Advance to Stalingrad

Hitler's Heroes During the Advance to Stalingrad

Knight's Cross Generals on the Eastern Front, 6 December 1941–2 February 1943

Jeremy Dixon

FRONTLINE BOOKS

First published in Great Britain in 2025 by
Frontline Books
An imprint of Pen & Sword Books Limited
Yorkshire – Philadelphia

ISBN 978 1 03610 158 9

A CIP catalogue record for this book is
available from the British Library

Typeset by Mac Style
Printed in the UK by CPI Group (UK) Ltd, Croydon, CR0 4YY.

The Publisher's authorised representative in the EU for product safety is Authorised Rep Compliance Ltd., Ground Floor, 71 Lower Baggot Street, Dublin D02 P593, Ireland.
www.arccompliance.com

For a complete list of Pen & Sword titles please contact

PEN & SWORD BOOKS LIMITED
47 Church Street, Barnsley, South Yorkshire, S70 2AS, England
E-mail: enquiries@pen-and-sword.co.uk
Website: www.pen-and-sword.co.uk
or
PEN AND SWORD BOOKS
1950 Lawrence Road, Havertown, PA 19083, USA
E-mail: uspen-and-sword@casematepublishers.com
Website: www.penandswordbooks.com

Dedicated to Nathan, Emma, Amelia and Ethan Pearce

Contents

Acknowledgements

I would like to thank Paul Budden for proof-reading the book and offering advice and for his continued support, and I must also thank my mum and dad, sister and nephews for their support. I would also like to thank my friends: Ann Driscoll, Jo Robinson, Jo Jeffrey, Angela Green, Nick Isles, Hazel Kirby, Jackie Snowling, Carol Ryan, Lisa Hunt, Liz Ross, Jane Budgen, Bev Drew, Vanessa Gardner, Lois Farnie, Lauretta Kelly, Linda Hurd, Paul Spendlove, Colin Harris, Alex Curran, Nathan Pearce, Debra and Dave Mills.

Introduction

This is the second of a four-volume work that describes how German officers who held the rank of General won the highest award for bravery and command, the Knight's Cross. This second volume describes how the 149 generals – one *Generalfeldmarschall*; two *Generaloberst*; thirty-eight full generals; fifty-three *Generalleutnants* and fifty-five *Generalmajors* – won their Knight's Cross and higher grades during the Soviet campaign.

On 22 June 1941 Germany invaded the Soviet Union, the largest land offensive in history. It was code-named Operation Barbarossa, named after a twelfth-century Holy Roman Emperor and German king. The Germans had been secretly massing troops near the Soviet border from February 1941 in preparation for Hitler's attack. The Germans attacked with more than 3 million troops, which included 690, 000 Axis troops, and using 600,000 vehicles, 750,000 horses, over 3,500 tanks and 1,830 aircraft. Hitler's aim was to conqueror the Soviet Union and repopulate it with German citizens. He planned to use Soviet prisoners as forced labour for the war effort.

German forces at Stalingrad from 6 December 1941 until 2 February 1943

Army Group North
Commander-in-Chief *Generalfeldmarschall* Wilhelm Ritter von Leeb
from 18.1.1942 *Generalfeldmarschall* Georg von Küchler

Commander of the 16th Army *Generaloberst* Ernst Busch

Commander of the 18th Army *Generaloberst* Georg von Küchler
from 16.1.1942 *General der Kavallerie* Georg Lindemann

Commander of Panzer Group 4 (redesignated 4th Panzer Army from 2 January 1942)
Generaloberst Erich Höepner
from 8.1.1942 *General der Infanterie* Richard Ruoff
from 31.5.1942 *Generaloberst* Hermann Hoth

Wilhelm von Leeb.

Georg von Küchler.

Ernst Busch.

Erich Hoepner.

Fedor von Bock.

Günther von Kluge.

Gotthard Heinrici.

Walter Model.

Army Group Centre

Commander-in-Chief *Generalfeldmarschall* Fedor von Bock
from 19.12.1941 *Generalfeldmarschall* Günther von Kluge

Commander of the 4th Army *Generalfeldmarschall* Günther von Kluge
from 19.12.1941 *General der Gebirgstruppe* Ludwig Kübler
from 20.1.1942 *General der Infanterie* Gotthard Heinrici
from 6.6.1942 *General der Infanterie* Hans von Salmuth
from 15.7.1942 *Generaloberst* Gotthard Heinrici

Commander of the 9th Army *Generaloberst* Adolf Strauss
from 15.1.1942 *General der Panzertruppe* Walter Model

Commander of the 2nd Panzer Army *Generaloberst* Heinz Guderian
from 25.12.1941 *Generaloberst* Rudolf Schmidt

Commander of Panzer Group 3 *General der Panzertruppe* Georg-Hans Reinhardt
(from 1.1.1942 known as 3rd Panzer Army)

Army Group South/Army Group B
Commander-in-Chief *Generalfeldmarschall* Walter von Reichenau
from 12.1.1942 *Generalfeldmarschall* Fedor von Bock

from 9.7.1942 known as Army Group B
Commander-in-Chief *Generaloberst* Maximilian von Weichs

Commander of the 6th Army *Generalfeldmarschall* Walter von Reichenau
from 30.12.1941 *General der Panzertruppe* Friedrich Paulus (later *Generalfeldmarschall*)

Commander of the 17th Army *General der Infanterie* Carl-Heinrich von Stülpnagel
from 5.10.1941 *Generaloberst* Hermann Hoth
from 20.4.1942 *General der Infanterie* Hans von Salmuth
from 1.6.1942 *Generaloberst* Richard Ruoff

Commander of the 11th Army *General der Infanterie* Erich von Manstein
(did not exist after 21.11.1942)

Walter von Reichenau.

Hermann Hoth.

Richard Ruoff.

Erich von Manstein.

On 6 December 1941 Soviet forces under the command of General Georgy Zhukov began the Soviet counteroffensive from Moscow. The exhausted German forces under the command of *General der Panzertruppe* Georg-Hans Reinhardt, commander of the 3rd Panzer Group, were caught by surprise and forced to retreat. The Soviet 30th Army had managed to break through the 3rd Panzer Army lines north-east of Klin and attacked the headquarters of the 56th Panzer Corps. The Germans began to pull back from the Moscow area, and elsewhere German Army Group North had pulled out of Leningrad. There was now heavy fighting inside Tikhvin, where the German 18th Army were allowed by Hitler to pull back to the Volkhov. There was a real danger of the 3rd Panzer Group being encircled by the Soviet 30th Army, and elements of the Soviet 16th Army pushed the 4th Panzer Group west towards Istra. On the southern wing the Soviet 50th Army had been held back by the 296th Infantry and 3rd Panzer Division, but by 9 December the Red Army had recaptured Tikhvin and the German 18th Army had now retreated to the Volkhov.

Georg-Hans Reinhardt.

Walter von Brauchitsch.

Heinz Guderian.

In an effort to slow the Soviet advance the Germans had blown up the Istra Dam on 11 December, which halted the progress of the Soviet 15th and 16th Armies. The German 1st Panzer Group and the 6th and 17th Armies were on the defensive as Red Army units began to cross both the Mius and Donets Rivers. Within a few days the German I. and XXXVIII. Army Corps had failed to prevent the Soviets from establishing a bridgehead, which threatened the German plans to recapture Leningrad. With Army Group Centre in grave danger and the 4th Army on the verge of collapse, Hitler relieved the Commander-in-Chief of the Army *Generalfeldmarschall* Walter von Brauchitsch of his command and took over command of the Army himself.

By Christmas Day 3,700 civilians had starved to death in Leningrad and the daily death rate was 1,500. That same day *Generaloberst* Heinz Guderian, commander of the 2nd Panzer Army, was dismissed by Hitler and replaced by *General der Panzertruppe* Rudolf Schmidt. On the 29th Kerch and Feodosia were recaptured by Soviet forces and as a result the German XXXXII. Army Corps was forced to withdraw. So far the Germans had lost 302,000 troops in Russia and the *Luftwaffe* had lost 2,100 aircraft with another 1,300 damaged.

On New Year's Day 1942 the Red Army offensive in the Ukraine began and its forces advanced towards Kursk. The German 9th Army, under the command of *Generaloberst* Adolf Strauss, together with the 4th Army of *General der Gebirgstruppe* Ludwig Kübler, continued to repel the Russians. Attacks involving both armies continued for the next few days and on 10 January the German 6th Army under *General der Panzertruppe* Friedrich Paulus counter-attacked around the area of Kharkov. Two days later, as the Soviets threatened to cut off 100,000 troops near Demyansk, *Generalfeldmarschall* Wilhelm von Leeb requested permission to retreat. Hitler, of course, refused, whereupon Leeb resigned and was immediately replaced by *Generaloberst* von Küchler. Although the German 9th Army still held Rzhev, the 4th Panzer Army was pushed back and the 16th Army, under *Generaloberst* Ernst Busch, was forced to retreat, thus exposing the rear of Army Group Centre.

On 17 January *Generalfeldmarschall* Walter von Reichenau, Commander-in-Chief of Army Group South died from a stroke and heart attack, and was replaced by *Generalfeldmarschall* Fedor von Bock. The following day Soviet forces under General Timoshenko launched a fresh offensive against the Germans, and two days later the German 4th Army was forced out of Mozhaisk. Hitler reacted by replacing its commander, *General* Kübler, with *General der Infanterie* Gotthard Heinrici. By the 24th the Soviets had smashed through German positions in the Ukraine, and four days later the German XXXXVI. Corps mounted a counter-attack near Rzhev.

On 8 February about 90,000 German troops near Demyansk were surrounded by the Soviet 1st Shock and 11th Armies. The Germans had to rely on the *Luftwaffe* for supplies of food and ammunitions. It was estimated that the troops inside the Demyansk Pocket required 305 tons of supplies daily, and at least 150 aircraft were required to supply them. However the Junkers Ju 52 transport aircraft used to drop supplies was to have little fighter protection, and the daily supply drops began on 12 February. On 27 February the Red Army begins a new offensive against the 11th Army, but it was a disaster with the Soviets suffering heavy losses in men and tanks at the hands of the German artillery and *Luftwaffe*. By 19 March the Soviets had lost 130 tanks and the German 18th Army attacked the Soviet 2nd Shock Army near the Volkhov River, surrounding just over 130,000 troops. Two days later the German ground effort to relieve the pocket began, and on 19 April the Soviet 33rd Army was wiped out, with its commander, General Mikhail Efremor, killed during the fighting, together with another 95,064 Soviet soldiers killed and missing and 213,303 wounded.

The German XXXIX. Panzer Corps relieved the garrison at Kholm on 5 May, bringing to an end a 103-day siege. The defenders had lost 1,500 troops and in an effort to keep the garrison supplied the *Luftwaffe* lost 252 Ju 52s. On the 8th the German 11th Army launched Operation Bustard to destroy enemy forces in the Kerch Peninsula and the attack made a good start when the XXX. Army Corps attacked the Soviet 44th Army. Two days later the 22nd Panzer Division arrived in the area and the 51st Soviet Army was encircled, with the 44th Army almost destroyed. The Soviets launched their Kharkov Offensive on 12 May to push the German forces back to the River Dnieper but only advanced 6 miles. After only two to three days the Soviet Kharkov Offensive was running out of steam. North of Kharkov the German 3rd and 23rd Panzer Divisions continued their attacks, however success for the Soviets to the south of the city meant that if Krasnograd fell the German 6th and 17th Armies would be in danger of being overrun. By 19 May German troops had captured the Kerch Peninsula in the Crimea and taken 100,000 prisoners.

On 2 June *Generaloberst* Erich von Manstein's 11th Army attacked the heavily defended fortress of Sevastopol from the air as well as with an artillery bombardment. The fortress was built before the Crimean War and was also heavily defended with favourable mountainous terrain all around. The German 4th Mountain Division and the 8th Cavalry Brigade were supplemented by the Romanian VII. Corps and the bombardment involved 1,300 artillery pieces and *Luftwaffe* attacks. On 10 June the German 6th Army launched Operation Wilhelm, the planned destruction of the Soviet 28th Army near Volchansk to help with the smooth running of the forthcoming offensive into the Caucasus.

Five days later the 6th Army was successful and the 28th Army was defeated and pushed back over the River Donets. On 19 June the Soviets captured the German plans for their offensive into the Caucasus, code name Blue, when a German aircraft carrying the Chief of Operations of the 23rd Panzer Division, *Major* Joachim Reichel, was forced down. However, when the plans were given to Stalin he was convinced they were a German ploy and they were ignored. By 22 June, Army Group South was ready to launch Operation Blue, and three days later the Soviet 2nd Shock Army was annihilated and its commander General Vlassov captured. The disaster cost the Red Army 54,774 killed and missing, with 39,977 wounded.

On 28 June Operation Blue began as the 4th Panzer Army, supported by the 2nd Army, was faced by the Soviet 13th and 40th Armies. In the Crimea the German 50th Infantry Division took Inkerman, and on 2 July the Red Army retreated before the German advance, with the 4th, 17th, 24th and 40th Armies pulling back towards Voronezh. On 4 July the *Luftwaffe* attacked the Soviet 5th Tank Army and in the Crimea Sevastopol fell to the German 11th Army. *General der Infanterie* Erich von Manstein had taken 90,000 prisoners, together with 460 artillery pieces, 760 mortars and 155 anti-tank guns. The 4th Panzer and 6th Armies were sent east towards Stalingrad, from where they would sweep south in support of Army Group A. On 11 July Hitler ordered the 1st and 4th Panzer Armies to converge at Kamensk and Millerovo before they pushed into the Caucasus, and the 6th Army then advanced on Stalingrad. Hitler believed that the Red Army had been defeated west of the Don, and two days later the 4th Panzer Army and the XXXX. Panzer Corps linked up at Boguchar, trapping 14,000 prisoners. Hitler thought this signalled the end of the Red Army resistance and all supplies were directed to the two panzer armies. The 6th Army was left stranded in the Don Elbow, which allowed the Soviets to build up their strength at Stalingrad.

On 20 July the 6th Army attacked the Soviet 62nd and 64th armies, inflicting heavy losses, and the armies broke apart the next day. Pleased by this success, Hitler issued Directive No. 45: 'The next task of Army Group A is to encircle enemy forces which have escaped across the Don in the area south and south-east of Rostov, and destroy them …' However, a few days later the 6th Army ran out of fuel and ground to a halt. On the 30th, near Stalingrad Soviet forces launched a counter-attack with the 1st and 4th Tank Armies, resulting in a tank battle with XIV. Panzer Corps. The *Luftwaffe* pummelled the two Soviet armoured units and they suffered heavy losses. On 5 August the 4th Panzer Army attacked the Soviet 57th and 64th Armies south-west of Stalingrad, but became bogged down and was stopped by an enemy counter-attack. Four days later the Soviet 62nd Army was encircled by the 16th and 24th Panzer

Divisions and Kleist's panzers entered Maikop. The Germans now planned to start pumping oil right away but they found the oil fields were burning, sabotaged by the retreating Soviets.

On 15 August a new offensive by the German 6th Army shattered the Soviet 1st Guards and 4th Tank Army in the Don Elbow. The city of Stalingrad was now the focus of the campaign as each side reinforced its armies. To the south, the 4th Panzer Army unleashed the 14th and 24th Panzer Divisions together with the 29th Panzer Grenadier Division against the south-western approaches to Stalingrad. The city that had Stalin's name would become an obsession of Hitler's and he risked everything to capture it. On 23 August the *Luftwaffe* launched a massive air raid against Stalingrad, a total of 600 bombers conducting 4,000 sorties over two days. Oil storage tanks along the River Volga burst into flames and fires broke out in the city, with up to 40,000 people killed. On 30 August the German LI. and VIII. Army Corps secured the Don–Volga land bridge as the XXXXVIII. Panzer Corps advanced within just 30 miles of Stalingrad. On 1 September the 62nd and 64th Soviet Armies in the north of Stalingrad attacked the XIV. Panzer Corps, but the operation was a shambles, with the Soviets suffering greatly at the hands of the German artillery. The attack was called off.

On 4 September the German 11th Army on the Volkhov advanced and General Manstein deployed the XXVI. Army Corps on the northern wing and the XXX. Army Corps in the south to contain the Soviet threat. Three days later the German LI. Army Corps of the 6th Army attempted to reach Stalingrad city centre, its aim to take the Mamayev Kurgan Hill, whose heights held a strong position over the city. Both sides soon realised that 'he who holds the hill holds the city!' On 9 September the LI. Army Corps approached Mamayev Kurgan in Stalingrad, and the Soviet 62nd Army was attacked in the north by the XIV. Panzer Corps and in the south by the XXXXVIII. Panzer Corps. Hitler relieved *Generalfeldmarschall* Wilhelm List from command of Army Group A for not achieving more and decided to take over the command of the Army Group himself. The German 6th Army and 4th Panzer Army continued to push their way to Stalingrad.

On 13 September a massive assault began at Stalingrad and the fighting raged throughout the night. The following day the assault continued, backed by massive artillery fire and *Luftwaffe* aircraft. During the night, the Soviet 13th Guards Rifle Division crossed the river, establishing a small bridgehead, and the *Luftwaffe* dropped mines in the River Volga. In Stalingrad the Soviets were forced out of the nail factory and fighting continued around Mamayev Kurgan and the grain elevator. Two days later the Soviet 284th Rifle Division crossed the Volga at Stalingrad and, together with the 95th Rifle Division, drove the

Germans back to the railway station. The German 6th Army regrouped for a fresh attack, and *Generaloberst* Paulus directed the offensive against the factory district with a fresh assault on against the Red October factory. On 5 October the Red Army unleashed a 300-gun barrage against the German units in the factory area of Stalingrad that resulted in heavy casualties. Four days later fighting was temporarily halted in Stalingrad as the Germans were exhausted. Fighting resumed a day later and during the night the Germans reached the factory and broke through to the Volga and in the Caucasus, where Group *Ruoff* failed to breach Red Army defences at the Black Sea. By the 18th the Germans had taken the tractor factory and had wiped out the 37th Guards Division and also attacked the Barrikady factory, fighting every inch of the way. Three days later the German 79th Infantry Division was repulsed from the Red October and Barrikady factories. On 22 October the first snow fell at Stalingrad and the Soviet 64th Army launched an attack and linked up with the 62nd Army. Plans for the Soviet counteroffensive around Stalingrad, code-named Uranus, were gathering pace.

On 11 November the 6th Army commenced its final offensive at Stalingrad with artillery and air strikes. It succeeded in taking most of the Red October factory, and by the evening the Soviet 62nd Army occupied three small pockets along the Volga. In Stalingrad, the German assaults were annihilating the 62nd Soviet Army and the group at Rynok and Spartakovka was reduced to 300 troops at the hands of the 16th Panzer Division. Cause for concern for *Generaloberst* Paulus was the Soviet build-ups to the north-west of Stalingrad, which had been picked up by *Luftwaffe* reconnaissance. On 19 November Operation Uranus began when the Romanian 3rd Army were attacked, and by the end of the day they had suffered 55,000 casualties. Paulus was ordered to restore the northern flank, and used his three panzer divisions. The next day Hitler created Army Group Don, led by *Generalfeldmarschall* Erich von Manstein, which was ordered to safeguard positions and restore the 6th Army's flanks. On 23 November, 27,000 Romanian soldiers surrendered and that signalled the end of the 3rd Army, which had suffered more than 90,000 casualties. Red Army units linked up at Kalach, trapping the German 6th Army, and *Generaloberst* Paulus put his forces into a defensive posture as part of the grandly titled Fortress Stalingrad. However, he had serious problems – a desperate shortage of infantry, treeless and shelter-free areas, lack of fuel and shortage of ammunition. *Luftwaffe* commander-in-Chief Hermann Göring assured Hitler that the *Luftwaffe* could supply the Stalingrad Pocket with everything they required. *General der Infanterie* Kurt Zeitzler, Chief of the General Staff, did not believe this boast. It was estimated that the trapped 6th Army needed at least 355 tons of supplies daily – by 14 December they had been supplied with only 150 tons!

By 19 December, with the 11th Panzer Division fending off Soviet attacks, Hermann Hoth's 6th Panzer Division had reached the River Myshkova and was only 30 miles from Stalingrad. Manstein signalled the code word Thunderclap, ordering Paulus to break out and link up with his force. Hitler, however, ordered Paulus to stand firm. The following day, Manstein tried to get Hitler to agree to the breakout as the 17th Panzer Division was down to just eight tanks. On New Year's Eve Hitler ordered an evacuation from the Caucasus, with the XXXX. Panzer Corps withdrawing. By the New Year the Soviets were moving closer and closer to Stalingrad and on 2 January 1943 another airfield fell to them, further reducing the number of *Luftwaffe* relief flights to Stalingrad. On the 8th General Konstantin Rokossovsky offered surrender terms to Paulus at Stalingrad. The terms he offered were favourable – all personnel who surrendered could retain their uniforms and rank insignia, decorations and personal belongings. Hitler, however, forbade any surrender.

On 10 January the Don Front of 281,000 troops, 257 tanks and 10,000 artillery pieces commenced Operation Ring, the destruction of the 6th Army at Stalingrad. The Soviets launched a series of blistering attacks over the next twenty-four hours and the 6th Army was torn apart. The attacks continued against the German troops in Stalingrad and so far had incurred 26,000 casualties, although Paulus had lost 60,000 troops as well as a huge amount of weapons. On 24 January Hitler sent a message to Paulus ordering him to fight to the end, 'Surrender is forbidden. The 6th Army will hold their positions to the last man and last round …' Two days later, however, the German 297th Infantry Division inside the Stalingrad Pocket surrendered to the Soviets and what was left of the 6th Army was now trapped in two small pockets.

By the 29th the fighting had calmed down around Leningrad, and the Soviet South-western Front commenced its operation to outflank the German Army Group Don. The following day, Hitler promoted Paulus to the rank of *Generalfeldmarschall*, a cynical move to prompt him to commit suicide rather than surrender. However, on 31 January Paulus surrendered Stalingrad and Hitler was disgusted. On 2 February the fighting at Stalingrad came to an end. The 6th Army had suffered 150,000 dead and another 90,000 taken prisoner, including one Field Marshal, 243 Generals and 2,000 officers. Only 6,000 German soldiers ever returned to Germany.

Knight's Cross Recipients

Recipients in order of being awarded.

NB: Underlined Christian names are those the subject chose to be known by.

Johannes Friedrich Gustav BLOCK

General der Infanterie

* 17 November 1894, Büschdorf, Saxony
+ 26 January 1945, Kielce, Poland

Knight's Cross: Awarded as *Oberst* and Commander of Infantry Regiment 202 of the 75th Infantry Division on 22 December 1941 for his leadership during the unstoppable forward advance during bad weather and difficult road conditions. His regiment drove over the course of twelve days for almost 225 miles, a remarkable achievement; they then attacked the Russian-held city of Sumy, with the success credited to Block. Shortly after he took command of the 294th Infantry Division he took part in the battle to recapture Kharkov and the Donets as part of the 6th Army. In September he was promoted to *Generalmajor* and took part in the Soviet winter offensive in late 1942

Johannes Block entered Army service as a war volunteer with Field Artillery Regiment 75 in August 1914. He was wounded the following year and in June was transferred to Replacement Battalion of Fusilier Regiment 36 as a *Fahnenjunker-Gefreiter*. Commissioned as a *Leutnant* in May 1916 while serving with Infantry Regiment 146 and twelve months later he transferred to Reserve Infantry Regiment 208 as an assault detachment commander. Block remained in the Army after the war, serving as a company commander with his old wartime regiment.

while attached to the 8th *Luftwaffe* Field Division during the retreat from the Volga. Promoted to *Generalleutnant* in January 1943, he saw action along the River Mius area and at Stalino [now Donetsk]. His division was later encircled at Taganrog, where they sustained heavy losses during the breakout.

In August 1919 Block joined the Freikorps Napoleon as an adjutant, which later became Rifle Regiment 40. From October 1920 he served with Infantry Regiment 2 and in November the following year he took part in the Beer Hall Putsch, part of Hitler's plan to overthrow the Bavarian Government, and would later be awarded the Blood Order of the Nazi Party.

Knight's Cross with Oakleaves: Awarded on 22 November 1943, to become the 331st recipient as *Generalmajor* and Commander of the 294th Infantry Division while attached to the XVII. Army Corps for his distinguished leadership during the fighting between the Rivers Don and Donets. He and his division also achieved great success during the defensive battles along the River Mius during the summer of 1943. The Oakleaves were personally presented to Block by Hitler during a ceremony at the Wolf's Lair, Rastenburg, in late 1943. He was appointed temporary commander of the VIII. Army Corps in April 1944 and was attached to Army Group North Ukraine until June. He was at the same time temporary commander of the XIII. Army Corps on the Eastern Front, taking over from *General der Infanterie* Arthur Hauffe while he was on leave. On 15 June he was appointed temporary commander of the LVI. Panzer Corps, and the appointment became permanent the following month. From June until August, the Soviet offensive Operation Bagration cleared German forces from the Belorussian and Eastern Polish areas. Block was promoted to *General der Infanterie* in August 1944 and continued to withdraw the LVI. Panzer Corps through Poland and into Germany as the Soviet advance continued. By November his headquarters had moved to Warsaw and in January 1945 they were in Weichsel, and the fighting became bloodier as the massive German withdrawal continued. During the fighting at the Baranov Bridgehead near Kielce on the Vistula, in southern Poland, Block was hit by gunfire and killed.

Ehrenfried-Oskar Martin Anton BOEGE

General der Infanterie

* 11 November 1889, Ostrowo, Posen
+ 31 December 1965, Hildesheim, Lower Saxony

Knight's Cross: Awarded as *Oberst* and Commander of Infantry Regiment 7 while attached to the 28th Infantry Division on 22 December 1941 in recognition of achieving great deeds of bravery on his own initiative within the area of VIII. Army Corps on 22 and 27 June 1941. He was credited with his swift thrust to the Njemen River north of Grodno, the battle near Vyazma and later took part in the Battle of Smolensk. He was promoted to *Generalmajor* in April 1942 and took over as Commander of 197th Infantry Division. He continued to see action during the invasion of the Soviet Union in Gzhatsk and Rzhev. Promoted to *Generalleutnant* in January 1943, he was assigned to a commanding general's course and in February 1944 he was given the leadership of the XXXXI. Panzer

Anton Boege entered the Army in September 1913 as a *Fahnenjunker* with Infantry Regiment 62 and by August 1914 he was a platoon leader with the rank of *Leutnant*. He was awarded both classes of the Iron Cross during the war and was promoted to *Oberleutnant* in April 1918. He remained in the Army after the war, serving with various infantry regiments, and by the beginning of the Second World War had risen to the rank of *Oberstleutnant*. He was for a time Deputy Commandant of *Führer* Headquarters, Alderhorst. He served with Infantry Regiment 161 during the Battle of France, where he won the Bar to the Iron Cross 1st and 2nd Classes.

Corps. Shortly after he was promoted to *General der Infanterie* and in June 1944 he took over as the commanding general of the XXXXIII. Army Corps.

Knight's Cross with Oakleaves: He became the 594th recipient on 21 September 1944 as *General der Infanterie* and Commanding General of the XXXXIII. Army Corps for actions in the Courland area. It was during this time that his command succeeded in recapturing the Estonian city of Ērgļi. Boege was appointed Commander-in-Chief of the 18th Army on 30 January 1945 and was captured by Soviet troops five months later. He was sentenced to twenty-five years' hard labour, but was released in October 1955 with serious health problems and settled in Hildesheim.

Alexander RATCLIFFE

Generalmajor

* 17 August 1890, Munich, Bavaria
+ 30 April 1979, Gauting, Bavaria

Knight's Cross: Awarded on 22 December 1941 as *Oberst* and Commander of Infantry Regiment 192 while attached to the 56th Infantry Division for actions during the invasion of the Soviet Union. After action during the invasion of France and Belgium, Ratcliffe took his regiment to the Soviet Union and as part of the main spearhead his regiment crossed the Bug River on rubber rafts during the opening stages of the campaign. He took part in the advance and retreat from Moscow, seeing action in the battles of Kovel and Kiev, with his command later suffering heavy casualties near Orel in 1942. From August he was delegated with the leadership of Division Staff No. 407 while attached to Military District VII, Munich. Between October and November 1942 Ratcliffe was Commander of Division No. 407 in Augsburg, and from December he was appointed Commandant of Braunschweig in Lower Saxony. From 23 March 1944 he served as Commandant of Orsha in Belarus and during the summer the Red Army encircled the German garrison and captured Vitebsk and Orsha as part of the Minsk offensive. Ratcliffe was wounded and taken prisoner by the Soviets. He was released four years later and returned to Germany.

Erwin RAUCH

Generalleutnant

* 19 October 1889, Berlin
+ 26 February 1969, Kirchenlamitz

Knight's Cross: Awarded on 22 December 1941 as *Generalmajor* and Commander of 123rd Infantry Division, part of the II. Army Corps, for his leadership and bravery in a number of battles during the drive towards Leningrad. In January 1942 his division formed the southern flank of Army Group North during the Soviet winter offensive, but had to cover 50 miles of open space due to a shortage of German troops. Rauch was promoted to *Generalleutnant* in November 1942, but his division was crushed by four Soviet armies and the remnants of his command managed to escape to the Demyansk and Kholm pockets. His command was not freed until February 1943, when his division was reformed and later that year took part in the Battle of Zaporozhe in the Ukraine. He entered the Reserves in January 1944 and the following month was appointed Commander of the 343rd Infantry Division in Brittany, where he was responsible for guarding a sector of the Atlantic coast near Brest. When the Allies broke through the Normandy front in August 1944 his division formed part of the German garrison in the siege of Brest. On 18 September Rauch was wounded near Brest and captured by US troops, being released on 5 June 1947.

Erwin Rauch was the brother-in-law to Hitler's Deputy, Rudolf Hess. He entered the Army in September 1908 and was commissioned as a *Leutnant* in January 1910. He served as a Platoon Leader from 1913 and two years later he was promoted to *Oberleutnant* and served as a regimental adjutant. From February 1917 until just after the war he served as a General Staff Officer and ended the war with the rank of *Hauptmann*. In November 1938, now with the rank of *Oberst*, he served as Commander of Infantry Regiment 2 in Allenstein and was awarded both classes of the Iron Cross in September and October 1939.

Maximilian Ludwig Julius Franz FRETTER-PICO

General der Artillerie

* 6 February 1892, Karlsruhe, Baden
+ 4 April 1986, Kreuth am Tegensee

Knight's Cross: Awarded on 26 December 1941 as *Generalmajor* and Commander of the 97th Infantry Division of the XXXXIX. Mountain Corps for actions during the capture of a bridgehead on 31 August 1941 on the Russian Front. He then ordered his troops to capture the high ground near Podgora in the Soviet Union and the attacked continued throughout the night, by which time the heights had been taken by the Germans. On 15 January 1942 Fretter-Pico was promoted to *Generalleutnant* and from December was confirmed as Commanding General of the XXX. Army Corps. He continued to see action on the Eastern Front and was promoted to *General der Artillerie* on 1 June 1942, and appointed Commander of the Army Detachment *Fretter-Pico*.

Maximilian Fretter-Pico entered Army Service with Baden Field-Artillery Regiment 1 in September 1910 and was wounded and hospitalised during the First World War. He was awarded both classes of the Iron Cross and ended the war with the rank of *Hauptmann*. He remained in the Army after the war, serving in the Reich Ministry of Defence and then as Chief Supply Officer of the 1st Cavalry Division from October 1930. When the Second World War began he held the rank of *Oberst* and was Chief of the General Staff of the XXIV. Army Corps, seeing action during the invasion of Poland from September 1939.

Knight's Cross with Oakleaves: He became the 368th recipient on 16 January 1944 as *General der Artillerie* and Commanding General of the XXX. Army Corps while attached to the 1st Panzer Army for his determined leadership on the Soviet Front. Fretter-Pico particularly distinguished himself during the winter battles between Don and the Donez and in the battles near Izyum in the summer of 1943. His command prevented an enemy breakthrough on 19 December 1943 with five rifle divisions and other special formations. During the battle the Soviets lost eighty-three tanks and Fretter-Pico and his Corps pushed back the enemy. On 25 May 1944 he was personally presented with the Oakleaves by Hitler at the Berghof on the Obersalzburg. From July he was delegated with the leadership of the 6th Army and from September 1944 was named as Commander-in-Chief of

Army Group *Fretter-Pico* with the 6th Army and 2nd Hungarian Army. From late March 1945 he was appointed to the Reich War Court in Torgau against *General der Panzertruppe* Walter Fries, who had been accused of retreating without fighting against orders west of Warsaw on the west bank of the Vistula. General Fries was later acquitted of all charges. On 30 March 1945 Fretter-Pico took command of the Replacement IX. Army Corps and on 22 April he surrendered his command to the Americans.

Robert MARTINEK

General der Artillerie

* 2 February 1889, Gratzen, Austro-Hungary
+ 28 June 1944, Berezino, Soviet Union

Knight's Cross: Awarded on 26 December 1941 as *Generalmajor* and Commander of 267th Infantry Division while attached to the VII. Army Corps for his part in the halting of the Soviet advances near Moscow during the winter offensive. Martinek personally fought with his men and while serving so closely he was able to ensure that the Soviet breakthrough would fail. From January 1942 he was delegated with the leadership of the 7th Mountain Division in Lapland between June 1942 until July. When he returned to his division he was assigned as Higher Artillery Commander to the 11th Army and took part in the conquest of Sevastopol. In December he was delegated with the leadership of the XXXIX. Panzer Corps and saw action near Rzhev in the Soviet Union as part of the 9th Army. In January 1943 he was promoted to *General der Artillerie* and his command of the corps was confirmed as permanent.

Knight's Cross with Oakleaves: He became the 388th recipient on 10 February 1944 as *General der Artillerie* and Commanding General of the XXXIX. Panzer Corps as part of the 4th Army

Robert Martinek was commissioned as a *Leutnant* with the Austrian Army in May 1910 and from 1914 he was a riding instructor with the Royal 8th Field Artillery Brigade. He saw action during the war as a Battery Commander with Artillery Regiment 24 and saw action in Serbia, Russia and Italy, ending the war with the rank of *Hauptmann*.

for conducting defensive battles successfully in the areas near Orsha and Mogilev, both in Belarus, during the winter of 1943–44. Martinek was briefly delegated with the temporary leadership of the 9th Army in March 1943, and on 24 February 1944 was presented with the Oakleaves personally by Hitler at the Berghof on the Obersalzburg. At the beginning of the Soviet offensive in June, the German forces found themselves fighting a losing battle. On 28 June the Soviets bombed the German positions in Berezina, Belarus, and the headquarters of the XXXIX. Panzer Corps took a direct hit. Martinek was fatally wounded in the head by shrapnel, and his orderly buried his body in Tscherwen in Belarus on 30 June 1944, where he still lies today.

In March 1938 Martinek transferred to the German Army with the rank of *Oberst* and was appointed Artillery Commander 35 in Karlsruhe from August. He saw action at the beginning of the war as Artillery Commander 7, while attached to the VII. Army Corps with the rank of *Generalmajor*.

Fritz Albert Otto SCHLIEPER

Generalleutnant

* 4 August 1892, Koldromb, Posen
\+ 4 June 1977, Nuremberg, Bavaria

Knight's Cross: Awarded on 27 December 1941 as *Generalleutnant* and Commander of 45th Infantry Division while attached to the 2nd Army for the part he played in the capture of Brest-Litovsk. He later saw action at Pinsk, Gomel and at Tula near Moscow, putting up fierce resistance against a strong Soviet counteroffensive from December 1941. From 15 April 1942 Schlieper was appointed head of the German Army Mission in Slovakia and German General at the Slovak Ministry of Defence. From August 1944 he was Commander of Special Staff II in the Army High Command until the German surrender in May 1945, and remained in Allied captivity until his release on 24 December 1947. He was the brother of *Generalmajor* Franz Max Schlieper and he was awarded the Knight's Cross on 21st September 1944 as Commander of Grenadier Brigade 1132.

Friedrich-Georg Wilhelm Karl Hermann Gotthard EBERHARDT

Generalleutnant

* 15 January 1892, Straβburg, France
+ 9 September 1964, Wiesbaden

Knight's Cross: Awarded on 31 December 1941 as *Generalleutnant* and Commander of the 60th Motorised Infantry Division, part of the III. Army Corps, for his bravery and leadership during a phenomenal victory near Rostov on the Eastern Front. He led his division during an attack against a strong Soviet force and his goal was to eliminate the threat on the corps flank which was achieved. Eberhardt '... smashed the enemy and pursued the survivors ... it was his actions that made it possible for the rest of Corps to reach their objective.' From March to May 1942 his division took part in the Battle of Kharkov and then advanced towards the Donets and Don, then ultimately towards Stalingrad. In July 1942 Eberhardt took over as commander of the 38th Infantry Division and from December his division was transferred to northern France, where it became part of the occupation force. From January his division was transferred to Saint-Nazaire to protect the coastline, and in March 1943 his division was transferred to the Eastern Front to be deployed on the west bank of the Donets. From mid-September 1943 Eberhardt was appointed Commander of the 174th Reserve Division and was stationed in Lublin, Poland, mainly on occupation duty, and from early August 1944 until December he commanded the 286th Security Division and remained in Poland. On 15 December he was transferred to the Reich War Court as a judge, where he took part in courts-martial cases. Eberhardt surrendered to the Allies at the end of the war and remained in captivity until mid-1947.

Friedrich-Georg Eberhardt entered Army service in March 1910 and was attached to the War School until July 1911, being commissioned as a *Leutnant* two months later. He saw action during the First World War and was taken ill in September 1915 and again in April 1917. By the end of the war he had risen to the rank of *Rittmeister* and continued to serve in the Army with the infantry and artillery, being promoted to *Major* in February 1931 and to *Oberstleutnant* in September 1933. From October 1935 he was Commander of Infantry Regiment 44 with the rank of *Oberst*, and in August 1939 he commanded the 60th Infantry Division with the rank of *Generalmajor* and was awarded the Bar to the Iron Cross 1st and 2nd Classes.

Hasso Eccard von MANTEUFFEL

General der Panzertruppe

* 14 January 1897, Potsdam, Brandenburg
+ 24 September 1978, Reith im Alpbachtal, Tyrol, Austria

Hasso von Manteuffel joined the Army in 1908 as a cadet in Naumberg and attended the Cadet Institute at Berlin-Lichterfelde from 1911 until February 1916. He joined the 5th Squadron of the Hussar Regiment and saw action during the First World War as a *Leutnant* and was wounded at the Battle of the Somme in October 1916. He served the rest of the war as an Ordnance Officer with the 6th Infantry Division and was awarded both classes of the Iron Cross.

Knight's Cross: Awarded on 31 December 1941 as *Oberst* and Commander of Rifle Regiment 6, part of the 7th Panzer Division, for the capture of the bridge over the Moscow–Volga Canal without damaging it on 28 November 1941. He later saw action during the battles of the Minsk Pocket, at Smolensk and Moscow, and the division suffered such heavy losses that it was sent to France in May 1942 to rest and refit. From early November he took part in the occupation of Vichy France as part of the 7th Panzer Division and then later until February 1942 he was in the *Führer* Reserve. From February until the end of April 1943 he was Commander of Division von Manteuffel, being promoted to *Generalmajor* the next month. Just before it was ready to leave for North Africa, Manteuffel fell ill from exhaustion and spent the next five months recovering. He took command of the 7th Panzer Division on 16 August 1943 and saw action near Kharkov until September. His troops then crossed the Dnieper River in a bid to clear Soviet bridgeheads but this failed.

Knight's Cross with Oakleaves: He became the 332nd recipient on 23 November 1943 as *Generalmajor* and Commander of 7th Panzer Division while attached to the LVII. Panzer Corps for the recapture of Zhitomir on the Russian Front. The counter-attack had begun on 14 November and continued to advance on Kiev-Zhitomir, which was taken two days later. Manteuffel had been wounded by a Soviet air attack and was taken to an aid station to be treated, but refused to be evacuated to a hospital. He later saw fierce fighting at Kharkov, Belgorod and along the Dnieper River and at Kiev, where his division was eventually forced by superior numbers to give way. Manteuffel,

Manteuffel remained with the Army after the war, serving with Cavalry Regiment 25 from May 1919, and went on to serve with Mounted Regiment 3 until the end of September 1932. Promoted to *Major* in 1936, he was appointed Staff Officer with the 2nd Panzer Division and he trained cadets. Promoted to *Oberstleutnant* in April 1939, he went on to command the 3rd Motorcycle Battalion from June 1940. From May 1941 he was Commander of the I. Battalion of the 7th Rifle Regiment and was awarded the Iron Cross 1st and 2nd Classes during the heavy fighting near Smolensk in the Soviet Union.

however, made a successful counter-attack and Zhitomir was taken, Hitler was overjoyed, and awarded Manteuffel the Oakleaves, presenting them to him personally at Rastenburg in December 1943.

Knight's Cross with Oakleaves and Swords: He became the fiftieth recipient on 22 February 1944 as *Generalmajor* and Commander of the 7th Panzer Division while still attached to the LVII. Panzer Corps and was awarded for further successes in the Zhitomir-Kiev area. He was responsible for repelling a Soviet thrust near Korosten, in the Ukraine, on 20 November 1943 and within another two days his division had advanced 40 miles. Three days later, Manteuffel personally led an attack against Malin, and despite hostile resistance his men reached the centre of the village and destroyed twenty-five Soviet tanks. In February 1944 Manteuffel was delegated with the leadership of the 16th Panzer Grenadier Division and was for a time almost encircled by a Soviet force. However, he managed to free his division without losing a single weapon and for that he was promoted to *Generalleutnant.* He continued to see action against Soviet forces that launched an offensive in May in an attempt to break through to the oilfields of Ploesti. Manteuffel led a counter-attack and together with the *Luftwaffe* destroyed 250 tanks and brought the Soviet advance to a halt. As a result, he was awarded the Swords and on 14 May was able to travel to Hitler's home, the Berghof on the Obersalzburg, where he was presented with them. In September he was promoted to *General der Panzertruppe* and was transferred to the Western Front as Commander-in-Chief of the 5th Panzer Army.

Knight's Cross with Oakleaves, Swords and Diamonds: He became the twenty-fourth recipient on 18 February 1945 as *General der Panzertruppe* and Commander-in-Chief of the 5th Panzer Army, part of Army Group B, for his success during the Ardennes Offensive and for constructing a stable front west of the Rhine. On 28 February he was summoned to Berlin, where Hitler presented him with the Diamonds, and a few days later he was appointed Commander-in-Chief of the 3rd Panzer Army on the Eastern Front. He held a position on the Oder Front until 26 April and two days later *Generalfeldmarschall* Wilhelm Keitel accused the Commander-in-Chief of Army Group Vistula, *Generaloberst* Gotthard Heinrici, of failure on the Neustrelitz–Neubrandenburg Road. This was in the presence of Keitel, who threatened to replace him with Manteuffel, but Manteuffel refused as he did not agree with the charges against Heinrici. On 3 May Manteuffel reached the British lines, where he surrendered his entire command and was imprisoned first by the British and then the Americans, being released on 31 December 1947.

Wilhelm Josef Ritter von THOMA

General der Panzertruppe

* 11 September 1891, Dachau, Bavaria
+ 30 April 1948, Dachau, Bavaria

Knight's Cross: Awarded on 31 December 1941 as *Generalmajor* and Commander of 20th Panzer Division, part of LVII. Army Corps, for his leadership during the drive on Moscow that began on 15 November 1941. It was also awarded for the holding of a new defensive position on the Ruza River despite the heavy winter conditions. The Germans advanced on Moscow from the north and the south, but with the freezing temperature, fierce local counter-attacks the German advance was slow. On 6 December the Soviets launched the first of a series of major counteroffensives that forced the Germans from Moscow. On 1

August Thoma was promoted to *Generalleutnant* and the following month he was delegated with the leadership of the German *Afrika Korps* after its former commander *General der Panzertruppe* Walther Nehring had been wounded, when a British aircraft bombed his command vehicle during the Battle of Alam Halfa. During this command he was delegated with the temporary leadership of Panzer Army Afrika for only two days while Rommel was on sick leave. On 1 November 1942 he was promoted to *General der Panzertruppe* and continued to command the German Afrika Korps until he was captured by British troops commanded by Captain Grant Allen Singer west of El Alamein, and was held in British captivity until 25 November 1947.

Friedrich Wilhelm Eduard Kasimir Dietrich von SAUCKEN

General der Panzertruppe

* 16 May 1892, Fischhausen-Samland, East Prussia
+ 27 September 1980, Munich, Bavaria

Knight's Cross: Awarded on 6 January 1942 as *Generalmajor* and *Führer* of the 4th *Panzer* Division while attached to the LIII. Army Corps for his leadership during heavy fighting on the Russian Front during the winter of 1941–42. On 28 December 1941, after some fierce fighting against a vastly superior Soviet force that broke into the German-occupied areas of Chmelewaja and Khmelevaya, Saucken and his troops crushed the Soviet forces. However, during the fighting Saucken was seriously wounded. While recovering in hospital, in recognition of his bravery and leadership he was presented with the Knight's Cross by the Commander-in-Chief of Army Group Centre *Generalfeldmarschall* Günther von Kluge. After a period of convalescence, Saucken took command of the Army School for Fast Troops in August 1942. He was promoted to *Generalleutnant* in April 1943 and the following month took command of the 4th Panzer Division.

Dietrich von Saucken entered the Army in October 1910 with the East Prussian Grenadier Regiment 'King Friedrich-Wilhelm I' No.3 in Königsberg and was commissioned as a *Leutnant* in June 1912. He served with this regiment during the First World War, was promoted to *Oberleutnant* in August 1917 and was awarded both classes of the Iron Cross.

Knight's Cross with Oakleaves: Saucken became the 281st recipient on 22 August 1943 as *Generalleutnant* and Commander of 4th Panzer Division, part of the XXXXVI. Panzer Corps, for operations during Operation Kutuzov, a counteroffensive operation launched by the Soviets as part of the fighting in Kursk. During the course of the fighting his division took over an area south of Orel and his troops destroyed sixty-two Soviet tanks, which weakened the enemy so much that their plans for a breakthrough had to be abandoned. This earned Saucken the Oakleaves, which were presented personally by Hitler in late August at the Wolf's Lair in East Prussia.

Knight's Cross with Oakleaves and Swords: Awarded on 31 January 1944, the forty-first recipient, as *Generalleutnant* and Commander of 4th Panzer Division while still attached to the XXXXVI. Panzer Corps for his success against the Soviets during the defensive battles in and around Gomel, Belarus and near Kalinkavichy in the Ukraine. On 25 May 1944 Saucken flew to the Berghof, Berchtesgaden, where Hitler presented him with the Swords, together with at least another nine army officers, including *General der Artillerie* Maximilian Fretter-Pico, *Oberst* Ernst-Günther Baade and *Generalleutnant* Friedrich Schulz. Saucken was then granted some leave and on 31 May 1944 he was delegated with the leadership of the III. Panzer Corps. From 29 June he took command

Saucken remained in the Army after the war, serving with Prussian Mounted Regiment 2 between April 1925 and April 1934 and then becoming a tactics instructor at the War School in Hannover with the rank of *Oberstleutnant*. From October 1936 he served as Commander of Mounted Regiment 2 with the 1st Cavalry Brigade and in September 1940 he served as Commander of the 4th Rifle Brigade with the rank of *Oberst*.

of the XXXIX. Panzer Corps, which played a decisive role against Soviet troops in East Prussia. On 1 August he was promoted to *General der Panzertruppe* and in December he established a new command, Panzer Corps *Grossdeutschland*, and he soon inflicted heavy losses on the Soviets. His troops destroyed one hundred Soviet tanks, however the Soviets were quick to get replacements and were soon strong enough to push back the Germans. His command came under the control of the 9th Army, whose front had already been broken by the enemy and which was in full retreat. Saucken was told to remain in the rear of the advancing enemy and was asked to attend *Führer* Headquarters at the Wolf's Lair in Rastenburg on 12 March 1945 and explain the current situation. As a result he was given command of the 2nd Panzer Army but, lacking in fuel and air support, his battered command faced a superior enemy.

Knight's Cross with Oakleaves, Swords and Diamonds: Awarded on 8 May 1945, the twenty-seventh recipient, as *General der Panzertruppe* and Commander-in-Chief of Army Headquarters East Prussia for his leadership and accomplishments throughout the war, with particular emphasis on his role in the battles for East Prussia. He had by now been given command of Army East Prussia – the new name given for the remnants of two armies. His forces were able to prevent total encirclement but only a small part of his forces could be saved the following night. One of his missions was to hold the enemy until 300,000 refugees had escaped the area, however this was not possible. On 8 May he was informed that he had been awarded the Diamonds to his Knight's Cross by Hitler's successor, *Grossadmiral* Karl Dönitz. The following day Saucken was captured by Soviet troops, who flew him to Moscow on the 16th for interrogation. He spent almost three years in the notorious Lubyanka Prison and later in various other prisons, for a time in solitary confinement. He was informed that he had been sentenced to twenty-five years' hard labour, however he was released after a general amnesty on 9 October 1955 and returned to Germany.

Karl von OVEN

General der Infanterie

* 29 November 1888, Berlin-Charlottenburg
+ 20 January 1974, Singen, Hohentwiel

Knight's Cross: Awarded on 9 January 1942 as *Generalleutnant* and Commander of 56th Infantry Division, part of the LIII. Army Corps, for his actions during the advance and retreat from Moscow. He took part in the battles of Kovel,

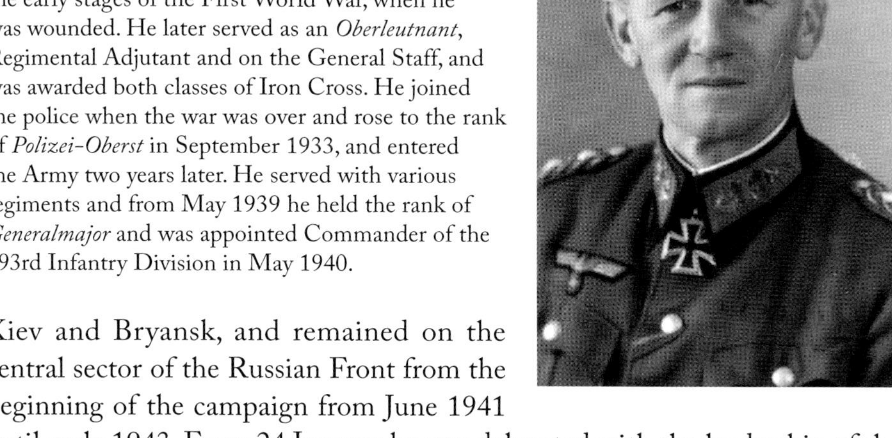

Karl von Oven entered the Army with Guard Regiment 3 in Berlin from February 1908, and was commissioned as a *Leutnant* the following year. He served as an adjutant with a Fusilier Battalion during the early stages of the First World War, when he was wounded. He later served as an *Oberleutnant*, Regimental Adjutant and on the General Staff, and was awarded both classes of Iron Cross. He joined the police when the war was over and rose to the rank of *Polizei-Oberst* in September 1933, and entered the Army two years later. He served with various regiments and from May 1939 he held the rank of *Generalmajor* and was appointed Commander of the 393rd Infantry Division in May 1940.

Kiev and Bryansk, and remained on the central sector of the Russian Front from the beginning of the campaign from June 1941 until early 1943. From 24 January he was delegated with the leadership of the XXXXIII. Army Corps and saw action in Demyansk. With his promotion to *General der Infanterie* in April 1943 his command was confirmed. From July he saw action in Nevel as part of the 16th Army and later saw action near Narva in Estonia. From March 1944 he entered the Reserves. From May 1944 until March 1945 he commanded Field Jäger Command II, part of Army Group Courland on the Eastern Front. He surrendered to Allied forces in May 1945 but little is known about his time in captivity.

Johann Hermann MEYER-RABINGEN

Generalleutnant

* 7 August 1887, Rotenburg, Hannover
+ 21 February 1961, Melle, Lower Saxony

Knight's Cross: Awarded on 12 January 1942 as *Generalleutnant* and Commander of 197th Infantry Division, part of the VII. Army Corps, for actions during the offensive battles around Moscow. From April until September he was in the *Führer* Reserve and was then appointed Commander of the 159th Reserve Division in Vichy France. In early 1944 his division was performing garrison duties in the Arcachon area on the Bay of Biscay coast and then at Bordeaux, where he was stationed during D-Day. From July 1944 he took over as Commander of Replacement Division Nr. 404, being stationed in Poland, where he served as a judge at Reich Court Martial hearings. From 21 November 1944 until 28 January 1945 he participated in the session of the 3rd Senate of the Reich Court Martial of *Generalleutnant* Gustav Heistermann von Ziehlberg, who was sentenced to death on 19 November 1944 for disobedience in the field, and was hanged in Berlin on 2 February 1945. On 29 January 1945 Meyer-Rabingen was appointed Commandant of Fortress Frankfurt am Oder and from March he returned as Commander of the 404th Replacement and Reconnaissance Division. Shortly after Hitler killed himself at the end of April, Meyer-Rabingen and his men surrendered to the Soviets on 8 May 1945.

Hubertus-Maria Ritter von HEIGL

Generalmajor

* 10 November 1897, Siegenburg, Bavaria
+ 24 January 1985, Munich, Bavaria

Knight's Cross: Awarded on 13 January 1942 as *Oberstleutnant* and Commander of Pioneer Battalion 70 (motorised) while attached to Army Pioneer Brigade 70 for actions near the village of Eupatoria, near Sevastopol in the Soviet Union. He fought together with his battalion for four days during bitter combat in below zero temperatures using specialised combat equipment. His forces crushed all Soviet resistance and killed 600 Red Army troops, 1,300 partisans and took 203 Red Army prisoners. He was promoted to *Oberst* on 1 March 1942 and in April he transferred to the Staff of the Pioneer Leader of the 11th Army on the Eastern Front. He saw action on the Kerch Peninsula, the conquest of Crimea and later saw action during the heavy fighting near Leningrad and entered the Reserves from

Hubertus-Maria Ritter von Heigl entered Army service in July 1915 with Bavarian Infantry Regiment 4 and was commissioned as a *Leutnant* in June the following year. He saw action during the First World War and was awarded both Classes of the Iron Cross and the Wound Badge in Black. He stayed in the Army after the war, serving in various infantry regiments before being taken ill and spending some months in hospital before being appointed adjutant of a training battalion attached to Infantry Regiment 21 in October 1924. From July 1936 until the beginning of the Second World War he served as an instructor in the War School and the War Academy in Berlin, before being transferred to command Motorised Pioneer Battalion 70.

April 1943. From early 1944 he served as General of Pioneers with Army Centre and from January 1945 he served in a similar capacity with Army Group North under *Generaloberst* Dr Lothar Rendulic. He was promoted to *Generalmajor* on 20 April 1945 and served as General of Pioneers with Army Group North West until the end of the war, when he surrendered to British forces.

Smilo Walther Hinko Oskar Constantin Wilhelm Freiherr von LÜTTWITZ

General der Panzertruppe

* 23 December 1895, Strasburg, Alsace
+ 19 May 1975, Coblenz, Rhineland-Palatinate

Knight's Cross: Awarded on 14 January 1942 as *Oberst* and Commander of Rifle Regiment 12 while attached to the 4th Panzer Division for his courage during the defensive successes in the central sector of the Eastern Front. In October 1941 his command was responsible for attacking enemy forces at Orel and the following month took part in the fighting south-east of Tula. From March 1942 he served as Commander of Rifle Brigade 4 and from 5 July his command was renamed Panzer Grenadier Brigade 4. On 14 July he was delegated with the leadership of the 23rd Infantry Division, which was sent to Amiens in France to reform as the 26th Panzer Division. This new unit trained in France for about a year and Lüttwitz was promoted to *Generalmajor* in October 1942, taking his new command to Italy in August 1943 as part of the LXXVI. Panzer Corps. Promoted to *Generalleutnant* in October 1943, he saw action at Anzio from early January 1944 as part of the 14th Army.

Smilo von Lüttwitz entered the Army as an officer candidate in August 1914 with the 2nd Grand Ducal Hessian Lifeguard Regiment 24 in Darmstadt. In June 1915 he was commissioned as a *Leutnant* and during the First World War he served as an Ordnance Officer with the General Staff of the Army and as a Regimental Adjutant. He remained in the Army after the war and by December 1935 had risen to the rank of *Major* and was serving as an adjutant of the 1st Regiment of Motorised Combat Troops. From May 1940 he was Commander of Rifle Regiment 12, part of the 4th Panzer Division and saw action during the invasion of France and Belgium.

Knight's Cross with Oakleaves: He became the 426th recipient on 16 March 1944 as *Generalleutnant* and Commander of the 26th Panzer Division as part of the LXXXVI. Army Corps for his division's successful defence against an attack by New Zealand troops on 7 December 1943 on the eastern sector of the Italian Front. Lüttwitz was personally presented with the Oakleaves by Hitler at the Berghof in April 1944. He was wounded in the face by shrapnel on 17 February and the following month his right eye developed a serious infection. For a time he was at risk of losing his sight and his stay in hospital was extended.

Knight's Cross with Oakleaves and Swords: Awarded on 4 July 1944 to become the seventy-sixth recipient as *Generalleutnant* and while still Commander of the 26th Panzer Division as part of the XIV. Panzer Corps for his outstanding leadership during the heavy fighting north of Rome. He particularly distinguished himself on 1 July during the counter-attack that retook Saline di Volterra, a village in Tuscany, and was presented with the Swords by Hitler at the Berghof in late July. Towards the end of July he took command of the XXXXVI. Panzer Corps and saw action during the defensive battles near the Vistula River in Poland. On 1 September Lüttwitz was promoted to *General der Panzertruppe* and from 21 September was delegated with the leadership of the 9th Army and saw action during the Warsaw Uprising. On 19 January 1945 he was relieved of his command by Hitler for ordering the unauthorised evacuation and retreat from Warsaw. He then served with the Reich War Court, which involved sentencing deserters to prison or the death sentence. From 31 March he was appointed Commanding General of the LXXXV. Army Corps on the Western Front. His corps put up a tough resistance against US forces, but on 4 April the Americans broke through into Thuringia and from the 15th Lüttwitz's command was in full retreat. From 19 April the 11th Panzer Division under *Generalmajor* Horst Freiherr Treusch von Buttlar-Brandenfels began to separate from the corps and moved towards Bad Königswart in Czechoslovakia. On 4 May the division surrendered to US troops and the following day Lüttwitz surrendered his corps. He remained in Allied captivity until his release on 30 June 1947.

Gustav-Adolf Ernst Friedrich Karl von ZANGEN

General der Infanterie

* 7 November 1892, Darmstadt, Hesse
+ 1 May 1964, Hanau am Main, Hesse

Knight's Cross: Awarded on 15 January 1942 as *Oberst* and Commander of Infantry Regiment 88 of the 15th Infantry Division for actions on the Russian Front near Mogilev. On 26 July 1941 he led his regiment in a decisive role in the prevention of the attempted breakout of two Soviet rifle divisions from the Mogilev Garrison. He was further recognised for his regiment 'mopping up' the forested area south-west of the city and clearing the area of the Soviet troops. He was promoted to *Generalmajor* in February 1942 and went on to see action with his division in south Vyazma until early May of that year, when his unit was transferred to Brittany, France, for a refit. Promoted to *Generalleutnant* in January 1943, he returned with his division to the Soviet Union the following month but from early April he was appointed Commanding General of the LXXXIV. Army Corps and was on occupation duty in Saint-Lô, north-western France, until the end of July. Promoted to *General der Infanterie*, he took over as Commanding General of the LXXXVII. Army Corps in Liguria, north-west Italy, from August 1943. On 12 July 1944 he was ordered to report to *Führer* Headquarters in Rastenburg, where they discussed the defence of the south. Zangen was told to make contact with *Generalfeldmarschall* Albert Kesselring and discuss the building of a fortress but nothing came from this as the Allies were approaching fast.

Knight's Cross with Oakleaves: He became the 647th recipient on 5 November 1944 as *General der Infanterie* and leader of the 15th

Gustav von Zangen entered the Army in February 1910 as an officer candidate with Infantry regiment No. 117 and was commissioned as a *Leutnant* two years later. He saw action during the First World War as a platoon leader and later as an adjutant, and was promoted to *Hauptmann* in 1915. He left the Army in 1920 and joined the police for a time but was accepted back into the Army in August 1935 with the rank of *Oberstleutnant*. In November 1938, now with the rank of *Oberst*, he was Commander of Infantry Regiment 88, part of the 15th Infantry Division. He saw action in Poland and later in France, during which time he was awarded both classes of the Bar to the Iron Cross.

Army while attached to Army Group B for his command during two months of fierce fighting near the Scheldt Estuary in northern France. During this time he not only denied the Allies the use of the port of Antwerp for a sustained period but was also able to prevent the destruction of his forces, which ensured the stability of the northernmost sector of the German front line. He was presented with his Oakleaves in November 1944 by Hitler at his Wolf's Lair headquarters at Rastenburg. In late 1944 and early 1945 he led his troops at Aachen and after the failure of the Ardennes Offensive he saw action in the area around Cologne. On 17 April 1945 he surrendered the 15th Army to US forces in the Ruhr Pocket area. Zangen was released from captivity in 1948.

Gerhard 'Gerd' Helmuth Detloff Graf von SCHWERIN

General der Panzertruppe

* 23 June 1899, Hannover
+ 29 October 1980, Rottach-Egern, Bavaria

Knight's Cross: Awarded on 17 January 1942 as *Oberst* and Commander of Motorised Infantry Regiment 76 while attached to the 20th Infantry Division for actions in Mga near Leningrad between 30 August and 5 September 1941. He later led his regiment during the battles of Tichvin, Volkhov and Staraya Russa, and in the Siege of Leningrad, which was a decisive three-day battle that culminated in the fall of Schlüsselburg. Between 17 February and 18 April 1942 he was delegated with the leadership of the 254th Infantry Division as part of the 18th Army in the Soviet Union. From July he was delegated with the leadership of the 8th Jäger Division and was promoted to

Gerhard Graf von Schwerin trained as an officer from 1908 and later he attended the Cadet Institute at Berlin-Lichterfelde. He served during the First World War with Guard Regiment 2 and was commissioned as a *Leutnant* in June 1915 and saw action in the field as a platoon leader, a company leader and as an adjutant. He left the army in March 1920 but returned six years later with Infantry Regiment 3 and continued training. From October 1937 served as a company commander with Infantry Regiment 17 with the rank of *Major*. He saw action during the invasion of France and the Low Countries from May 1940 as temporary Commander of Rifle Regiment 86 and was awarded the Bar to the Iron Cross 1st and 2nd Classes.

Generalmajor in October 1942. In the following month he took over command of the 16th Motorised Infantry Division.

Knight's Cross with Oakleaves: He became the 240th recipient on 17 May 1943 as *Generalmajor* and Commander of the 16th Motorised Infantry Division, part of the XXIX. Army Corps, for his leadership during the retreat from the Caucasus in the winter of 1942–43. His greatest accomplishment was the destruction of the Soviet 4th Guard Mechanized Corps in heavy fighting in the Soviet Union between 18 and 23 February 1943. From 20 May his command was renamed the 16th Panzer Grenadier Division and Schwerin was promoted to the rank of *Generalleutnant* in June that same year.

Knight's Cross with Oakleaves and Swords: Awarded on 4 November 1943 to become the forty-first recipient as *Generalleutnant* and Commander of the 16th Panzer Grenadier Division, part of the 1st Panzer Army, for his leadership during the retreat from Mius and for his leadership during the fighting for the Zaporozhye Bridgehead in the Ukraine. He continued to see action in the Soviet Union and took part in the withdrawal near Nikopol. From January 1944 he saw action in Mykolaiv in the Ukraine as part of the 6th Army. He was decorated with the Swords personally by Hitler at the Berghof on the Obersalzburg in March 1944. From September, Schwerin was Battle Commandant of Aachen, which was defended by his command, the 116th Panzer Division, which had been badly mauled during the fighting at Mortain in north-western France. On 14 September, Schwerin withdrew his troops during the heavy fighting near Aachen against the orders of Hitler. He was immediately relieved of his command and faced a court marital for treason. Without the support of both *Generalfeldmarschalls* Gerd von Rundstedt and Walter Model he would have been given the death sentence. Instead he received a severe reprimand. He was fortunate that the Gestapo did not find out about his knowledge of the 20 July 1944 plot against Hitler, otherwise he could have been executed. In December he was recalled to duty and was appointed Commander of the 90th Panzer Grenadier Division and just two weeks later he took command of the LXXVI. Panzer Corps. He was promoted to *General der Panzertruppe* in April 1945 but towards the end of the month his command was virtually destroyed by an Anglo-American force in Italy, where he surrendered to British forces on 26 April. He remained in Allied captivity until 24 December 1947.

Paul Robert Ludwig Fritz SEYFFARDT

Generalleutnant

* 4 March 1894, Weilburg, Hessen-Nassau
+ 20 September 1979, Baden-Baden

Knight's Cross: Awarded on 17 January 1942 as *Oberst* and Commander of Infantry Regiment 111 as part of 35th Infantry Division for actions during the heavy fighting near Gzhatsk in Smolensk. Towards the end of March 1942, Seyffardt was delegated with the leadership of the 205th Infantry Division fighting as part of the 9th Army in the Soviet Union. In June he was promoted to *Generalmajor* and was confirmed as Commander of his division and continued to see action near Yelikije-Luki in the Soviet Union. Promoted to *Generalleutnant* in January 1943, he remained divisional commander until November, when he entered the Reserves. From February 1944 he served as Commander of the 348th Infantry Division guarding the Channel coast until the autumn, when the Allies broke through to Normandy and crossed the Seine River, attacking the 15th Army from the rear. Seyffardt took his command to Normandy in August, where it suffered heavy losses and where Seyffardt was captured by US troops on 9 September 1944. He was taken to a prisoner-of-war camp in Clinton, Mississippi, where he was held until 1947.

Kurt CUNO

Generalleutnant

* 27 August 1896, Zweibrücken, Bavaria
+ 14 July 1961, Munich, Bavaria

Knight's Cross: Awarded on 18 January 1942 as *Oberst* and Commander of Panzer Regiment 39 while attached to the 17th Panzer Division for actions on the Russian Front. He had the mission of defending against Soviet forces that had attacked the 2nd Army near Szuchinitschi, but later he had to pull back when they became surrounded by a much larger enemy and lost control of an important railway station. He soon succeeded in pushing back the Soviets with minimal losses and using his initiative he recaptured the station. In doing so he laid the groundwork for a future attack against enemy forces that had penetrated deep into the area between the 2nd and 4th Panzer Army. In June 1943 Cuno attended a divisional leaders course and was promoted to *Generalmajor* in July 1943, taking over command of the 233rd Reserve Panzer Division the

Kurt Cuno entered Army service in February 1915 as a *Fahnenjunker* and from December fought with the Bavarian Engineer Regiment. He was commissioned as a *Leutnant* in April 1916 and was awarded both classes of the Iron Cross later that year. He remained with the Army after the war and was promoted to *Major* in June 1935. From October 1937 he took command of the I. Battalion of Panzer Regiment 25 and was promoted to *Oberstleutnant* in February 1938.

following month. His command was stationed in Denmark and from May 1944 he was appointed General of Motor Transport Affairs for Field and Replacement. Promoted to Generalleutnant in August of that year, he remained in Denmark until the end of the war. In June 1945 he went into Allied captivity, being released in June 1947.

Curt von JESSER

Generalmajor

* 4 November 1890, Wadowice, West Galicia, Austro-Hungary
+ 17 August 1950, Baden, Vienna

Knight's Cross: Awarded on 18 January 1942 as *Oberst* and Commander of Panzer Regiment 36 as part of the 14th Panzer Division for actions in Kharkov and later in the drive across the Don. From May 1942, Jesser was Commander of Fast Troops in Military District XIII, Nuremberg. On 1 December he was promoted to *Generalmajor* and delegated with the leadership of the 386th Motorised Infantry Division, which

Curt von Jesser entered the Austrian Army as a cadet in August 1909 and saw action as a company commander with Rifle Regiment 6 from May 1915. He was awarded the Iron Cross 2nd Class during the war and ended the war with the rank of *Hauptmann*, remaining in the army after the Armistice. In June 1923 he served as battalion adjutant with Infantry Regiment 5 and two years later he served as company commander with the rank of *Hauptmann*. In March 1938 he transferred into the German Army and from February 1940 was attached to Panzer Regiment 36 with the rank of *Oberst* and saw action during the invasion of Poland.

was stationed in southern France. From early March 1943 he was in the *Führer* Reserve and later attached to Army Group D. From 24 August he took over as temporary leader of the 155th Reserve Panzer Division in France while it was training, and from early September he once again entered the Reserves. In January 1944 he was attached to the Staff of the Military Commander in France, *General der Infanterie* Carl-Heinrich von Stülpnagel. From February 1945 he was Commandant of Fortress Section Styria in Austria, and was arrested by Allied troops in October 1945. He remained in Allied captivity until his release on 17 March 1949.

Ludwig Felix Hermann KIRSCHNER

Generalmajor

* 12 June 1904, Bayreuth, Bavaria
+ 11 February 1945, near Saybusch, Poland

Knight's Cross: Awarded on 18 January 1942 as *Major* and Commander of the I. Battalion of Infantry Regiment 436, part of the 132nd Infantry Division, for actions on the Soviet Front. On 15 January 1942 Kirschner and his battalion were deployed as a lead German unit during the attack on Feodosia on the Crimean coastline. Two days later his troops made a breakthrough of the Soviet lines and with just over 150 men made it to the coastal road north of Sarigöl. In doing so they completed the German encirclement of Feodosia itself. He was promoted to *Oberstleutnant* in August 1942 and from 15 October he was delegated with the leadership of Infantry Regiment 72.

Ludwig Kirschner entered the police service as an officer candidate in May 1925 and after his training he served in Munich as a *Polizei-Leutnant*. A few years later he served in Nuremberg and was promoted to *Polizei-Oberleutnant* in January 1934. In March 1936 he transferred into the Army as an *Oberleutnant*, serving in the III. Battalion of Infantry Regiment 110, and from May that year he was appointed company commander.

Knight's Cross with Oakleaves: He became the 135th recipient on 28 October 1942 as *Oberstleutnant* and Commander of Infantry Regiment 72, part of the 46th Infantry Division, for his outstanding command in the Caucasus Mountains during October after the failed German advance to Tuapse in the Soviet Union. Kirschner took part in the Siege of Sevastopol and in the Caucasus campaign.

He was promoted to *Oberst* on 10 June 1943 and later saw action in the Kuban, the Donets, the Battle of Dnepropetrovsk and in the retreat through the southern Ukraine. From November Kirschner was appointed Commander of the Battalion Leaders School in Antwerp, and from August 1944 he was Commander of the Grenadier Instruction Brigade and placed at the disposal of the Army High Command. The following month he went on a divisional leaders course and from November he was given the leadership of the 320th Volksgrenadier Division, which had been formed with the remnants of other shattered units. On 30 January 1945 Kirschner was promoted to *Generalmajor* and his command was confirmed and he saw action near Cracow in Poland, where his unit was crushed. It was reduced to only battle group strength and saw action in Poland, where on 11 February Kirschner was killed in action.

Kirschner then attended various courses and in November 1938, now with the rank of *Hauptmann*, he was appointed company commander with Infantry Regiment 104. In August 1941 he was promoted to *Major* and appointed Commander of the I. Battalion of Infantry Regiment 436, seeing action in Kiev as part of the 6th Army.

Karl Hermann ARNDT

Generalleutnant

* 10 March 1892, Gross-Kauer, Glogua in Silesia
\+ 30 December 1981, Balve-Langenholthausen, North Rhine-Westphalia

Knight's Cross: Awarded on 23 January 1942 as *Oberst* and Commander of 511th Infantry Regiment, attached to the 293rd Infantry Division, for operations in the Soviet Union. In June 1941, he had taken part in the fighting at Brest-Litovsk, then later at Kiev and Bryansk. During the fighting east of Kiev his command held back two enemy divisions that were trying to break through the German lines by utilising a bridgehead in the area. Arndt ordered his regiment to launch a counter-attack, and directed the attack from a roof of a house despite the close proximity of enemy artillery fire. The house was hit and crumbled beneath him but he escaped unharmed. In January 1943 Arndt

Karl Arndt joined the Army as a student in April 1908 and later served during the First World War. He was wounded and captured by the British in September 1918. He stayed in the Army after the war and was commissioned as a *Leutnant* in June 1919, serving in various Reichswehr Regiments. He was appointed company leader in November 1923 and promoted to *Oberleutnant* the following month. In January 1936 he was briefly in hospital after a car accident and then served as a *Major* on the staff of Infantry Regiment 68. Promoted to *Oberstleutnant* in December 1937, he was serving as Commander of the II. Battalion during the invasion of Poland in September 1939.

took over as Commander of the 293rd Infantry Division, seeing further action in the Soviet Union and where he was promoted to *Generalmajor* on 10 March. He fought in the Battle of Kursk in July again at Bryansk in August, and later at Kharkov, where his division suffered heavy losses. On 8 November he was promoted to *Generalleutnant* and made Commander of the 359th Infantry Division, which had been hastily put together from the remnants of the 293rd Infantry Division. Mobilised in the area of Radom in Poland, in early 1944 it was assigned to southern Russia as part of the 4th Panzer Army. Its job was to defend the position west of Tarnopol against heavy Soviet attacks in April 1944 and it later saw action in southern Poland.

Knight's Cross with Oakleaves: Arndt was awarded the Oakleaves on 1 February 1945, to become the 719th recipient as *Generalleutnant* and Commander of the 359th Infantry Division, attached to the 17th Army, for his part in halting a Soviet breakthrough near Cracow by superior Soviet forces. On 25 April he was appointed Temporary Commander of the XXXIX. Panzer Corps, with his headquarters in Berlin. Arndt was captured by US forces at his headquarters on 8 May 1945 and was imprisoned at Dachau, the site of the Nazi concentration camp, where he remained until 5 July 1947.

Eberhard von KUROWSKI

Generalleutnant

* 10 September 1895, Stettin
+ 11 September 1957, Stanzach, Austria

Knight's Cross: Awarded on 23 January 1942 as *Oberst im Generalstab* and Chief of the General Staff of the XXXX. Army Corps while attached to the 4th Army for actions on the Russian Front. He saw action during the attack in the area of Roslavl in the Soviet Union together with Panzer Group 4 and later joined forces with the 10th Panzer Division rearguard action to take Kirov and Mosalsk. In early October his corps captured Vyazma and closed the pocket around Soviet units in the area but during the following days had to defend itself against strong attacks. In late November the temperature dropped below minus 35 degrees, causing high levels of frostbite among the Germans, while the Soviets had been fully equipped with warm clothing since mid-November. From 10 May 1942 Kurowski was Chief of the General Staff of the 2nd Panzer Army and on 1 June was promoted to *Generalmajor*. He saw action during the defensive fighting in the area north-east of Orel and later in the defensive fighting in the area of Army Group Centre. He entered the Reserves from April 1943

Eberhard von Kurowski entered Army service as an officer candidate with Foot Guards Regiment 1 in August 1914 and was commissioned as a *Leutnant* in October the following year. He was awarded both classes of the Iron Cross, was wounded six times during the war and was awarded the Wound Badge in Gold. He remained in the Army after the war, serving mainly with Infantry Regiment 9, and from October 1935, now with the rank of *Major*, he served on the General Staff of X. Army Corps. He served as Chief of Operations on the General Staff of the 21st Infantry Division from November 1937 and at the beginning of the Second World War he was serving as an *Oberstleutnant* and Chief of Operations on the General Staff of the XXI. Army Corps under General der Infanterie Nikolaus von Falkenhorst, seeing action in Poland.

and returned as Commander of the 110th Infantry Division on 1 June 1943 with the rank of *Generalleutnant*. He saw action in the Soviet Union as part of the LV. Army Corps near Zhizdra and from September to April 1944 he saw action during trench warfare in the Rahachow area and later during the retreat via Bobruisk and Mogilev. Later his division fought in the area around Pronya, then east of Orscha and was later deployed near Gorky, taking part in defensive battles. He later moved west across the Dnieper River with his division where it was almost decimated in the Minsk Pocket. On 12 July 1944 he and most of his command was captured by the Soviets, and remained as a prisoner until his release on 6 October 1955.

Hermann SCHULTE-HEUTHAUS

Generalmajor

* 15 January 1898, Klein-Weissensee
+ 26 December 1979, Berlin

Knight's Cross: Awarded on 23 January 1942 as *Oberstleutnant* and Commander of Motorcycle Infantry Battalion 25 while attached to 25th Infantry Division for actions on the Central Sector of the Russian Front. From 24 March until 14 September 1942 he served as Adjutant on the General Staff of Panzer Army *Afrika* under the command of *Generalfeldmarschall* Erwin Rommel and in April that year was promoted to *Oberst*. From February 1943 he served briefly as Adjutant of Army Group Afrika, and after five weeks with the Reserves he attended Panzer School I from May 1943. In July he was appointed Commander of Fusilier Regiment *Grossdeutschland* and in September he was seriously wounded and had to have his right arm amputated. He returned to active duty with Replacement Brigade

Hermann Schulte-Heuthaus entered the Replacement Battalion of Grenadier regiment 4 in October 1914 and later served as ordnance officer, battalion and regimental adjutant with the rank of *Leutnant*. He left the Army in 1919 and entered civilian life, returning in September 1934 with the rank of *Hauptmann*. He was appointed company commander of various units and from August 1939 he was assigned to the Infantry School in Potsdam with the rank of *Major*. From February 1940 he served in France as Commander of I. Battalion with Infantry Regiment 1 until he was wounded on 26 May 1940.

Grossdeutschland in March 1944. From 16 October he was delegated with the leadership of Panzer Grenadier Division *Brandenburg*, seeing action on the Eastern Front, and in March 1945 his command was confirmed when he was promoted to *Generalmajor*. He saw action in Hungary, the Protectorate and Silesia and ended the war at battle group strength with the 4th Panzer Army. Most of the division surrendered to the Soviets, except for a small group including Schulte-Heuthaus who managed to surrender to the Americans.

Martin STRAHAMMER

Generalmajor

* 13 November 1890, Gösting, Austro-Hungary
+ 2 May 1945, Viadana di Calvisano, Italy

Knight's Cross: Awarded on 30 January 1942 as *Oberstleutnant* and Commander of Panzer *Jäger* Battalion 20, part of the 170th Infantry Division, for his bravery and actions in the Soviet Union. On 22 January he was leading a battle group near Sudak on the south coast of the Crimea against superior forces and managed to crush all resistance in the area. On 1 April 1942 he was promoted to *Oberst* and from September he led Infantry Regiment 266 and took part in the winter fighting during the withdrawal near Rzhev and in the Battle of Kursk. From May 1943 he took command of Grenadier Regiment 146, part of the 65th Infantry Division, seeing action in Antwerp until August, when his command was sent to Italy.

Martin Strahammer entered Austrian Infantry Regiment 24 in 1912 and three years later he served as company leader, carrying on throughout the war and rising to the rank of *Oberleutnant* in 1918. He served with the Army after the war and in March 1938 he transferred into the German Army and was Commander of Anti-tank Battalion 240 from November 1939 with the rank of *Oberstleutnant*. He later served with the 170th Infantry Division while attached to a Panzer Battalion, seeing action in Denmark and France.

Knight's Cross with Oakleaves: He became the 545th recipient on 11 August 1944 as *Oberst* and Commander of Grenadier Regiment 146 while attached to 65th Infantry Division for his part in the defensive fighting at the beachhead in Nettuno in Italy. He also took part in the withdrawals north of Rome, where he fought with great courage and outstanding leadership.

Strahammer was personally decorated with the Oakleaves on 7 November 1944 by *SS-Reichsführer* Heinrich Himmler in Posen. From early January 1945 he was delegated with the deputy leadership of the 98th Infantry Division and from February he took command of the 114th *Jäger* Division, seeing action in the Battle of Bologna. He was promoted to *Generalmajor* in April when his command was confirmed, and although his command fought well it was down to only 984 soldiers – less than two battalions in strength. In late April his command surrendered to the Americans but on 2 May Strahammer was shot near Brescia in Italy while trying to escape.

Karl Richard Albert BRITZELMAYR

Generalmajor

* 26 May 1894, Passau, Lower Bavaria
+ 9 March 1968, Landshut, Bavaria

Knight's Cross: Awarded on 2 February 1942 as *Oberstleutnant* and Commander of Infantry Regiment 217 while attached to the 57th Infantry Division during the invasion of the Soviet Union. On 22 January 1942 Britzelmayr and his regiment captured the village of Solntsevo near Kursk following a tough battle, in temperatures of minus 35 degrees. When the attack threatened to bog down the street fighting, he placed himself at the head of his troops, which inspired them and they succeeded in defeating the enemy forces. The capture of Solntsevo enabled the southern wing of the 2nd Army to make successful attacks and close gaps in which the enemy was pouring its forces and eliminate the threat. In June Britzelmayr was promoted to *Oberst* and continued to see

Karl Britzelmayr entered Army service in August 1913 as an officer candidate and at the beginning of the war he was a senior non-commissioned officer with Bavarian Infantry Regiment 16. He was severely wounded later that month and in October he was commissioned as a *Leutnant*. Shortly after he was awarded the Iron Cross 2nd Class. By the end of the war he had been promoted to *Oberleutnant* and had been awarded the Iron Cross 1st Class. He retired from active service in June 1919 and entered civilian life. He joined the Army again in October 1935, and saw action in Poland as Commander of III. Battalion of Infantry Regiment 179 with the rank of *Major*.

action in the Soviet Union, being delegated with the temporary leadership of the 57th Infantry Division from mid-December 1942. Returning to his old command in January 1943, he continued to see action in the Soviet Union and was awarded the German Cross in Gold on 9 June. From September he was attached to a company leaders' course in Sissonne, and the following month he became Commander of the Company Leaders' School. From May 1944 he attended the 11th Divisional Leaders Course and from September was delegated with the leadership of the 347th Security Division. Promoted to *Generalmajor*, he took command of the 19th *Volksgrenadier* Division and in December he led his troops during heavy fighting on the Saar front. In early February 1945 US troops launched an attack against the already weakened defences of his division, but his troops managed to hold their positions in front of the West Wall. By 24 March he had under his command just 400 men and two days later the division was disbanded. He surrendered to US troops on 30 April and remained in Allied captivity until June 1947.

Alfred KUZMANY

Generalmajor

* 24 October 1893, Dorna-Watra, Bukowina, Austro-Hungary
+ 4 October 1961, Vienna, Austria

Knight's Cross: Awarded on 2 February 1942 as *Oberstleutnant* and Commander of Infantry Regiment 338 while attached to the 208th Infantry Division for his actions near Orel. Promoted to *Oberst* shortly after being informed of his award, he continued to see action on the Russian Front until April 1942 when he was transferred to the Reserves, where he remained for the next two months. In June he was named Commandant of Ulm

Alfred Kuzmany entered the Austrian Army with Infantry Regiment 5 in October 1913 as a *Leutnant* and was severely wounded in the Carpathians in February 1915. In July 1916 he returned to duty as a platoon and then company commander with the rank of *Oberleutnant*, staying in the Army after the war. In March 1938 he transferred into the German Army with the rank of *Major* and was assigned to Infantry Regiment 134 as Second Personnel Officer to the General Commanding XVIII. Army Corps. Promoted to *Oberstleutnant* in June 1939, he was assigned as Commander of the III. Battalion of Infantry Regiment 484.

and was promoted to *Generalmajor* on 30 January 1945, remaining in Ulm until the end of March. He was then named as Commandant of Linz in Austria, where he surrendered to US troops in June 1945. He remained in captivity until his release on 17 April 1947.

Alexander MÖCKEL

Generalmajor

* 25 March 1896, Giessen, Hesse
+ 24 March 1945, Graben-Neudorf, Baden

Knight's Cross: Awarded on 6 February 1942 as *Oberstleutnant* and Commander of Infantry Regiment 517 while attached to 295th Infantry Division for actions in the Dnieper area in the Soviet Union. Later he took part in the encirclement at Uman and fought across the Ukraine and Donets, only to be turned back by the Soviet winter. He was promoted to *Oberst* on 1 January 1943 and from March was Commander of Grenadier Regiment 517 while attached to the 295th Infantry Division. Möckel was due to be flown out from Stalingrad, because of typhus, but became involved from 31 March 1943 in the organisation of the new 295th Infantry Division, which had been destroyed at Stalingrad. When the new division was formed it served in northern Norway, where Möckel stayed until October 1944 when he attended the 15th Divisional Leaders Course. From 29 December he was delegated with the leadership of the newly formed 16th *Volksgrenadier* Division, which had been decimated by the US 7th Army in France. He was promoted to *Generalmajor* in March 1945 and appointed Commander of his division, where he saw action in southern Alsace. Möckel was killed on 24 March when his headquarters was bombed.

Alexander Möckel joined the Army in August 1914 as a war volunteer and fought with Infantry Regiment 116 as a company leader as a *Leutnant*. After the war he entered the Hessian Protection Police and from August 1934 he served with the Army as *Hauptmann* and Commander of the 3rd Company of Infantry Regiment 15 in Kassel. He later took command of the 11th Company with Infantry Regiment 82 and from March 1939 he served as tactics instructor at the War School in Hannover.

Maximilian de ANGELIS

General der Artillerie

* 2 October 1889 in Budapest, Hungary
+ 6 December 1974 in Graz, Austria

Maximilian de Angelis joined the Austrian Army in August 1910 as a twenty-year-old *Leutnant*. During the First World War he was an *Oberleutnant* with Field Cannon Regiment 42, serving with distinction in Galicia and Southern Poland. He ended the war in an Italian prison with the rank of *Hauptmann*, and stayed in the Army after the war, joining the Austrian Army. Promoted to *Major* on 1 January 1921, five years later he became a General Staff officer with the 3rd Brigade Command in St Pölten.

Knight's Cross: Awarded on 9 February 1942 as *Generalleutnant* and Commander of the 76th Infantry Division, part of the XXXIV. Army Corps, for his part in the prevention of the Soviet breakthrough near Artemovsk in Ukraine on 18 January 1942. A week later Angelis took over as Commander of the XXXXIV. Army Corps and was promoted to *General der Artillerie* on 1 March. He briefly took command of the reformed 6th Army while *Generaloberst* Karl-Adolf Hollidt was on leave. At this time he took part in the fierce fighting in the Western Caucasus area.

On 1 September 1939, the day Germany invaded Poland, Angelis was appointed Commander of the 76th Infantry Division and was assigned to the area south of Bad Kreuznach, Germany. From December his division was relocated to the Trier area. At the beginning of the Western Campaign in May 1940 he led his division during the fighting through Luxembourg and into France. He led his forces into the area south-east of Sedan and into northern France, where they saw heavy action, and during the second phase of the campaign his division fought on the west bank of the Meuse and into Verdun.

Knight's Cross with Oakleaves: He became the 323rd recipient of the Oakleaves on 12 November 1943 as *General der Artillerie* and Commanding General of the XXXXIV. Army Corps. It was awarded in recognition of his relentless pursuit of the enemy as far as the Western Caucasus and for his role in holding the Kuban Bridgehead despite facing larger and stronger enemy forces. He was personally presented with the Oakleaves by Hitler at his headquarters the Wolf's Lair in Rastenburg, East Prussia, on 15 December 1943. Later that month his command became part of the 17th Army and he saw action near the River Dnieper before handing his command over to *Generalleutnant* Friedrich Köchling in April 1944. In July he took command of the 2nd Panzer Army, and took part in the defence of Belgrade, which included the battles around the Danube and Dran Rivers, during the withdrawal from the Dalmatian coastal area. From early 1945 he took part in the defence and then retreat from Kärnten and Steiermark in southern Austria. He surrendered to US troops in May 1945, and in April 1946 was handed over to Yugoslavian authorities, who sentenced him to twenty years' imprisonment. Then in March 1949 he was sent to the Soviet Union, who tried and sentenced him twice to twenty-five years' imprisonment. However, he was released on 11 October 1955 following a general amnesty.

Adolf SINZINGER

Generalleutnant

* 29 January 1891, Suben, Austro-Hungary
\+ 15 June 1974, Wels, Austria

Knight's Cross: Awarded on 9 February 1942 as *Oberst* and Commander of Infantry Regiment 257 while attached to 83rd Infantry Division for his bravery and leadership during the defence of the Soviet town of Velizh in Smolensk. From 17 February he took over the leadership of the 83rd Infantry Division and took part in the defensive battles as part of Army Group Centre. His command was confirmed

Adolf Sinzinger joined the Austrian Army in August 1910 as a cadet and was commissioned as a *Leutnant* from May 1913. He saw action during the First World War, was wounded in December 1914 and promoted to *Oberleutnant* the following year. He remained in the Army after the war and by 1936 had been promoted to the rank of *Oberst*. Two years later he entered the German armed forces and was assigned to the staff of Infantry Regiment 89.

in April, when he was promoted to *Generalmajor*. From mid-December he took command of the 377th Infantry Division, which had been decimated during the fighting in Stalingrad, and in January 1943 Sinzinger was promoted to *Generalleutnant*. After a period in the Reserves he was appointed Commandant of Vienna on 15 March 1944. He was part of the conspiracy against Hitler in July 1944 and was arrested on 29 July and taken into custody, where he remained until he was freed by US troops on 31 January 1945.

Paul Franz Heinrich DANHAUSER
Generalleutnant

+ 2 August 1892, Regensburg, Bavaria
+ 11 December 1974, Landshut, Bavaria

Knight's Cross: Awarded on 10 February 1942 as *Oberst* and Commander of Infantry Regiment 427 while attached to the 129th Infantry Division for his bravery and outstanding leadership qualities while fighting in the Soviet Union. He and his regiment had acquitted themselves very well while fighting in the combat area of Smolensk and Vyazma along the Dnieper River area. On 7 January 1942 his regiment had been sent south, where his command created a bridgehead as far as the Osuga railroad. Here Danhauser repulsed a major Soviet attack and was finally awarded the Knight's Cross. He was delegated with the leadership of the 256th Infantry Division just after receiving the award and in April he was promoted to *Generalmajor*, with his command of the division confirmed in August. He saw action with his division in Smolensk while attached to the 9th Army until he was transferred to the Reserves for a rest. Promoted

Danhauser entered the Army in July 1911 with Bavarian Infantry Regiment 15 and attended the War School in Munich from October 1912. He was commissioned as a *Leutnant* the following year and served with the Bavarian Brigade Replacement Battalion at the beginning of the First World War. Promoted to *Oberleutnant* in January 1917, he served as an adjutant before leading the I. Battalion of Bavarian Replacement Regiment 1 from September 1918. He was awarded both classes of the Iron Cross during the war and remained in the army after the war, entering the *Wehrmacht* in 1935 with the rank of *Major* with the War Ministry.

to *Generalleutnant* in March 1943, he was appointed Commander of the 271st Infantry Division in December that year as part of the LXXXVIII. Army Corps in the Netherlands. From October 1944 he was temporary Commander of Military District XII, with his headquarters in Wiesbaden. At the end of the war he was taken into custody by the Americans and remained in captivity until his release in June 1947.

Hans Oskar Karl HAHNE

Generalmajor

* 30 November 1894, Berlin
+ 24 June 1944 near Vitebsk, Soviet Union

Knight's Cross: Awarded on 10 February 1942 as *Oberst* and Commander of Infantry Regiment 507 while attached to the 292nd Infantry Division during the Soviet winter offensive and the drive towards Moscow. Hahne was personally presented with the award by Infantry Division Commander *Generalleutnant* Willy Seeger. He saw action during the defensive actions of 1942, which included the Rzhev withdrawal and the Battle of Kursk, where his regiment and the division sustained heavy casualties. He entered the Reserves in January 1944 and from 14 March was delcgated with the leadership of the 197th Infantry Division and took part in very heavy action during the summer of 1944. The division broke up in July 1944 and Hahne was reported as missing in action near Vitebsk. His body has never been discovered.

Hans Hahne entered Army service as a war volunteer in August 1914 and was appointed an officer candidate in May 1915. He served as an adjutant with Reserve Infantry Regiment 209 from May 1915 as a *Leutnant der Reserve* and was acting regimental adjutant from September 1918. He rejoined the Army after the war and served as an orderly officer, adjutant and from 1927 he was a welfare officer with Infantry Regiment 9. Promoted to *Major* in October 1935, he served as an instructor at the War School in Hannover, and was Commander of the II. Battalion of Infantry Regiment 371.

Günther PAPE

Generalmajor

* 14 July 1907, Düsseldorf
+ 21 January 1986, Düsseldorf

Knight's Cross: Awarded on 10 February 1942 as *Major* and Commander of the III. Motorcycle Infantry Battalion while attached to 3rd Panzer Division for his outstanding bravery while fighting on the Russian Front. On 30 January 1942 his battle group stormed a village before his tanks had arrived, inflicting heavy losses on the Soviets and capturing their commander. From August he was Commander of Panzer Grenadier Regiment 394 while still attached to the 3rd Panzer Division and took part in the campaign in the Caucasus. He was promoted to *Oberstleutnant* on 30 September 1942.

Günther Pape entered a training squadron with Mounted Regiment 15 in Paderborn from April 1927 and was commissioned as a *Leutnant* in February 1932. In October 1934 he served with the II. Battalion of Mounted regiment 16 in Eisenach and was Adjutant of the III. Motorcycle Battalion from October 1935. In September 1941 he was promoted to *Major* and named Commander of the III. Motorcycle Battalion with the 3rd Panzer Division, seeing action in the Soviet Union.

Knight's Cross with Oakleaves: He became the 301st recipient on 15 September 1943 as *Oberst* and Commander of Panzer Grenadier Regiment 394 while attached to the 3rd Panzer Division for his achievements during the heavy fighting near Belgorod in the Soviet Union and was wounded on 5 July, the first day of Operation Citadel. He was presented with the Oakleaves personally by Hitler at his Military Headquarters, the Wolf's Lair in Rastenburg. From October 1943 he was head of the Regimental leaders training course at the Panzer School in Bergen and from August the following year he attended the 13th Divisional Leaders Course at Hirschberg. From 4 September he was delegated with the leadership of Panzer Grenadier Division *Feldherrnhalle* and saw action in Hungary. From December his command was renamed Panzer Division *Feldherrnhalle* and Pape was promoted to *Generalmajor* at the same time. His command was almost destroyed during the fighting in Budapest and during the last months of the war saw action in Brno, Czechoslovakia, where he surrendered to US troops on 9 May 1945. He was released from Allied captivity on 13 May 1947 and joined the ranks of the *Bundeswehr*, rising to the rank of *Brigadegeneral*.

Wolfgang Julius Max Richard Hermann THOMALE

Generalleutnant

* 25 February 1900, Lissa, Posen
+ 20 October 1978, Peine, Lower Saxony

Knight's Cross: Awarded on 10 February 1942 as *Oberstleutnant* and Commander of Panzer Regiment 27 while attached to the 19th Panzer Division for actions during the fighting at Bialystok, Minsk and Smolensk encirclements. Promoted to *Oberst* in March 1942, he transferred to the Staff of the Chief of Armaments and Commander of the Reserve Army, *Generaloberst* Friedrich Fromm. From March 1943 Thomale served as Chief of Staff to the Inspector of Panzer Troops *Generaloberst* Heinz Guderian, and was promoted to *Generalmajor* in February 1944. From July he acted as Inspector General of the *Wehrmacht* and, although he had knowledge of the plot against Hitler, he was never charged with anything and remained Chief of Staff with the Inspector of Panzer Troops until the end of the war. Promoted to *Generalleutnant* in March 1945, he surrendered to US troops in May 1945 and was a prisoner of war at Camp Ritchie in Maryland in the United States until his release on 15 November 1946.

Wolfgang Thomale entered the Army with Guard Grenadier Regiment 5 in March 1918 and was commissioned as a *Leutnant* in October 1919. He later served with Motor Detachment 3 and later with 6 in Hannover. From October 1934 was attached to the 1st Panzer Regiment in Zossen. He was promoted to *Major* in 1937 and served as adjutant of the 3rd Panzer Brigade in Berlin until May 1938, when he served as Group Leader in the Weapons Department of Panzer Troops, Cavalry and Army Motorization in the General Army Office in Berlin.

Wend Hans Georg Herbert Egmont Christoph von WIETERSHEIM

Generalleutnant

* 8 April 1900, Neuland, Löwenburg
+ 19 September 1975, Bad Honnef, North-Rhine Westphalia

Knight's Cross: Awarded on 10 February 1942 as *Oberstleutnant* and Commander of Rifle Regiment 113 while attached to the 1st Panzer Division in recognition of his command's defensive fighting at Kaliningrad in the Soviet Union on the

Wend von Witersheim entered the Army as an officer candidate in August 1918 and was assigned to Hussar Regiment 4. He was commissioned as a *Leutnant* in September 1919 and was assigned to the 2nd Company of Mounted Regiment 12 from October 1923, being promoted to *Oberleutnant* four years later. In January 1934 he was appointed Commander of the 3rd Company with Mounted Regiment 4 in Potsdam and was promoted to *Rittmeister*, and four months later he took command of the 1st Company of Motor Vehicle Battalion 3 in Wünsdorf. In October 1937 he was appointed adjutant on the staff of the 3rd Panzer Division and was promoted to *Major* in December 1938.

night of 19–20 October 1941. A Soviet breakthrough would have resulted in the recapture of an important railway bridge over the Volga and Wietersheim had personally gathered together reserve forces and led them in the counter-attack. He was promoted to *Oberst* on 20 April 1942 and continued to lead his regiment during the fierce fighting on the Eastern Front.

Knight's Cross with Oakleaves: He became the 176th recipient on 12 January 1943 as *Oberst* and Commander of Panzer Grenadier Regiment 113 while still part of the 1st Panzer Division and once again led an important counter-attack with a battle group at the end of November 1942. The Oakleaves were personally presented to him by Hitler at *Führer* Headquarters in Rastenburg together with *Oberst* Maximilian von Edelsheim. On 10 August 1943 Wietersheim was named as the Commander of the 11th Panzer Division and took part in the successful defensive fighting in the mid-Dnieper region. He was promoted to *Generalmajor* in November and saw action at Cherkassy from February 1944.

Knight's Cross with Oakleaves and Swords: Awarded on 26 March 1944 to become the 58th recipient as *Generalmajor* and Commander of 11th Panzer Division, part of the XXXXVII. Panzer Corps, for his outstanding leadership during the battles on the southern sector of the Eastern Front from late 1943 to early 1944. He was presented with the Swords by Hitler at the Berghof on the Obersalzburg together with twelve other officers, including Generals Erich Brandenberger, Friedrich Mieth, Helmuth Weidling and Werner Frost. His unit suffered heavy losses and was moved to southern France for refitting, being stationed at Toulouse for a time. In July his unit conducted delaying operations up the Rhône Valley against Allied forces that had landed in southern France. He was promoted to *Generalleutnant* in July, saw action in Alsace, took part in the defence of the Belfort Gap and later saw action in the Ardennes. In October 1944 his command tried to overrun the US bridgehead at Remagen with only 4,000 men, twenty-five tanks and eighteen pieces of artillery, but by then he was in command of one of the strongest panzer divisions left on the Western Front. Later his unit was transferred to Army Group G on the southern sector of the front in March 1945 and escaped the encirclement in the Ruhr Pocket. His division distinguished itself in many battles and finally surrendered to the US 90th Infantry Division on 5 May near Wallern, Bavaria.

Heinrich Friedrich WIESE

General der Infanterie

* 5 December 1892, Nordhastedt, Schleswig-Holstein
+ 11 February 1975, Giessen, Hesse

Friedrich Wiese entered the Army in August 1914 as a war volunteer and with his training complete he was assigned to Infantry Regiment 84. He was commissioned as a *Leutnant* in November 1915 and later served as a company officer with Machine-Gun Company 3. He was awarded both classes of the Iron Cross. When the war ended he joined the police, rising to the rank of *Polizei-Major.* He rejoined the Army in October 1935 and was assigned to Infantry Regiment 69 in Hamburg.

Knight's Cross: Awarded on 14 February 1942 as *Oberst* and Commander of Infantry Regiment 39 while attached to the 26th Infantry Division for actions on the Russian Front. On the morning of 2 January 1942 Soviet forces made several failed frontal attacks against Wiese and his regiment and finally infiltrated his forces through wooded and swampy terrain that had been considered impassable. The situation seemed hopeless for Wiese and his troops since there were no telephone connections and the German radios had failed because of the bitter cold. Wiese ordered an immediate breakout of the encirclement and through his skills as a commander and the bravery of his men he was responsible for this being a success, thus saving his troops from total destruction. On 11 April he was appointed Commander of the 26th Infantry Division, seeing action on the central sector of the Russian Front, where in September he was promoted to *Generalmajor*. He was promoted to *Generalleutnant* on 21 January 1943, and later fought during the beginning of the Battle of Kursk. From August he took command of the

Wiese was promoted to *Oberstleutnant* in June 1938, serving as Commander of the I. Battalion with Infantry Regiment 116, and he saw action on the Western Front, where he was awarded the Bar to the Iron Cross 1st and 2nd Classes.

XXXV. Army Corps in the area south of Bryansk and was promoted to *General der Infanterie* on 1 October 1943.

Knight's Cross with Oakleaves: He became the 372nd recipient on 24 January 1944 as *General der Infanterie* and Commanding General of the XXXV. Army Corps as part of the 9th Army for his leadership skills, once more on the Eastern Front. He particularly distinguished himself during the evacuation of the Gomel Bridgehead against overwhelming odds and his defeat of all Soviet breakthrough attempts during December 1943 in the area south-west of Zhlobin. He was decorated with the Oakleaves by Hitler at his Military Headquarters in Rastenburg on 13 February 1944. From June 1944 he was delegated with the leadership of the 19th Army in south-eastern France and from late 1944 he saw action in the Rhône Valley and into Alsace-Lorraine. On 19 March 1945 he was appointed Commander of the VIII. Army Corps and fought against Soviet forces in Warsaw as part of the 9th Army. They later pushed through towards Silesia, where on 8 May he surrendered his command to US troops. He was released from captivity on 26 June 1947.

Hermann Carl Albert HARRENDORF
Generalmajor

* 18 May 1896, Altona, Schleswig-Holstein
+ 27 March 1966, Hamburg

In June 1915 Hermann Harrendorf entered Army service as a war volunteer with Infantry Regiment 31 and served as a platoon and company leader. He rejoined the Army in October 1933 with Infantry Regiment 6 with the rank of *Leutnant der Reserve* and later trained as a platoon leader. He served with Infantry Regiment 469 in France and Belgium from June 1940 with the rank of *Hauptmann der Reserve*, and was awarded the Bar to the Iron Cross 2nd Class in May 1940.

Knight's Cross: Awarded on 16 February 1942 as *Hauptmann der Reserve* and Commander of the III. Battalion of Infantry Regiment 469 of the 269th Infantry Division for his part in the Battle of the Volkhov, south-east of Leningrad. At the beginning of the winter of 1942 his regiment, together with the whole division, was sent to Norway for rest and refit while remaining there on occupation duty. Harrendorf, however, was transferred to be the Training Director of a *Luftwaffe* Field Division from 18 December 1942, and from the end of March 1943 he attended a Regimental Leaders' Course in Döberitz. Promoted to *Major* in July 1943, he was delegated with the leadership of Fusilier Regiment 334 and he took over as Commander on 1 September with the rank of *Oberstleutnant.* He served on occupation duty in Trondheim, Norway, and was then transferred to the lower Adriatic coast of Montenegro in Yugoslavia. Later he served in the Balkans area, where the division suffered heavy losses in the withdrawal from Montenegro to Sarajevo. In April 1944 Harrendorf was promoted to *Oberst* and attended the 15th Divisional Leaders Course from October that year. In December he was delegated with the leadership of the 96th Infantry Division and was fighting Soviet troops in Slovakia. On 30 January 1945 he was promoted to *Generalmajor* and his command was confirmed while seeing heavy fighting in the Hungarian campaign. He took part in the heavy fighting near Vienna until the war ended. He surrendered to western forces and remained in captivity until his release on 14 May 1948, being fortunate not to be handed over to the Soviets.

Philipp KLEFFEL
General der Kavallerie

* 9 December 1887, Birkenfelde, Posen
+ 10 October 1964, Coburg, Bavaria

Knight's Cross: Awarded on 17 February 1942 as *Generalleutnant* and Commander of the 1st Infantry Division, attached to the XXVIII. Army Corps, for actions on the Russian Front. From the beginning of the Soviet campaign from June 1941, Kleffel led his division during the heavy battles into the Baltic States during the drive on Leningrad. By October his command had been reduced by two thirds but he continued to see action on the northern sector of the Soviet Front, primarily as part of the 18th Army. For his success and leadership he was personally presented with the Knight's Cross by *General der Kavallerie* Georg Lindemann, Commander of the 18th Army. He was named as the Commanding General of the L. Army Corps in January 1942 and in March was promoted to *General der Kavallerie*, seeing action during the Siege of Leningrad. He was transferred to the *Führer* Reserve in September 1943 and reported sick until January 1944, when he returned to active duty. From 15 January he took over as Acting Commanding General of the Replacement XI. Army Corps and Commander of Military District XI in Kassel. From April he was attached to the Special Staff I of the Army High Command, and from July he was named as Commanding General of General Command *Kleffel*, seeing service in the Netherlands. He remained in Holland until the end of the war, serving briefly as Commanding General of the XXX. Army Corps from December 1944 until April 1945. At the same time he was delegated with

Philipp Kleffel entered the Army as an officer candidate in November 1905 and was commissioned as a *Leutnant* in May 1907. He served as regimental adjutant of Ulanen Regiment 4 at the beginning of the First World War and later served with the Cavalry before becoming a General Staff Officer in April 1917. He remained in the Army after the war and served as Chief of Operations on the Staff of the Inspector of Cavalry and on the staff of the Infantry Leader in Potsdam. In October 1935 he was promoted to *Oberst* and the following year he was serving as Commander of Mounted Regiment 14 in Ludwigslust, and in 1938 served as Higher Cavalry Officer 4. From August 1939 he was Chief of the General Staff of the Replacement IX. Army Corps with the rank of *Generalmajor*, and from April 1940 he took command of the 1st Infantry Division and saw action during the invasion of Belgium.

the temporary leadership of the 25th Army and saw defensive action against approaching Allied forces. He surrendered as part of the General Staff of the Commander-in-Chief Netherlands under *Generaloberst* Johannes Blaskowitz to Lieutenant General Charles Foulkes of the I. Canadian Corps at Wageningen on 6 May 1945.

Rudolf Ernst Philipp August Joachim *Freiherr* von ROMAN

General der Artillerie

* 19 November 1893, Bayreuth, Bavaria
+ 18 February 1970, Schernau-Dettelbach, Bavaria

Rudolf von Roman served with the 6th Royal Bavarian Field Artillery Regiment as an *Oberleutnant* during the First World War where he was awarded the Iron Cross 1st and 2nd Classes. He later served as an adjutant in the *Reichswehr* after the war and was promoted to *Hauptmann* in June 1924. From April 1931 he served with Artillery Leader VII in Munich. From October 1935 he was Commander of the II. Battalion of Artillery Regiment 53 and from August 1939 he was Commander of Artillery Regiment 10. As an *Oberst*, he saw action during the invasion of Poland, where he was awarded the Bar to the Iron Cross 1st and 2nd Classes.

Knight's Cross: Awarded on 19 February 1942 as *Generalmajor* and Commander of 35th Infantry Division, part of the V. Army Corps, for actions on the Russian Front. He saw heavy action from mid-December 1941 against strong Soviet forces, who attacked his position during the advance on Moscow with ten tanks. Under his leadership, the Germans repelled the attack. His forces destroyed five tanks, and his stand against the Soviet forces gave the V. Army Corps the victory they needed. After the German breakthrough near Volokolamsk, Roman and his division pushed forward towards the Moscow–Volga Canal, north-west of the Soviet capital, and he was awarded the German Cross in Gold.

Knight's Cross with Oakleaves: He became the 313th recipient on 28 October 1943 as *General der Artillerie* and Commanding General of XX. Army Corps while attached to the 2nd Army for his distinguished command during the heavy defensive battles around Gomel in September. He was presented with the Oakleaves by Hitler at the Wolf's Lair in Rastenburg in early November.

At the beginning of September, Roman was promoted to *Generalleutnant* and shortly after was delegated with the leadership of the XX. Army Corps. By November he had been promoted to *General der Artillerie* and his command was confirmed. From May until December 1944 he fought along the Bug River area and into East Prussia, finally seeing his last action in the Heiligenbeil Pocket in March 1945. In April he went on leave, and was then supposed to have taken over the command of the XIV. Army Corps but this was never confirmed. The following month he was captured by US forces and remained in Allied captivity until June 1947, when he returned home to Bavaria.

Theodor SCHERER

Generalleutnant

* 17 September 1889, Höchstädt, Bavaria
+ 17 May 1951, Ludwigsburg, Württemberg

Knight's Cross: Awarded on 20 February 1942 as *Generalmajor* and Commander of 281st Security Division while attached to the XXXIX. Army Corps for his outstanding leadership during the Battle of Kholm. In January 1942 he had just 5,000 troops and was surrounded by the Soviets, however his troops possessed no anti-tank guns and the Soviet artillery bombardments had destroyed most of the houses, leaving the Germans without adequate shelter in the bitter cold. The Soviet snipers would pick off German troops on a regular basis, however Soviet tactics never changed and soon Scherer was able to predict where and when an attack would happen. Crucially, the Germans were able to radio for supporting artillery fire from outside the pocket, and as Scherer's forces were basically in a fortress they managed to hold the town for more than one hundred days. As the Soviets advanced through the narrow streets in their tanks the Germans laid traps and destroyed many of them.

Theodor Scherer entered the Royal Bavarian Infantry Regiment 12 in July 1908 and then attended the War School and was commissioned as a *Leutnant* in October 1910. He saw action during the First World War with a machine gun company and was later appointed platoon leader with the rank of *Oberleutnant*. From July 1916 he was a prisoner of war when he was captured by British troops and spent the remainder of the conflict in Holland. He then joined the Bavarian State Police from October 1920, rising to the rank of *Major* in July 1932, and later served in the Eichstädt Police School.

From October 1935 Scherer served with the German Army, rising to the rank of *Oberst* in January 1937 as Battalion Commander with Infantry Regiment 111 in Baden-Baden. In April 1938 he was appointed Commander of Infantry Regiment 56 with the rank of *Oberst* and served in France, where in June 1940 he was awarded both classes of the Bar to the Iron Cross.

Knight's Cross with Oakleaves: He became the 92nd recipient on 5 May 1942 as *Generalmajor* and Commander of the 281st Security Division as part of the 16th Army for his leadership of the defenders of Kholm. The fighting continued in Kholm for almost two more weeks and they were supported by a massive artillery barrage and Stuka dive-bombers until finally a relief force broke through. The relief force found Scherer at his makeshift headquarters in the town with only 1,200 men still fit for action. They had held the town for 107 days and had launched 2,000 individual assaults against Soviet positions. Scherer was decorated with the Oakleaves on 17 May by Hitler at his headquarters in Rastenburg. On 5 September Scherer took command of the 34th Infantry Division and saw brief action in the Soviet Union. Promoted to *Generalleutnant* on 1 November, the following day he was named as Commander of the 83rd Infantry Division and saw action in the Soviet Union as part of Army Group Centre. A few days after he took command the city of Velikiye Luki was encircled by Soviet forces and 7,500 men were trapped. The LIX. Army Corps was unable to mount a rescue and the 8th Panzer Division was ordered to break through but failed. Further attempts were made by Scherer's own forces, which fought for four long weeks until finally a battle group broke through and the pocket fell on 16 January 1943. Only a few hundred German soldiers escaped and Scherer was one of them. After time in the Reserves he was appointed Inspector of Coastal Protection and made *Wehrmacht* Commander *Ostland* under the command of *General der Panzertruppe* Werner Kempf in April 1944. In early 1945 he was appointed Commander of Battle Group Schere in the Posen area and from early April he was made responsible for the defence of the Elster River area. He was later put in charge of the southern sector of the Elbe under *General der Panzertruppe* Maximilian Reichsfreiherr von Edelsheim. He surrendered to Allies in May 1945 and was kept in Allied captivity until 17 May 1951.

Otto KOHLERMANN

Generalleutnant

* 17 February 1896, Magdeburg
\+ 27 February 1984, Augsburg

Knight's Cross: Awarded on 22 February 1942 as *Oberst* and Artillery Commander 129 for actions on the Russian Front. From early May he was delegated with the leadership of the 60th Motorised Infantry Division, saw action in Kharkov and took part in the battles on the Don. On 1 July Kohlermann was promoted to *Generalmajor* and took over the division as its official commander, taking charge in the drive to the Volga and in the Stalingrad street fighting. Kohlermann managed to get out before the division surrendered to the Soviets in February 1943 and helped to create a second 60th Motorised Infantry Division in France. It was officially activated in March and received the honorary title of

Otto Kohlermann entered the Army in July 1914 as an officer candidate with Field Artillery Regiment 66 and served in the war as a platoon leader and later as a battery commander. He was awarded the Iron Cross 1st and 2nd Classes and ended the war with the rank of *Oberleutnant*, remaining in the Army after the war. By October 1934 he was Commander of the II. Battalion of Artillery Regiment 5 and was promoted to *Major* the following year. When the war began in September 1939 he was the Commander of Experimental Battalion within the Artillery School and was promoted to *Oberst* in September 1940. In December he was appointed Artillery Commander 10 and saw action during the invasion of the Soviet Union.

Feldherrnhalle because it contained a high number of SA Brownshirt volunteers. It was redesignated a Panzer Grenadier Division in May and Kohlermann was promoted to *Generalleutnant* in July 1943. In August it was sent to southern France during the period of vacillation of the post-Mussolini Italian government, while the Italian 4th Army evacuated the area and returned home. Towards the end of 1943 Kohlermann took his division to the Eastern Front, where it saw action in the Soviet Union. In April 1944 he was relieved of his command and rested until May. Kohlermann then took over as Higher Coastal Artillery Commander South-West, part of Army Group C, in Italy, where in May 1945 he surrendered to Allied troops.

Hans de SALENGRE-DRABBE

Generalleutnant

* 21 October 1894, Sigmaringen, Prussia
\+ 25 August 1944 near Tiraspol, Soviet Union

Knight's Cross: Awarded on 22 February 1942 as *Oberst* and Commander of Infantry Regiment 457 while attached to the XXXXIV. Army Corps for his command during success in repelling heavy Soviet tank attacks over a period of seven days. His command experienced heavy losses during their own counter-attacks and through his exemplary leadership they remained in control and fought with great skill. Salengre-Drabbe led his troops from the beginning of the Soviet campaign in June 1941 and later saw action in the Battles of the Uman and Kiev Pockets, where hundreds of thousands of Soviet troops were taken prisoner. From May 1942 he saw action in the Battle of Kharkov, where the German division he was attached to suffered heavy losses. By the autumn of 1942 the 257th Infantry Division to which his regiment was attached moved to France

Hans de Salengre-Drabbe entered the Army in March 1914 and served as a *Leutnant* with Infantry Regiment 2 during the First World War as platoon leader and company leader. He later served as an adjutant and was promoted to *Oberleutnant* in October 1918, remaining in the army after the war. From October 1935 he served as Commander of the I. Battalion of Infantry Regiment 43 in Insterburg with the rank of *Major*. From August 1938 he was adjutant to the Chief of the Army Weapons Office and was promoted to *Oberst* in June 1940.

for rest and refit. From 18 January 1943 he attended the Divisional Leaders Course in Berlin and from 24 February he took command of the 384th Infantry Division in France. He was promoted to *Generalmajor* in May and towards the end of the year he saw action in the Soviet Union, where he was involved in the Dnieper bend battles, the Battle of Krivoy Rog and in the Nikopol Bridgehead. Promoted to *Generalleutnant* in January 1944, Salengre-Drabbe took part in the fighting in Uman and in the retreat to the Bug River. He was killed in action near Tiraspol on the eastern bank of the Dniester River on 25 August 1944.

Werner SANNE

Generalleutnant

* 5 April 1889, Berlin
+ 26 September 1952, camp hospital in Krasnopolye, Soviet Captivity

Knight's Cross: Awarded on 22 February 1942 as *Generalmajor* and Commander of 100th Light Infantry Division while attached to III. Army Corps for actions during the Soviet winter offensive. Sanne fought at Uman and Kiev, with his command heavily involved in the sweep across the Odessa. On 1 April 1942 he was promoted to *Generalleutnant* and saw action during the Battle of Kharkov, in the encirclement and Battle of Staryyoskol, the drive to the Volga and in the fighting at Stalingrad. In fact, his command was destroyed at Stalingrad and Sanne himself was taken prisoner by the Soviets on 31 January 1943. He died while in captivity in the prison camp hospital on 26 September 1952.

Werner Sanne entered the Army with Infantry Regiment 117 from October 1908 and was commissioned as a *Leutnant* in June 1910. He later served as a battalion adjutant and company leader, and was promoted to *Oberleutnant* in February 1915. During the war he was awarded both classes of the Iron Cross. He remained in the Army after the war and from October 1935 served as Commander of Infantry Regiment 57, part of the 9th Infantry Division, with the rank of *Oberstleutnant*.

Theodor Josef Maria Ferdinand Hubert Freiherr von WREDE

Generalleutnant

* 3 November 1888, Hamburg-Wandesbek
+ 30 March 1973, Bonn, North Rhine-Westphalia

Theodor von Wrede entered the Army as a *Fahnenjunker* in Ulan Regiment 5 in March 1907 and was commissioned the following year. He saw action during the First World War and later served in the *Reichswehr*. He was a *Major* when Hitler came to power. A member of the military attaché branch in the 1930s, he was military attaché to Budapest from 1937. In October 1939 he assumed command of the 393rd Infantry Division, which he led until May 1940. It consisted of men over the age of forty-five and was used as an occupation force in Poland. He assumed command of the 290th Infantry Division from June 1940, which he led in the final stages of the French campaign.

Knight's Cross: Awarded on 22 February 1942 as *Generalleutnant* and Commander of 290th Infantry Division while attached to X. Army Corps for his success during the fighting in the Soviet Union, where his forces defeated every Soviet attack during a five-week period. He had commanded this division since October 1940 and remained in France as part of the occupation force until he saw action during the invasion of the Soviet Union leading his division as part of the LVI. Panzer Corps. It was an effective fighting unit and played a major role in the capture of Daugavpils. In the winter of 1941 his division took part in heroic resistance against the Soviet 34th Army south of Lake Ilmen and was very nearly wiped out. On 1 May 1945 Wrede was seriously wounded and hospitalised for many months. In December 1944 he was discharged from the army on medical grounds.

Werner Heinrich Bernhard von ERDMANNSDORFF

General der Infanterie

* 26 July 1891, Bautzen, Saxony
+ 5 June 1945, Ljubljana, Yugoslavia

Knight's Cross: Awarded on 27 February 1942 as *Oberst* and Commander of Motorised Infantry Regiment 30 and leader of the 18th Infantry Division

Werner von Erdmannsdorff entered the Army in October 1910 and in 1912 he was commissioned as a Leutnant and shortly after the start of the First World War he was wounded. He served primarily with Jäger Battalion 13 and ended the war as an *Oberleutnant* after winning both classes of the Iron Cross. He remained in the Army after the war and in 1930 served as tactics instructor at the Infantry School in Dresden as *Hauptmann*. At the beginning of the Second World War he held the rank of *Oberst* and was awarded the Bar to the Iron Cross 1st and 2nd Classes during the Polish Campaign.

(Motorised) for actions on the Russian Front. Erdmannsdorff had already distinguished himself during the defence of Tikhvin near Leningrad and during the retreat near the Volkhov River in Novgorodsky in December 1941. In more recent events it was his regiment that had held the city of Staraya Russa against a vastly superior enemy and for this he was awarded the Knight's Cross. In March 1942 Erdmannsdorff was promoted to *Generalmajor* and continued to be attacked by the Red Army with no rest. In January 1943 he was promoted to *Generalleutnant*. By May he was involved in trench warfare until his command could be evacuated the following month, when his command was renamed the 18th Panzer Grenadier Division. They reorganised, and from 21 July his division was transferred to Army Group Centre, then to the Reserves. From December he survived with the Military Replacement Inspector in Dresden. On 10 August 1944 Erdmannsdorff was delegated with the leadership of the LXXI. Army Corps and led them as the occupation force in northern Norway. On 9 October he took over as leader of the LXXXXI. Army Corps, part of Army Group E in Salonika and Serbia. On 30 January 1945 he was promoted to *General der Infanterie* and became the official Commander of the LXXXXI. Army Corps, which became pinned down by the extreme weather and Soviet attacks. Towards the end of February 1945 divisions under his command carried out anti-partisan operations and according to records more than 7,000 partisans were killed and 199 more taken prisoner. On 8 May he finally surrendered to British troops and was extradited to Yugoslavia. He was murdered by partisans without a trial on 5 June 1945.

Ferdinand NEULING

General der Infanterie

* 22 August 1885, Bautzen, Saxony
+ 20 February 1960, Hildesheim, Rhineland-Palatinate

Knight's Cross: Awarded on 28 February 1942 as *Generalleutnant* and Commander of 239th Infantry Division, attached to the 6th Army, for actions during the heavy engagements in the Ukraine. He saw heavy fighting at Kharkov and on 1 January 1942 his division was disbanded, all his men were divided up among the other divisions, and Neuling himself was appointed leader of Group *Neuling*. In March he entered the Reserves and from September was he was appointed leader of the LXII. Reserve Corps and assigned to Berlin as Inspector of Military District III. In mid-October 1942 Neuling was promoted to *General der Infanterie* and was appointed Commander of the Berlin Military District. In August 1944 his corps was relocated to Le Bourg in France and then moved to the southern French Mediterranean coast between the Italian border in the east and the area between Marseille and Toulon. On 15 August Allied troops landed in his area and his battle group tried to delay the invasion, with bridges and roads also destroyed by the *Luftwaffe*. On the 18th the Allies surrounded the German headquarters and Neuling was taken prisoner by troops of the US 36th Division. He was held in captivity at a prisoner of war camp in Clinton, Mississippi, until June 1947.

Werner SCHULZE

Generalmajor

* 15 January 1895, Calbe, Schönebeck
+ 3 November 1966, Stuttgart

Knight's Cross: Awarded on 1 March 1942 as *Major der Reserve* and Commander of the II. of Infantry Regiment 510, part of the 293rd Infantry Division, for his leadership during heavy fighting in the defensive battles near Krasnyi in the Soviet Union between 15 January and 1 February 1942. He distinguished himself when a group of Soviet soldiers, well over company strength, succeeded in penetrating almost 1.3 miles behind enemy lines and Schulze on his own initiative launched an immediate counter-attack. They succeeded in destroying the Soviet force and prevented them from advancing further; soon after the Germans were able to launch a major counter-attack. From the end of July

Werner Schulze served with the Prussian Army from September 1913 and at the start of the First World War served as platoon leader with the 6th Company of Fusilier Regiment No. 36. He later served as adjutant of the II. Battalion and leader of a machine gun company, and was awarded both classes of the Iron Cross with the rank of *Leutnant*. He left the Army in 1923 but rejoined in January 1935 as a Reserve Officer. At the beginning of the Second World War he held the rank of *Hauptmann der Reserve* and was company commander of Replacement Battalion 479. From February 1941 he was battalion commander and saw action during the invasion of the Soviet Union, where he served as *Major der Reserve.*

1942 he was delegated with the leadership of the 503rd Infantry Regiment and from September he led the 551st Infantry Regiment, part of the 329th Infantry Division. He was promoted to *Oberstleutnant der Reserve* on 1 December and led his regiment in Demyansk. Later, as part of the 16th Army, he saw action in Staraya Russa in Novgorod until April 1944.

Knight's Cross with Oakleaves: He became the 557th recipient on 23 August 1944 as *Oberst der Reserve* and Commander of Grenadier Regiment 551 for his outstanding leadership during the defensive fighting near Demyansk and from March 1944 in the withdrawal from Ergli in Latvia. Between 18 July and 16 August he took command of the 329th Infantry when its Commander, *Generalleutnant* Johannes Mayer, was seriously wounded, seeing action in Latvia. He entered the Reserves at the end of September 1944 and from October until early December he was delegated with the leadership of the 131st Infantry Division when it withdrew to East Prussia. He was promoted to *Generalmajor der Reserve* on 30 January 1945 and his command of the 131st Infantry Division was confirmed while still fighting in East Prussia. In early April he took command of the 329th Infantry Division as part of the 16th Army in the Courland area around the Vistula River, where he surrendered his command to British troops on 8 May 1945. He remained in Allied captivity until 1948.

Dr Lothar RENDULIC

Generaloberst

* 23 October 1887, Wiener Neustadt, Lower Austria
+ 17 January 1971, Eferding, Upper Austria

Knight's Cross: Awarded on 6 March 1942 as *Generalleutnant* and Commander of 52nd Infantry Division while attached to the LVII. Army Corps for his success against Soviet forces near Yukhnov. During the intensive ten-day battle his division had to fight off thirty-three Soviet attacks, which they did without giving up an inch of ground. In July his command fought with partisans in the forest near Bryansk and later in Sukhinichi, where his troops stormed almost 3,000 bunkers. In November he was promoted to *General der Infanterie* and took command of the XXXV. Army Corps, seeing action in Orel as part of the 2nd Panzer Army.

Knight's Cross with Oakleaves: Awarded on 15 August 1943 to become the 271st recipient as *General der Infanterie* as Commanding General of XXXV. Army Corps as part of the 9th Army for his outstanding leadership during the defensive battles at Kursk following Operation Citadel. In July Rendulic was fighting in the Kursk area against a far superior force, and led his troops with great skill during the many defensive battles over a period of nine days, destroying 819 Soviet tanks. He was presented with the Oakleaves personally by Hitler at *Führer* headquarters in Rastenburg on 15 September 1943. In late August he had taken command of the 2nd Panzer Army, seeing action in the Balkans as part of Army Group F and in April 1944 he was promoted to *Generaloberst*. From June he became Commander-in-Chief of the 20th Mountain Army, seeing action in Lapland and later in Finland.

Lothar Rendulic entered the Austrian Army with the 6th Company of Infantry Regiment 'Georg I, King of the Hellenes' in August 1910 with the rank of *Leutnant*. He commanded the 10th Company of Infantry Regiment No. 99 from July 1914 and three months later he was seriously wounded and admitted to hospital. In March 1915 he entered the General Staff with the rank of *Oberleutnant* and remained in the Army after the war. He joined the Austrian National Socialist Party in May 1932, and in March 1938 he entered the German armed forces with the rank of *Oberst*. In April he was appointed Chief of the General Staff of the XVII. Army Corps and was promoted to *Generalmajor* in November 1939.

After his surrender, Rendulic was interned and tried in the Hostages Trial at Nuremberg, because of his involvement in reprisals against civilians in Yugoslavia. On 19 February 1948 he was found guilty of war crimes and sentenced to twenty years in prison, although he was cleared of charges concerning the scorching of Lapland. Based upon the recommendations of the Peck Panel, this sentence was later reduced to ten years, and on 1 February 1951 Rendulic was released from the military prison in Landsberg am Lech in Bavaria.

Knight's Cross with Oakleaves and Swords: He became the 122nd recipient on 18 January 1945 as *Generaloberst* and Commander-in-Chief of 20th Mountain Army for his leadership during the successful withdrawal from Finland. He fought with great courage and his men were outnumbered two to one by the Finns as the Soviets advanced in the north. On 18 January 1945, during one of the last award ceremonies in Berlin, he was presented by Hitler at the Reich Chancellery with the Swords. From late January he took over as Commander-in-Chief of Army Group North from *Generaloberst* Ferdinand Schörner, and a few days later he took command of Army Group *Courland*. In March he was ordered to take command of the defence of East Prussia by Hitler, who had great faith in Rendulic. On 6 April he was summoned to Hitler's bunker in Berlin and told to take command of Army Group South in Vienna, where the Soviets were about to take the city. On 6 May Rendulic ordered the remnants of his Army Group to fight their way westward to avoid capture by the Soviets.

Karl-Ludwig RHEIN

Generalleutnant

* 30 March 1894, Wetzlar
+ 27 March 1988, Wetzlar

Knight's Cross: Awarded on 6 March 1942 as *Oberst* and Commander of Infantry Regiment 439, attached to the 134th Infantry Division, for actions in the central sector of the Russian Front. From 22 February 1943, Rhein was delegated with the leadership of the 331st Infantry Division and saw action

Karl-Ludwig Rhein entered the Army as a war volunteer in November 1914 with Infantry Regiment Kaiser Wilhelm No. 116 and was later appointed platoon leader. He was commissioned as a *Leutnant* in September 1915 and later was awarded both classes of the Iron Cross, ending the war as an ordnance officer. He remained in the Army after the war and from October 1934 was serving as an instructor with the Infantry School in Dresden. From January 1935 he was with the War School in Munich. He served as a battalion commander with Motorised Infantry Regiment 86 from November 1938 and in January 1940 he served in a similar capacity with Infantry Regiment 382 with the rank of *Oberstleutnant*.

on the Russian Front. He was promoted to *Generalmajor* in May 1943 and his command of the division was confirmed. He continued to see action in the Soviet Union and was promoted to *Generalleutnant* in November. From January 1944 he entered the *Führer* Reserve until 25 April, when he returned to command the 331st Infantry Division. In mid-1944 his division was transferred to Calais and saw action in Normandy, and on one occasion he was trapped in the Falaise Pocket and managed to break out. He also participated in the early stages of the withdrawal through France. On 1 August he took over command of the 295th Infantry Division and saw action in Norway until January 1945, when Rhein was appointed Inspector of Infantry with the Chief of Army Armaments and Commander of the Replacement Army in Berlin, *SS-Reichsführer* Heinrich Himmler. Rhein surrendered to Allied forces in May 1945 and remained in Allied captivity until his release in mid-1947.

Georg KOSSMALA

Generalmajor

* 22 October 1896, Myslowitz, Silesia
+ 18 March 1945, Oberglogau, Silesia

Knight's Cross: Awarded on 13 March 1942 as *Oberst* and Commander of Security Regiment 3 while attached to the 285th Security Division for his personal courage and dogged determination against the Red Army during the fierce fighting on 16 January 1942 in the Demyansk Pocket From 23 February he was appointed commander of all German formations in the Demyansk area,

Georg Kossmala entered Army service as a war volunteer with Infantry Regiment 63 in August 1914 and was commissioned as a *Leutnant* three years later. He served as a platoon leader and company leader during the First World War and joined the police after the war. Promoted to *Polizei-Hauptmann* in April 1927, he transferred back into the Army in August 1935 with the rank of *Hauptmann*. He was attached to the Army Signals School and from January 1940 he was Commander of I. Battalion of Infantry Regiment 222 with the rank of *Oberstleutnant* and later transferred to Infantry Regiment 570.

where his regiment held their ground until they were ordered to pull back on 8 March. From August he was named as the Commander of Infantry Regiment 6 and continued to see action in the Demyansk area and at the front near Leningrad. He saw further action near Demyansk until March 1943, then being involved in the fighting near Staraya Russa, a town near Novgorod.

Knight's Cross with Oakleaves: He became the 435th recipient on 26 March 1944 as *Oberst* and Commander of Grenadier Regiment 6, part of the 30th Infantry Division, for continued actions on the Russian Front. On 23 January 1944 he took command of troops just west of Lake Ilmen, where numerous Soviet tanks were destroyed. Then from 29 February his regiment took part in the heavy fighting along the Panther Line between Krasnaya Gorka and Nomojowo. He was presented with the Oakleaves on 27 April 1944 personally by Hitler at his Berghof mountain retreat. From June 1944 he took command of the 30th Infantry Division as part of the XXVIII. Army Corps, seeing action near the shores of the Baltic Sea, and from August he took command of the 32nd Infantry Division. From October he was named Commander of the 344th Infantry Division and saw action in Aachen, Germany, and on 1 January 1945 he was promoted to the rank of *Generalmajor*. From January 1945 his command was based in Cracow, Poland, and from February he was based near Oppeln as part of the 1st Panzer Army. On 18 March he was killed in action near Oberglogau in Silesia and his body remains missing.

Franz GRIESBACH

Generalmajor

* 21 December 1892, Brück, Brandenburg
+ 24 September 1984, Lage, North Rhine-Westphalia

Knight's Cross: Awarded on 14 March 1942 as *Major* and Commander of I. Battalion of Infantry Regiment 391, attached to 170th Infantry Division, for actions in the Crimea. He led his battalion with great skill and captured Hill 175 despite fierce resistance, which enabled the regiment to continue the attack the following day. Griesbach showed great bravery and skill as a commander and his efforts were crucial in ensuring the fall of Feodosia, Crimea, on 18 January 1942. On 1 April 1942 he was promoted to *Oberstleutnant* and had been briefly delegated with the leadership of Infantry Regiment 391. From 17 April he was delegated with the leadership of Grenadier Regiment 399 and took part in the Siege of Sevastopol. He took part in the attacks that resulted in the fall of the Soviet naval fortress at Sevastopol and from August his command of the regiment was confirmed. In January 1943 he was promoted to *Oberst.*

Knight's Cross with Oakleaves: He became the 242nd recipient on 17 May 1943 as *Oberst* and Commander of Grenadier Regiment 399, part of the 254th Infantry Division, in recognition of his extreme courage at the head of his men during the fighting near Krasny Bor in the Soviet Union. He launched the counter-attack on his own initiative and fought at the front of his troops in a battle that lasted for five and a half hours. By the end of the fighting his troops had claimed 2,000 dead Soviet soldiers

Franz Griesbach entered Army service in April 1914 and was attached to Infantry Regiment 27. He was commissioned as a *Leutnant der Reserve* in August 1916. He won both classes of the Iron Cross during the war and left the Army in January 1919 and became a school teacher in the area of Magdeburg. He returned to the Army in April 1936 and was promoted to *Oberleutnant der Reserve* two years later and soon after was assigned to the II. Supplemental Battalion of Infantry Regiment 12. He commanded the 10th Company of Infantry Regiment 467 during the invasion of Poland and later was awarded both classes of the Bar to the Iron Cross for action in the Soviet Union as Commander of Infantry Regiment 391.

and many were seriously wounded, with 338 taken prisoner. He was personally presented with the Oakleaves by Hitler together with *Generalleutnant* Hans-Karl von Scheele, *Oberst* Karl Löwrich, *Oberst* Franz Griesbach, *Hauptmann* Erich Bärenfänger and four others at *Führer* Headquarters in Rastenburg. He saw action during the Siege of Leningrad and from February 1944 was delegated with the leadership of the 170th Infantry Division. However, just two days into his new position he was seriously wounded at Leningrad and was hospitalised.

Knight's Cross with Oakleaves and Swords: Awarded on 6 March 1944 to become the 53rd recipient while *Oberst* and still Commander of Grenadier Regiment 399 for actions near Leningrad in January 1944. He led a battle group at this time and his men destroyed sixty-nine enemy tanks between 16 and 18 January. His group ultimately managed to prevent a Soviet breakthrough south of Leningrad. He was presented personally by Hitler with his Swords on 25 May 1944 at the Berghof, together with eight other officers, which included *Generalleutnants* Dietrich von Saucken and Georg-Wilhelm Postel, *General der Artillerie* Maximilian Fretter-Pico and *Oberst* Ernst-Günther Baade. Promoted to *Generalmajor* on 1 August 1944, Griesbach remained in the Reserves until the end of the war. He returned to hospital, where on 27 April 1945 he was captured by Soviet forces and remained a prisoner until his release on 21 October 1949.

Gottfried Heinrich von ERDMANNSDORFF

Generalmajor

* 25 April 1893, Kamenz
+ 30 January 1946, Minsk, Soviet Union

Knight's Cross: Awarded on 20 March 1942 as *Oberst* and Commander of Infantry Regiment 171 as part of 56th Infantry Division for actions on the Russian Front. On 23 January 1942 Erdmannsdorff made the decision to break through the enemy to help the German attack west of Bolkhov by units of the LIII. Army Corps. It was a brave decision and on 25 January he had prevented the German attack from being broken near Koljana. Had he not made this decision it would have required a costly retake of the salient positions. In October Erdmannsdorff was given leadership of a newly formed 465th Division in France. In December he was promoted to *Generalmajor*, his command was confirmed and he then moved to Military District V in Stuttgart. Here he used his extensive wartime experiences and knowledge in training his troops for the next eighteen months. In April 1944 Erdmannsdorff was appointed

Gottfried von Erdmannsdorff entered the Army in February 1913 with the Royal Saxon Jäger Battalion 2 and was wounded in action in September 1914. He was awarded both classes of the Iron Cross and was wounded again in June 1918 and was awarded the Wound Badge. He ended the war with the rank of *Oberleutnant*. He remained in the Army after the war, serving with Infantry Regiment 10 for twelve years. By October 1936 he was an *Oberstleutnant* and from November 1938 served as Commandant of Erfurt. He saw action in Poland as part of the 14th Army and was awarded the Bar to the Iron Cross 1st and 2nd Class while a battalion commander with Infantry Regiment 171 in France.

Commandant of Fortress Position Mogilev and by June he was defending his position against a strong Soviet attack. A message was sent from the Commander of the 4th Army, *General der Infanterie* Kurt von Tippelskirch, 'to hold the town until the last man'. However, Erdmannsdorff later reported that his forces had been weakened and the Soviets were on the edge of the city. Two and a half hours later he reported the only part of the city still under his control was the centre and his troops were in hand-to-hand combat with Soviet troops. By August the city had fallen and Erdmannsdorff was captured by Soviet troops and later tried for war crimes. This included the deportation of 10,000 people, the destruction of villages, schools and churches and the shooting of disabled people. He was sentenced to death by a military tribunal on 29 January 1946 and executed the following day.

Wilhelm BEHRENS

Generalleutnant

* 23 August 1888, Berlin
+ 15 August 1968, Lotte near Osnabrück, Lower Saxony

Knight's Cross: Awarded on 27 March 1942 as *Oberst* and Commander of Infantry Regiment 106 while attached to the 15th Infantry Division for his leadership during the defence of the city of Iklinskoje, west of the Nara River. He took part in the attempts to push back the enemy and his troops managed to prevent a major crisis and a breakthrough on its southern flank. At this time the army was already facing an extreme threat of a breakthrough on its southern flank. If the enemy had also succeeded in breaking through at Iklinskoje then the entire

Wilhelm Behrens entered the Army as a *Fahnenjunker*, was commissioned as a *Leutnant* in June 1910 and served with Ulanen Regiment 1. In December 1915 he was promoted to *Oberleutnant* and made machine gun squad leader with the same regiment, which he served with throughout the First World War. Behrens remained in the Army after the war and served as Leader of the Volunteer Ulanen Battalion II from 1919. In March 1922 he was promoted to *Rittmeister* and transferred into Mounted Regiment 7. He served with three different regiments between October 1923 and September 1934, having been promoted to *Major* in October 1932. In June 1935 he was promoted to *Oberstleutnant* and from October served as Commander of the II. Battalion of Infantry Regiment 10.

withdrawal movement of the army's centre would have been jeopardised. The prevention of an enemy breakthrough at Iklinskoje was therefore of significant operational importance. In June he became Commander of Division 193 and was used to train other troops in battle. Two years later he entered the Reserves and was promoted to *Generalleutnant* on 1 September 1944. He retired from military service soon afterwards and was captured by Soviet forces shortly after the end of the war and kept in prison until 20 October 1949.

Karl <u>Friedrich</u> 'Fritz' Wilhelm SCHULZ

General der Infanterie

* 15 October 1897, Nettkow, Grünberg, Silesia, Poland
\+ 30 November 1976, Freudenstadt, Baden-Württemberg

Knight's Cross: Awarded on 29 March 1942 as *Oberst im Generalstab* and Chief of the General Staff of XXXXIII. Army Corps in recognition of his bravery during the heavy defensive battles near Kaluga in the Soviet Union during the winter of 1941–42. Towards the end of May 1942 Schulz was appointed Chief of the General Staff of the 11th Army while on the Eastern Front and was promoted to *Generalmajor* in July 1942. In November he was appointed Chief of the General Staff of the Army Group Don under the command of *Generalfeldmarschall* Erich von Manstein. From May 1943 he took over as Chief of the General Staff of Army Group South, being promoted to *Generalleutnant* from July and seeing action in the Soviet Union, once again under the command of Manstein.

Friedrich Schulz joined the Army as a war volunteer in September 1914, seeing action from May 1915 with the Reserve Field Artillery Regiment 52. From November 1916 he served as deputy battalion adjutant with the rank of *Leutnant* and ended the war as battalion adjutant. He remained in the Army after the war, serving with Infantry Regiment 8 until October 1930, when he transferred to the staff of the 4th Division in Dresden. From October 1935 he served as 1st General Staff Officer with the 23rd Infantry Division in Potsdam, rising to the rank of *Oberstleutnant* in February 1939. From April 1940 he served as Chief of the General Staff of the XXXXIII. Army Corps seeing action on the Channel Coast in France and later in the Soviet Union.

Knight's Cross with Oakleaves: He became the 428th recipient on 20 March 1944 as *Generalleutnant* and leader of III. Panzer Corps while attached to the 1st Panzer Army for his leadership during the battles near Cherkassy between November 1943 and January 1944. From mid-January to February he briefly took command of the LIX. Army Corps and in April he was promoted to *General der Infanterie* and appointed Commanding General of the XXXXVI. Panzer Corps. The following month he flew to the Berghof in Berchtesgaden to meet Hitler, where he was presented with the Oakleaves. He saw action near Stanislau as part of the 1st Panzer Army from March 1944 and entered the *Führer* Reserve in July before being appointed Commander-in-Chief of the 17th Army on 30 January 1945.

Knight's Cross with Oakleaves and Swords: Awarded on 26 February 1945 to become the 135th recipient as *General der Infanterie* and Commander-in-Chief of the 17th Army, part of Army Group Centre, for his army's defence of the industrial region of Upper Silesia. Following the Soviet breakthrough near Legnica in Poland, Schulz was eventually able to halt their advance and form a new defensive front upon which many Soviet attacks pushed back with heavy losses on both sides. Schulz proved a capable and brave commander during this time, and was described as an inspiration to his men. On 2 May he was appointed Commander-in-Chief of Army Group G before surrendering to US troops just four days later.

Walter JOST

Generalleutnant

* 25 July 1896, Rastatt, Baden
+ 24 April 1945 near Villadose, Province of Rovigo, Italy

Walter Jost entered the Army in August 1914 as a war volunteer with Field Artillery Regiment 30 and was commissioned as a *Leutnant* in September 1916. He served as an ordnance officer with Infantry Regiment 111 from May 1917 but soon returned to his regiment. He remained in the Army after the war, serving as adjutant with different regiments, and from October 1933 served as a company commander. Promoted to *Oberstleutnant* in August 1937, he later served as Commander of the III. Battalion of Infantry Regiment 75.

Knight's Cross: Awarded on 31 March 1942 as *Oberst* and Commander of Infantry Regiment 75, part of the 5th Light Infantry Division, and saw action while leading his regiment during the defensive battles of Rzhev in the Soviet Union. He later took part in Operation Bridge Strike, the liberation of the trapped German troops in the Demyansk Pocket, and Jost achieved remarkable success, seeing action and as usual leading his troops from the front. On 1 April the Commander-in-Chief of the 16th Army, *Generaloberst* Ernst Busch, personally presented Jost with his Knight's Cross. From June 1942 Jost took temporary command of the 5th Light Division while its commander *Generalmajor* Karl Allmendinger was on leave. On 15 July Jost was seriously wounded near Jaswry and admitted to hospital. He was still recovering in April 1943 when he was promoted to *Generalmajor*. Shortly after he was assigned General with Special Duties with the High Command of the *Wehrmacht* and from August he served as Chief of the Central Department. On 26 April 1944 he was appointed Commander of the 42nd *Jäger* Division, seeing action in northern Yugoslavia. Later he was transferred to Genoa, northern Italy, and from September saw combat in the Gothic Line campaign. He was promoted to *Generalleutnant* in December and saw action during the Battle of Bologna and in the final campaign in Italy. By March 1945 his command had a strength of fewer than 2,600 men and was finally crushed by British forces south of the Po River, the victim of another 'hold at all costs' order from Hitler. On 24 April Jost himself was killed near Villadose, Italy, and is buried in that country's German War Cemetery in Costermano sul Garda. His body is in Plot 3, Grave 593.

Hellmuth MÄDER

Generalmajor

* 5 July 1908, Rotterode, Thuringia
+ 12 May 1984, Coblenz, Rhineland-Palatinate

Knight's Cross: Awarded on 3 April 1942 as *Major* and Commander of III. Battalion of Infantry Regiment 522 while attached to the 297th Infantry Division for his outstanding bravery during the heavy fighting in the area north of Kharkov in the Soviet Union. From early July 1942 Mäder took command of Infantry Regiment 522 and saw action during the summer offensive in the Don region in central and southern Russia. He was promoted to *Oberstleutnant* on 1 September 1942 and saw action during the defeat at Stalingrad, where he was seriously wounded. He was transferred into the Reserves while recovering and promoted to *Oberst* in October 1943, but he did not return to front-line duty until January 1944 as Commander of Reserve Brigade *Narva*.

Hellmuth Mäder entered the *Landespolizei* in Bonn in April 1928. He was commissioned as a *Leutnant* in April 1933 and transferred into the Army in October 1935. He was named Commander of the 14th Company of Infantry Regiment 80 in June 1936 and was promoted to *Hauptmann* two years later. From September 1939 he served as 1st assistant adjutant on the General Staff of the 34th Infantry Division. He later served as Commander of the III. Battalion of Infantry Regiment 522.

Knight's Cross with Oakleaves: He became the 560th recipient on 27 August 1944 as *Oberst* and leader of Infantry Training Brigade of Army Group Weapons School North and Combat Commander of the City of Šiauliai in Lithuania for actions on the Eastern Front. On 26 July, following the Soviet summer offensive against Army Group North, the spearhead of the Soviet 3rd Guards Tank Corps reached the city of Šiauliai. Mäder assembled what forces he could find into a battle group and defended the city for one day and one night. On the night of 27–28 July the area was surrounded but with the help of reinforcements and the courage of his troops they managed to break out to safety. From October 1944 Mäder was delegated with the leadership of the 7th Panzer Division and from 21 November he attended a Divisional Commanders' course in Hirschberg.

Knight's Cross with Oakleaves and Swords: Awarded on 18 April 1945 to become the 143rd recipient as *Generalmajor* and Commander of *Führer* Grenadier Division *Grossdeutschland* while attached to the XXXIX. Army Corps for his command's success during the fighting in Lower Silesia. Promoted to *Generalmajor* in January, he took part in the defensive battles in Pomerania and in March saw heavy fighting in Lower Silesia during the Battle of Lubań. His forces linked up with the 8th Panzer Division and pushed back the attacking Soviets, capturing most of their weapons, which would be the last German operational victory in the East. In mid-April his forces took part in the fighting around Vienna, where in May 1945 he surrendered his command to US forces. However, he was handed over to the Soviets on 14 May and was sentenced to ten years' imprisonment, returning to Germany in October 1955. In September 1957 he entered the *Bundeswehr* and became Chief of the Troop Office from October 1960 until September 1968, reaching the rank of *Generalleutnant.*

Maximilian 'Max' Heinrich SACHSENHEIMER

Generalmajor

* 5 December 1909, Mühlbach, Baden
+ 2 June 1973, Merzhausen, Baden-Württemberg

Knight's Cross: Awarded on 5 April 1942 as *Hauptmann* and Commander of II. Battalion of Jäger Regiment 75, part of the 5th Light Infantry Division, for actions during fierce fighting in the Demyansk Pocket. Sachsenheimer led the attack from the front and secured the all-important Staraya Russa road, which was crucial in continuing the German attack in that sector. During October 1942 he fell seriously ill and had to be evacuated to a local hospital, where

Max Sachsenheimer entered the 2nd Company of the 14th Baden Infantry Regiment as a volunteer in April 1928 and attended various courses before being commissioned as a *Leutnant* in July 1934. He served as a platoon commander with Infantry Regiment Konstanz from October 1934 and was promoted to *Oberleutnant* in October 1937. In July 1941 he was serving as a battalion commander with the rank of *Hauptmann*. He was wounded during an enemy tank attack and had half of his hand torn off. He was treated at a field hospital by Professor Thiess, a hand specialist.

on 1 December he was promoted to *Major*. He finally returned to the front on 8 February 1943 as Commander of the II. Battalion of *Jäger* Regiment 75 and from April served as the Second General Staff Officer [Ib] on the General Staff of the 5th *Jäger* Division. In October he was assigned to a General Staff Training Course at Hirschberg and from March 1944 he was delegated with the leadership of *Jäger* Regiment 75.

Knight's Cross with Oakleaves: He became the 472nd recipient on 14 May 1944 as *Major* and leader of *Jäger* Regiment 75 while attached to the 5th *Jäger* Division for his leadership during the relief of Kovel in March 1944. He took part in various attacks and in close combat patrols from late March into April, and on 1 April he was promoted to *Oberstleutnant* and officially took command of the 75th *Jäger* Regiment. Sachsenheimer was presented with the Oakleaves personally by Hitler in a ceremony at the Berghof on the Obersalzburg on 31 May 1944. On 7 August he attended the 13th Divisional Leaders Course at Hirschberg and on 1 September he was promoted to the rank of *Oberst*. A few weeks later he took command of the 17th Infantry Division and in December he was promoted to *Generalmajor* and saw action in late 1944 in southern Poland.

Knight's Cross with Oakleaves and Swords: Awarded on 6 February 1945 to become the 132nd recipient as *Generalmajor* and Commander of 17th Infantry Division while attached to the 9th Army in recognition of his successful mission to recapture a poison gas factory at Dyhernfurth (Brzeg Dolny) near Breslau. This prevented the poison gas from falling into the hands of the Soviets and German chemistry experts soon rendered the poison stock harmless. He was presented with the Swords by *Generalfeldmarschall* Ferdinand Schörner, the Commander-in-Chief of Army Group Centre, on 12 February 1945. With most of his division smashed, he defended the Hirschberg–Bad Warmbrunn zone of Silesia with three regiments and some assorted troops, which included staff and students of the Army NCO School at Brno. In late April 1945 remnants of his division were surrounded in Czechoslovakia by US troops and Sachsenheimer surrendered on 8 May. He was in US captivity until April 1947.

Rudolf HOLSTE

Generalleutnant

* 9 April 1897, Oldendorf, Hesse-Nassau
+ 4 December 1970, Baden-Baden, Baden-Württemberg

Rudolf Holste entered Army service as war volunteer in August 1914 and was wounded a year later. From March 1916 he saw action with Field Artillery Regiment 62. He was awarded both classes of the Iron Cross and ended the war as a regimental adjutant with the rank of *Leutnant*. He remained in the Army after the war and served with Artillery Regiment 6 until November 1933. From October 1934 he served as adjutant of the Inspector of Cavalry, with the rank of *Hauptmann*. He later served with Artillery Regiment 11 and was awarded the Bar to the Iron Cross 1st and 2nd Classes for action during the Polish Campaign with Mountain Artillery Battalion 1.

Knight's Cross: Awarded on 6 April 1942 as *Oberst* as Commander of Artillery Regiment 73, attached to the 1st Panzer Division, in recognition of his outstanding leadership and personal bravery during the fierce fighting in February 1942 near Rzhev on the Russian Front. His regiment helped with the flanking thrust of the panzers during their drive into the rear of the enemy in support of the assaulting German infantry. In early July elements of the 1st Panzer Division helped in destroying or capturing more than 200 Soviet tanks, 590 guns and 1,300 anti-tank guns near Pushkeri. From January 1943 Holste was appointed commander of the 14th Motorised Infantry Division, taking part in the withdrawal from the Rzhev salient, and from February 1944 he was attached to Army Group North as a battle group commander.

Knight's Cross with Oakleaves: On 27 August 1944 he became the 561st recipient as *Oberst* and leader of the 4th Cavalry Brigade, attached to the 2nd Army, in recognition of his bravery and leadership during the defensive battles between 10 and 29 July 1944. He particularly distinguished himself during the tough defensive battles and showed extraordinary bravery, with his brigade playing an important role in the rescue of the retreating German units in the Brest-Litovsk area. He was presented with the Oakleaves by Hitler on 19 September 1944 at *Führer* Headquarters in Rastenburg. From October, Holste led his brigade as part of the 4th Army in East Prussia, and on 15 November he was promoted to *Generalmajor*. In April 1945 his command was upgraded and became the 4th Cavalry Division, seeing action in Styria, Austria, as part of the 2nd Panzer Army. On 20 April Holste took over the leadership of the XXXXI. Panzer Corps and two days later was ordered by *Generalfeldmarschall* Wilhelm Keitel, together with the forces under *SS-Obergruppenführer* Felix Steiner, to lead an attack against the Russians in the area north-west of Berlin. Holste was ordered to attack between Spandau and Oranienburg. By 27 April the Soviet forces encircling Berlin linked up and the German forces inside Berlin were now cut off. On 4 May Holste was promoted to *Generalleutnant* and just four days later he surrendered to the Allies.

Ernst MAISEL

Generalleutnant

* 16 September 1896, Landau
+ 16 December 1952, Schönau am Königssee

Knight's Cross: Awarded on 6 April 1942 as *Oberst* and Commander of Infantry Regiment 42, part of the 46th Infantry Division, for his leadership and bravery during the heavy fighting on the coast of the Kerch Peninsula in the Crimea. In September he joined the Reserves and was assigned as Department Chief in the Army Personnel Office in Berlin, and from January 1943 he became Head of the Office responsible for Army discipline. He was promoted to *Generalmajor* in June 1943 and from 1 October 1944 he was named as Deputy Head of the Army Personnel Office, with the rank of *Generalleutnant*. One of his responsibilities was to be court protocol officer of the Army Court of Honour that investigated Army officers involved in the 20 July 1944 plot to kill Hitler.

Ernst Maisel was a war volunteer and served in Flanders from 1915 with Bavarian Field Artillery Regiment 12. He later served as a battery officer with the 4th Battery of Field Artillery Regiment 12 and was wounded during the Battle of Somme. He was commissioned a *Leutnant* in August 1915 and continued to serve with Field Artillery Regiment throughout and after the war. Promoted to *Oberleutnant* in April 1925, he served as adjutant with Infantry Regiment 21 in Nuremberg until October 1935. When the Second World War began he was serving as Commander of the III. Battalion of Infantry Regiment 104 and saw action during the French Campaign.

It was in this capacity that, together with his superior *Generalleutnant* Wilhelm Burgdorf, he delivered a message personally to *Generalfeldmarschall* Rommel at his home on 14 October, telling him that Hitler knew of his involvement in the plot to kill him and that he should commit suicide in order to save his family from arrest. That same day Rommel left with both generals and took poison, although it was reported to the German people that Rommel had died in action from his wounds. He was given a state funeral, which Hitler did not attend. Maisel surrendered to US forces on 7 May 1945 and was released in March 1947.

Johann 'Hans' SCHLEMMER

General der Gebirgstruppe

* 18 January 1893, Nesselwang
+ 26 June 1973, Bad Kreuznach

Knight's Cross: Awarded on 21 April 1942 as *Generalmajor* and Commander of 134th Infantry Division while attached to the XXXXVII. Army Corps for his leadership in the difficult and bloody fighting near Orel in the Soviet Union from 28 January until 20 February. His division was able to repulse a total of fifty-nine Soviet tank attacks, which resulted in the Soviet 61st Army attempt to break through towards Orel being broken. Schlemmer led his division during the fighting at Bialystok, Bobruisk, Kiev and Bryansk. It suffered from a lack of supplies but remained in the front line until the spring of 1943.

Johann 'Hans' Schlemmer joined Engineer Battalion 2 of the Royal Bavarian Army in August 1913 as an officer candidate. During the First World War he fought with the Royal Bavarian Field Artillery Regiment 5 as a platoon leader and was commissioned as a *Leutnant* in December 1914. He remained in the Army after the war and from 1926 until 1928 he studied engineering at the Technical University in Berlin-Charlottenburg, graduating as an engineer in July 1930. Promoted to *Major* in August 1934, he was attached to the Reich Defence Ministry. From September 1939 he was Commander of Artillery Regiment 7 and was awarded the Bar to the Iron Cross 1st and 2nd Classes.

Knight's Cross with Oakleaves: He became the 369th recipient on 18 January 1944 as *Generalleutnant* and Commander of 134th Infantry Division while attached to the XXXXI. Army Corps for continued actions in the Soviet Union. In December 1943 his command attacked the Russian army forces west of Rechitsa, which lasted for several days. His troops kept up the pace until enemy forces pushed them away and halted their advance. The Oakleaves were presented to Schlemmer by Hitler at his headquarters in Rastenburg on 13 February 1944. Schlemmer was delegated with the leadership of the VIII. Army Corps from April 1944. From July he took command of the LXXV. Army Corps in northern Italy, where he saw action in the Alpine region of the front. He was promoted to *General der Gebirgstruppe* on 9 November and continued to see heavy action in Italy until the German capitulation. Schlemmer surrendered to US troops on 3 May and remained in captivity until his release on 17 June 1947.

Heinrich Gerhard Albert GÖTZ

Generalmajor

* 1 January 1896, Hannover
+ 31 January 1960, Oberaudorf, Bavaria

Knight's Cross: Awarded on 3 May 1942 as *Oberstleutnant* and Commander of Infantry Regiment 466, part of the 257th Infantry Division, for his successful holding of two strongpoints on the Russian Front. His regiment played a major role in the defence of the German military bases in the Donets area against fierce Soviet forces between 18 and 31 January 1942. Götz demonstrated how it was possible to hold strongpoints despite

Heinrich Götz entered the Reserves as a war volunteer in August 1914 and transferred into Infantry Regiment 74 in November. He became an officer candidate soon after, being commissioned as a *Leutnant* in May 1915. He saw action during the First World War, being awarded both classes of the Iron Cross, and remained in the Army until May 1925. He rejoined the Army in May 1925 as a *Hauptmann* and from October 1935 he was Commander of the 2nd Company of Infantry Regiment 9. From May 1938 he served as adjutant with the Staff of the 3rd Infantry Division with the rank of *Major*.

the cold and enemy superiority, and his success demonstrated to the entire front line a feeling of superiority over the Soviets. Promoted to *Oberst* in July, he then led his regiment during the battles of Voronezh and Kalach, but during the drive to Stalingrad his regiment, together with the entire division, was sent to Brittany in France to rest and refit. He returned with his regiment to Russia in April 1943 and was heavily engaged in the fighting, particularly at Dnepropetrovsk and Krivoy Rog among other battles. From January 1944 Götz was rested and attended two divisional leaders courses, and from May he was attached to Army Group North as a divisional commander. From late June 1944 he was delegated with the leadership of the 83rd Infantry Division and took part in the retreat through the Baltic States. On 23 August he took command of the 21st Infantry Division, taking part in the retreat from Leningrad. He was promoted to *Generalmajor* on 20 September and just five days later was seriously wounded by a gunshot to the head. Once Götz had recovered he returned as Commander of the 21st Infantry Division on 17 January 1945 and saw action in East Prussia.

Knight's Cross with Oakleaves: Awarded on 5 March 1945 to become the 765th recipient as *Generalmajor* and Commander of the 21st Infantry Division, part of the XXXXI. Panzer Corps, in recognition of his success in organising a battle group against Soviet forces in East Prussia. The group succeeded in fending off an attack by twenty-four Soviet tanks, which enabled many German troops to escape the area and avoid Soviet captivity by heading for the Anglo-American lines. Götz was promoted to *Generalleutnant* in April and took over command of Division Scharnhorst, seeing action west of Berlin until the end of the war. He surrendered to Allied troops on 9 May and was released from captivity in 1948.

Hans KÄLLNER

Generalleutnant

* 9 October 1898, Kattowitz, Upper Silesia
+ 18 April 1945 near Sokolnice, Olmütz, Bohemia & Moravia (Czechoslovakia)

Knight's Cross: Awarded on 3 May 1942 as *Oberst* and Commander of Rifle Regiment 736, part of the 19th Panzer Division, for his leadership and bravery during the fierce fighting west of Kaluga in the Soviet Union. During April 1942 a Soviet rifle division launched an advance that got within less than 2 miles of the German lines. In response Källner took command of the first

Hans Källner entered the Army Reserves as a war volunteer in June 1915 as a *Gefreiter*, and was commissioned as a *Leutnant* in October 1917 while serving with Reserve Dragoon Rifle Regiment 13. He left Army service in early 1919 and joined the police in May 1920 as a *Leutnant.* He later became a riding instructor with the mounted police in Potsdam with the rank of *Polizei-Oberleutnant*. He left the police and rejoined the Army in October 1935 with the rank of *Rittmeister* with Mounted Regiment 4. In October 1937 he was appointed Commander of the II. Battalion of Cavalry Regiment 4 and was promoted to *Oberstleutnant* in 1939, serving with Reconnaissance Battalion 11 while serving in Poland, where he was awarded the Bar to the Iron Cross 1st and 2nd Classes.

German battalion that arrived on the scene. He took back the villages that had been lost in a counter-attack and pushed the Soviet forces far enough away so they could no longer fire on the German lines. As a result the Soviet breakthrough attempt was halted. From July 1942 Källner was commander of the 19th Panzer Grenadier Brigade, and briefly in April he commanded a battle group. In early May he attended the 4th Divisional Leaders' Course in Berlin and from September took command of the 19th Panzer Division. He then saw heavy fighting near Kiev in November, during which time he was promoted to *Generalmajor*.

Knight's Cross with Oakleaves: He became the 392nd recipient on 12 February 1944 as *Generalmajor* and Commander of the 19th Panzer Division while attached to the XXXXVIII. Panzer Corps for actions during the heavy fighting near Zhitomir. He led his division during three days of bitter fighting against a Soviet breakthrough and his troops destroyed about fifty tanks and twenty guns despite inadequate logistical support. Källner was presented with the Oakleaves by Hitler on 27 April 1944 at the Berghof. His command formed part of General Hube's 'Floating Pocket' from April and later saw action more north after Army Group Centre was crushed. His force, together with two other panzer divisions, surprised and destroyed a Soviet tank corps north of Warsaw and thus halted the Soviet summer offensive of 1944. Shortly after Källner was promoted to the rank of *Generalleutnant*.

Knight's Cross with Oakleaves and Swords: Awarded on 23 October 1944 to become the 106th recipient as *Generalleutnant* and Commander of the 19th Panzer Division, part of the IV. SS-Panzer Corps, for his leadership north of Warsaw in August 1944. During this time his division succeeded in making it possible for other German forces to build a new defensive line on the western bank of the Vistula. The Swords were personally presented to him by Hitler in early November at the Reich Chancellery in Berlin. By early 1945 the 19th Panzer Division was only at battle group strength and was retreating through southern and eastern Poland, seeing action in the Baranov Bridgehead battles in January 1945. On 22 March Källner was delegated with the leadership of the XXIV. Panzer Corps and prevented a Soviet breakthrough near Głubczyce in Poland. In April he led his command to Sokolnice in Czechoslovakia, where he was killed in action.

Hans-Georg LEYSER

Generalmajor

* 19 June 1896, Worin, Brandenburg
+ 18 April 1980, Hannover, Lower Saxony

Knight's Cross: Awarded on 3 May 1942 as *Oberst* and Commander of Motorised Infantry Regiment 51 while attached to the 18th Motorised Infantry Division for actions during the Tikhvin Offensive during the invasion of the Soviet Union. His regiment was successful during the German objective of cutting off supply routes to Leningrad and that was the beginning of the German offensive towards an attack on Moscow. In mid-July 1942 Leyser entered the Reserves and from there was delegated with the leadership of the 29th Motorised Infantry Division while seeing action at Stalingrad. In November he was promoted to *Generalmajor* and his command was confirmed. He continued to see action at Stalingrad as part of the 6th Army under *Generaloberst* Friedrich Paulus. By the beginning of 1943 the Germans had lost the battle at Stalingrad and were surrounded by Soviet tank forces. Leyser stated, 'I observed the Soviets attack in a dispersed formation, but tank following tank, each covered with infantry and flying enormous red flags ...' The tanks were heavily armoured British-made Churchills. Leyser added, 'We felt like spectators of a great human drama in a giant theatre. Our infantry weapons were out of range and the few remaining anti-tank guns had little effect.' On 31 January 1943 Leyser surrendered to the 6th Army together with twenty-two generals, which included Paulus, now a *Generalfeldmarschall*. Leyser was released from captivity and returned to Germany on 20 October 1949.

Dietrich von MÜLLER

Generalleutnant

* 16 September 1891, Malchow, Mecklenburg-Schwerin
+ 3 January 1961, Hamburg

Knight's Cross: Awarded on 3 May 1942 as *Oberstleutnant* and Commander of Rifle Regiment 5 while attached to the 269th Infantry Division for his leadership during the defensive fighting near Pogost'e near Leningrad on 16 February 1942. He managed to salvage a critical situation, resulting in victory for his regiment against a large Soviet force supported by more than forty tanks. By preventing the Soviets from breaking through, Müller averted an extremely

Dietrich von Müller entered the Army in October 1912 with Jäger Battalion 3 and was commissioned as a *Leutnant* in June the following year. He served as an ordnance officer and company leader, and was wounded in March 1916 and promoted to *Oberleutnant*. He was awarded both classes of the Iron Cross. He was discharged from the Army in April 1920 and rejoined in January 1934 as a *Hauptmann*. Two years later he served as Commander of the 6th Company with Infantry Regiment 5. Promoted to *Major* in March 1938, he served as Commander of the II. Battalion of Infantry Regiment 5, part of the 2nd Infantry Division, and saw action in Poland, where he was awarded both classes of the Iron Cross and later took part in the invasion of the Soviet Union.

dangerous outcome, not just for the division but for the corps, and shortly after he was promoted to the rank of *Oberst*.

Knight's Cross with Oakleaves: He became the 272nd recipient on 16 August 1943, as *Oberst* and Commander of Panzer Grenadier Regiment 5, part of 12th Panzer Division, for his bravery and leadership in the Soviet Union. Between 13 and 20 July 1943 Müller played a major role in the success of his regiment in stabilising the front line despite heavy and bloody battles involving the 12th Panzer Division. His leadership prevented a Soviet attack on 14 July and two days later he led his regiment during a particular audacious attack when he drove through enemy lines with two panzer tanks and several armoured vehicles, rescuing his battalion which had been encircled by the Red Army. From August 1943, Müller was Chief of Tactical Training at the Panzer School in Krampnitz and later transferred to the Panzer School in Paris. From March 1944 he served on the Staff of the General Inspector of Panzer Troops under his friend, *Generaloberst* Heinz Guderian. He attended the 12th Divisional Leaders Course in Hirschberg from July 1944, and in August he was personally appointed Commander of the 16th Panzer Division by Guderian, despite Müller's low rank. Guderian's faith in Müller was soon justified; he became an excellent tank commander and a brilliant leader, and was known as 'the second Hube', a reference to Hans Hube, another renowned tank commander. On 9 November 1944 Müller was promoted to *Generalmajor*.

Knight's Cross with Oakleaves and Swords: Awarded on 20 February 1945 to become the 134th recipient as *Generalmajor* and Commander of 16th Panzer Division while attached to XXIV. Panzer Corps for his leadership during the Soviet winter offensive of early 1945. His division was encircled south of Kielce but he managed to escape the enemy and was later encircled yet again east of Sulejów, Poland, but once again managed to break out. From 19 February he was attached to the staff of Guderian, the General Inspector of Panzer Troops, and at the same time Müller commanded Panzer Division *Jüterbog*. From 5 March he was transferred back to command the 16th Panzer Division and saw action west of the Vistula, before then fighting in the retreat through Poland and into Czechoslovakia. On 20 April he was promoted to *Generalleutnant* and that same day he was captured by Czech partisans and handed over to the Soviets. They imprisoned him until 7 October 1955, when he returned to Germany.

Ernst Karl Paul MICHAEL

Generalmajor

* 28 April 1897, Weimar, Thüringia
+ 22 January 1944, Tuganitzky, Soviet Union

Knight's Cross: Awarded on 18 May 1942 as *Oberst* and Commander of Infantry Regiment 2 while attached to the 11th Infantry Division for actions during the invasion of the Soviet Union. From October 1942 his command was renamed the 2nd Grenadier Regiment and fought as part of the 18th Army in the Soviet Union in Volkhov and the area around Leningrad. From early May 1943 he attended the 4th Divisional Leaders Course in Berlin and remained in the *Führer* Reserve until November, when he was delegated with the leadership of the 205th Infantry Division. From 25 November he was Commander of the 9th *Luftwaffe* Field Division and was killed during heavy fighting near Tuganitzky in the Soviet Union on 22 January 1944. He was posthumously promoted to *Generalmajor*.

Johann-Heinrich ECKHARDT

Generalleutnant

* 3 November 1896, Böddiger, Melsungen
+ 15 May 1945, Vimperk, Czechoslovakia (Soviet PoW)

Knight's Cross: Awarded on 20 May 1942 as *Oberst* and Commander of *Jäger* Regiment 38 of the 8th Infantry Division in recognition for his

Johann-Heinrich Eckhardt entered the Army Reserves in April 1914 and after an officers' course transferred into Infantry Regiment 54 as a *Leutnant*. He briefly joined the *Freikorps* after the war and then returned to the Army in October 1920. From 1926 he was attached to the infantry and by August 1929 had been promoted to *Hauptmann*. At the outbreak of the Second World War he was an *Oberstleutnant*, serving as commander of the II. Battalion of Infantry Regiment 38. Eckhardt distinguished himself during the Polish Campaign as a battalion and regimental commander and was awarded both classes of the Bar to the Iron Cross. He was awarded the German Cross in Gold on 25 January 1942.

outstanding leadership and personal bravery during the fierce counter-attack on 23 March 1942 against Soviet forces near Podzepotschje in the Soviet Union. He launched a counter-thrust and took vital positions while under attack from heavy gunfire, setting an excellent example of bravery by a commanding officer. He continued to see heavy action against the Soviet army until July and his regiment withdrew from the area around Rostov on 13 July, leaving most of his vehicles due to a lack of fuel. He saw action again on 23 July as commander of the 211th Infantry Division when he captured a bridge near Kalach. From 23 August Eckhardt led his regiment during the attack on Stalingrad. On 1 October he was promoted to *Generalmajor* and led his division during action in Spas-Demensk; then while attached to the IX. Army Corps his command was deployed to the Vitebsk area.

Knight's Cross with Oakleaves: Awarded on 3 November 1944 to become the 644th recipient as *Generalleutnant* and Commander of the 211th Infantry Division while attached to the XXIII. Army Corps for his distinguished command during the defensive actions between the Bug and Narew Rivers. The main Soviet effort against the southern wing of his division on 2 September 1944 took place on both sides of the Ostrów to Różan and the Ostrów to Ostrołęka railway. On this day the Soviet attacks were eliminated in large part thanks to the personal efforts of Eckhardt himself. After the costly operations his division was converted to the 211th *Volksgrenadier* Division in November 1944 and saw action in West Prussia and from December in the General Government area of Poland. It was here that Eckhardt and his division surrendered to US troops on 8 May 1945. Just seven days later, Eckhardt died in the Winterberg prison camp, with the cause unknown.

Diepold Georg Heinrich Freiherr von LÜTTWITZ

General der Panzertruppe

* 6 December 1896, Krumpach-Trebnitz, Silesia
+ 9 October 1969, Neuberg an der Donau, Bavaria

Knight's Cross: Awarded on 27 May 1942 as *Oberst* and Commander of Rifle Regiment 59 while attached to the 20th Panzer Division for his outstanding leadership during his regiment's attack on Moscow in October 1941. In February 1942 his battle group and regiment was able to prevent two Soviet armies from achieving contact with German troops. In April his regiment defended against strong enemy attacks on the Ugra River near Smolensk, and in doing so he

Heinrich von Lüttwitz entered Army service with Ulanen Regiment 1 in August 1914 and was wounded near Verdun in October of that year. Promoted to *Leutnant* in December he returned to front-line duty on the Eastern and Western Fronts from March 1915. He was awarded both classes of the Iron Cross during the war and remained in the Army after the Armistice, serving with Mounted Regiment 8 from 1920 until September 1936 and rising to the rank of *Major*. From August 1939 he was serving as Commander of Reconnaissance Battalion I of the 1st Infantry Division and was wounded on 2 September and hospitalised for almost two weeks. He returned to front-line duty as Commander of Rifle Battalion 59 in July 1940 with the rank of *Oberstleutnant* and later that year served as Commander of Rifle Regiment 101.

made a major contribution to ensuring that a pocket containing a number of Soviet units could be liquidated. From the end of June 1942 he took command of Rifle Brigade 20 while attached to the 20th Panzer Division and took part in the Kursk offensive. On 10 October he took command of the division and saw action in the battles around Gshatsk, Orel, Toropez and Bryansk, being promoted to *Generalmajor* on 1 December 1942. He was then promoted to *Generalleutnant* in June 1943 but his command was defeated during the German summer offensive at Kursk. Lüttwitz went to the front to observe the battle and then filed his report. He was promptly added to the Reserve List from September 1943, where he remained until January 1944. From February he was appointed, on the suggestion of Heinz Guderian, as Commander of the 2nd Panzer Division and saw action in White Russia, arriving at Bobruisk on 1 February. During the following weeks he supervised the transfer of his new division to France, where he set up his new headquarters on the outskirts of Amiens and began to rebuild his battered division.

Knight's Cross with Oakleaves: He became the 571st recipient on 3 September 1944 as *Generalleutnant* and Commander of 2nd Panzer Division, part of the LVI. Panzer Corps, awarded for his efforts in directing German units through the corridor at Falaise to safety in late August 1944. He was personally presented with the Oakleaves by *SS-Reichsführer* Heinrich Himmler in Posen on 7 November 1944. From 5 September he was delegated with the leadership of the XXXXVII. Panzer Corps. On 9 November he was promoted to *General der Panzertruppe* and his command was confirmed. He later took part in the Battle of the Bulge and from April 1945 he took command of Army Detachment *von Lüttwitz*, seeing action in the Ruhr Pocket.

Knight's Cross with Oakleaves and Swords: He became the 157th recipient on 9 May 1945 as *General der Panzertruppe* and Commanding General of the XXXXVII. Panzer Corps while attached to the Parachute Army of Army Group H for actions in the Ruhr Pocket. The award recommendation from the Parachute Army headquarters arrived at the Army Personnel Office on 28 April 1945. Major Domaschk did not process the order as he thought that von Lüttwitz had been taken prisoner in the Ruhr Pocket along with the rest of Army Group B on 15 April 1945. The award was put 'on hold' and not processed, and therefore not approved. The award date and number were assigned by the Award Association of the Knight's Cross. The assumption made by the Army Personnel Office was correct: Lüttwitz had surrendered to the Americans on 16 April after the Ruhr Pocket collapsed. He remained in Allied captivity until his release on 1 July 1947.

Friedrich Hermann Rudolf ZICKWOLFF

Generalleutnant

* 1 August 1889, Bayreuth
+ 17 September 1944, Tübingen Hospital, Baden-Württemberg

Knight's Cross: Awarded on 2 June 1942 as *Generalleutnant* and Commander of 113th Infantry Division while attached to VII. Army Corps for his leadership during the defence against enemy attacks in the Kharkov area of the Russian

Friedrich Zickwolff entered the Army in July 1908 as an officer candidate and was commissioned as a *Leutnant* a year later. He served during the First World War with the 9th Company of Infantry Regiment 124 and from March 1915 served as company leader with the rank of *Oberleutnant*. He ended the war as a brigade adjutant with the rank of *Hauptmann* and had been awarded both classes of the Iron Cross. He stayed in the Army after the war and from October 1935 he served as Commander of Infantry Regiment 13. In October 1936, now with the rank of *Oberst*, he was Commander of Infantry Regiment 119. In August 1939 he was appointed Commander of the 227th Infantry Division and was promoted to *Generalmajor* in October 1939.

Front. He and his command played a leading role in the prevention of a Soviet breakthrough along the north-eastern edge of the salient, being vital for stabilising the German front line along the Berestova River for two days. Here he was able to threaten the northern flank of the Soviet advance, forcing them to divert forces to face his division, which sufficiently weakened the Soviet assault to a point that it was unable to capture Krasnograd. From September 1942 Zickwolff took command of the 343rd Infantry Division, which was formed in south-western Germany, and once formed it was sent to France in spring 1943, where it was responsible for guarding a sector of the Atlantic coast near Brest. On 25 August Zickwolff was seriously wounded during an attack by partisans in Brittany and was sent to Tübingen Hospital in central Baden-Württemberg, Germany, where he died in September 1944.

Maximilian SIRY

Generalleutnant

* 19 April 1891, Parsberg, Bavaria
+ 6 December 1967, Fulda, Hesse

Knight's Cross: Awarded on 13 June 1942 as *Generalmajor* and Commander of 246th Infantry Division as part of the 9th Army on the Russian Front in the Rzhev salient. Promoted to *Generalleutnant* on 21 January 1943, he later took part in the withdrawal from Rzhev and in May he was appointed Commander of Army Coastal Command North in Norway. In January 1945 his command was deployed to Mountain Higher Command 20 and was attached to Army Coastal Artillery Training Command Norway. Siry briefly transferred to the Reserves in February and in March he was assigned for a short period as commander of the 347th Infantry Division on the Western Front. In early April he was assigned to the Commander-in-Chief West *Generalfeldmarschall* Albert Kesselring of the *Luftwaffe*, and from May until August 1945 he was held in Allied captivity.

Werner KOLB

Generalmajor

* 27 July 1895, Burbach, Siegen
+ 18 February 1975, Neu Isenburg

Knight's Cross: Awarded on 27 June 1942 as *Major der Reserve* and Commander of the II. Battalion of Infantry Regiment 36 in recognition of his bravery and leadership during the fighting at the northern tip of the Russian industrial area, north-east of Artemovsk (known now as Bakhmut), near Krasnoyarsk. He later saw action at Rostov and in the Caucasus campaign of 1942–43. In April 1943 Kolb was promoted to *Oberstleutnant der Reserve* and from July he took over as commander of Grenadier Regiment 36, continuing to see action in the Caucasus and later in the Nikopol Bridgehead.

Knight's Cross with Oakleaves: He became the 514th recipient on 26 June 1944 as *Oberst der Reserve* and Commander of Grenadier Regiment 36 for his achievements during the defensive battles on the southern sector of the Eastern Front in late 1943 and 1944. On 30 September 1943 his regiment was forced to move to new positions, where they pushed back a Soviet force of six rifle divisions and three tank brigades. In January 1944 Kolb was promoted to *Oberst der Reserve* and was presented with the Oakleaves by Hitler at *Führer* Headquarters in Rastenburg in August. During the fierce defensive battles over the Dniester near the Romanian border he had to retreat when his regiment was almost wiped out and he managed to escape capture by the Soviets. From November 1944 he was Commander of the 9th *Volksgrenadier* Division and saw action during the Ardennes Offensive in late 1944. He continued to fight in the West, opposing the Americans who were pushing across Luxemburg and then southern Germany. In February 1945 Kolb was promoted to *Generalmajor*

Werner Kolb entered the Army Reserves as a war volunteer with Infantry Regiment 55 in August 1914 and saw action while attached to Infantry Regiment 158. He was commissioned as a *Leutnant* in November 1915 and served as a platoon leader and later as an adjutant and court officer. He left the Army at the end of the war and studied engineering. He entered the Reserve Army in 1936 and saw action as a company commander with Infantry Regiment 16 from September 1939. From December 1940 he was Commander of the II. Battalion of Infantry Regiment 36, now with the rank of *Hauptmann der Reserve*.

der Reserve and from April remnants of his command were attached to the 352nd *Volksgrenadier* Division and defended Franconia and Nuremberg. On 8 May Kolb and his staff surrendered to the Americans and Kolb remained a prisoner until his release on 20 December 1947.

Moritz Otto Wilhelm Heinrich von DREBBER

Generalmajor

* 12 February 1892, Oldenburg, Lower Saxony
+ 30 May 1968, Oldenburg, Lower Saxony

Knight's Cross: Awarded on 30 June 1942 as *Oberst* and Commander of Infantry Regiment 523 while attached to the 297th Infantry Division for actions on the Russian Front. In June he led a combat group consisting of his own Infantry Regiment 523, a rifle battalion, an artillery battalion, two tank destroyer companies and two engineer battalions. His combat group was deployed south of the Donets to establish a bridgehead in support of the 14th Panzer Division in crossing the Velykyi Burluk River in the Ukraine. His troops captured the bridgehead by surprise within two hours and the Soviet defenders were eliminated, which left the way clear for the Panzer Division. On 11 June, without waiting, Drebber continued to advance and by the following day his men had cleared a minefield of its 2,000 mines. Drebber and his men crossed swamps at chest height all without vehicle support and all while being constantly threatened by Soviet gunfire. It was reported that without Drebber's extreme actions the enemy would have escaped. He took 1,660 prisoners and captured thirty-six artillery guns. In January 1943 Drebber was promoted to *Generalmajor* and given command of the 297th Infantry Division, part of the IV. Army Corps at Stalingrad. He was captured by Soviet forces on 25 January and was not released until 21 January 1949.

Moritz von Drebber joined the 91st Infantry Regiment in March 1911, and after his training he was commissioned as a Leutnant in May the following year. He was appointed company leader with the 79th Reserve Infantry Regiment in September 1914, but two weeks later was wounded and hospitalised. From 1935 he was a battalion commander with Infantry Regiment 58 and was promoted to *Oberstleutnant* in June 1935. From August 1939 he commanded Infantry Regiment 327 and was awarded the Bar to the Iron Cross in November and the Bar to the Iron Cross 1st Class in France in June 1940.

Karl Albert Kurt BRENNECKE

General der Infanterie

* 16 December 1891, Ringelheim, Hannover
+ 30 December 1982, Bonn, North Rhine-Westphalia

Kurt Brennecke entered Army service as an officer candidate with Infantry Regiment 15 in February 1910, and he was commissioned as a *Leutnant* in August 1911. He served with the same regiment throughout the war and was promoted to *Hauptmann* in August 1918. He was awarded both classes of the Iron Cross. He stayed in the Army after the war, attending various courses, and from October 1935, now an *Oberst*, he served as Chief of the General Staff of VII. Army Corps. At the beginning of the Second World War he was serving as Chief of Staff of the 4th Army with the rank of *Generalmajor* and was during this time awarded the Bar to the Iron Cross 1st and 2nd Classes.

Knight's Cross: Awarded on 12 July 1942 as *General der Infanterie* and Commanding General of the XXXXIII. Army Corps, attached to the 4th Army, for his outstanding personal bravery during the fighting to destroy the enemy around Podlipki in north-eastern Poland. He continued to see heavy action in the Soviet Union until 27 January 1943, when he fell ill and was transferred into the *Führer* Reserve. From June 1943 he served as the Commander of Courses for Divisional Commanders and Commanding Generals in Berlin. Due to heavy bombing, the courses were moved to Hirschberg, the Infantry School at Döberitz, and finally Neustadt and Bad Wiesse on Lake Tegernsee in the Bavarian Alps. It was here that he surrendered to American troops on 8 May 1945, and he remained a prisoner until 31 March 1948.

Dietrich KRAISS

Generalleutnant

* 16 November 1889, Stuttgart, Württemberg
+ 2 August 1944, near Saint-Lô, Normandy, France

Knight's Cross: Awarded on 23 July 1942 as *Generalmajor* and Commander of 168th Infantry Division while attached to the XXIX. Army Corps for

Dietrich Kraiss entered Army service as a *Leutnant* with Infantry Regiment 126 in March 1909 and served as a platoon leader and later as a battalion leader during the First World War. Promoted to *Hauptmann* in 1918, he remained in the Army after the war, serving with Infantry Regiment 13 and then attached to the Reich Defence Ministry until September 1934. From October 1935 he was battalion commander in Infantry Regiment 119 and from October 1937 he was Commander of Infantry Regiment 90 in Hamburg with the rank of *Oberst*.

actions during the early stages of Case Blue, the German summer offensive against the Soviet Union. During the advance on the town of Stary Oskol his forces identified a strong Soviet force nearby and from 5 July he led forward elements of his command against the enemy forces, which destroyed them. He continued to see action near Kharkov and around Voronezh, and was promoted to *Generalleutnant* in October 1942. From early 1943 he saw heavy action in the Belgorod sector. Towards the end of March 1943 he was rested and placed in the Reserves, serving with Military District Command X, and from mid-May Kraiss served as Commander of the newly formed 355th Infantry Division. After completing his training, he took his division to the Crimea in July 1943, and first saw combat near Kharkov in southern Russia from September. From early November that year he took command of the 352nd Infantry Division in Normandy, where it had been formed as part of the 7th Army.

Knight's Cross with Oakleaves: He became the 549th recipient, posthumously, on 11 August 1944 as *Generalleutnant* and Commander of the 352nd Infantry Division for actions during the Normandy battles during the Allied invasion of France. Elements of his command saw action on Omaha beach and fought well despite being heavily outnumbered and outgunned by the Allied forces. While the neighbouring division had evacuated their positions by the end of the first day, the troops under Kraiss prevented the Americans from breaking through to Saint-Lô. On 2 August 1944, during what would be the decisive battle by the Americans to reach Saint-Lô, Kraiss was mortally wounded and was rushed to an aid station, where he died the same day.

Richard Adolf DANIEL

Generalmajor

* 24 December 1900, Anspach, Usingen
+ 4 May 1986, Neumünster, Schleswig-Holstein

Knight's Cross: Awarded on 25 July 1942 as *Oberstleutnant* and Commander of Infantry Regiment 391, part of the 170th Infantry Division, in recognition of his bravery and leadership during the heavy fighting in the Soviet Union. On 29 June 1942 Daniel led his regiment in a breakthrough of the inner fortification of Fortress Sevastopol's southern front. Then, without waiting for orders or other units, he thrust forward and in doing so laid the groundwork for a swift attack

Richard Daniel entered Army service in April 1916 at the age of seventeen as a pupil with the Unteroffizier Preparatory School in Annaburg. He entered the police in October 1919, where he remained until October 1933, and with the rank of *Polizei-Hauptmann* he transferred into the Army. From October 1937, with the rank of *Hauptmann*, he commanded the 6th Company of Infantry Regiment 46.

In October 1939 Daniel was appointed commander of the I. Battalion of Infantry Regiment 401 and served in Denmark and France before taking part in the invasion of the Soviet Union. There, in July 1941, he was awarded the Iron Cross 1st and 2nd Classes.

towards the south, taking control of important roads. He later saw action in the area around Leningrad and was promoted to *Oberst* on 30 November 1942. From early November 1943 he served as an instruction officer for regimental leaders at the Infantry School in Döberitz and from July 1944 he was delegated with the leadership of the 45th Grenadier Division. In October he was promoted to *Generalmajor* and his command became the 45th *Volksgrenadier* Division, part of the 9th Army on the Eastern Front.

Knight's Cross with Oakleaves: Awarded, without a recipient number, as *Generalmajor* and Commander of the 45th *Volksgrenadier* Division while attached to the VIII. Army Corps on 30 April 1945 for actions on the Eastern Front. On the night of 14–15 February 1945 his division pushed toward Strzelin, a town in Lower Silesia, in the midst of ongoing enemy attack. On 15 February the enemy penetrated into the German sector, captured the town of Campen and threatened a flank of his division. Daniel immediately rushed to the threatened area, and in doing so the Soviets attacked again. Daniel personally led three assault-gun vehicles in a counter-attack and managed to strike at the unsuspecting Soviet force and recapture the town. This personal intervention by Daniel laid the groundwork for further counter-attacks, which he led with a battalion and once again pushed the enemy out of the area. On 16 February the enemy made another attack and *Generalmajor* Daniel rallied an armoured company with three assault-gun vehicles and once again pushed the enemy back. He was solely responsible for ensuring the defensive front did not collapse and his forces destroyed seventy-nine enemy tanks. On 18 March 1945 Daniel was severely wounded and hospitalised for the rest of the war. He was taken into custody by the British on 8 May and was not released until July 1947.

Kurt OPPENLÄNDER

Generalleutnant

* 11 February 1892, Ulm, Württemberg
+ 17 March 1947, Garmisch-Partenkirchen, Bavaria

Knight's Cross: Awarded on 25 July 1942 as *Generalmajor* and Commander of 305th Infantry Division while attached to the VIII. Army Corps for actions near Kharkov on the Russian Front. On 31 October 1942 Oppenländer was relieved of his command after being found drunk and was transferred into the Reserves, when it was discovered he was ill and he was admitted to hospital. He was promoted to *Generalleutnant* in August 1943 and the following month was appointed Commandant of Cracow in Poland. On 1 June 1944 he was delegated with the leadership of the 198th Infantry Division but was relieved from duty on 5 August that same year because of physical and nervous exhaustion, and after being caught drunk on duty once again. He was admitted to hospital in Badenweiler. In November that year he disturbed a National Socialist Women's League meeting in a drunken state and was arrested and charged with undermining the war effort. In February 1945 all charges were dropped by the courts but in early March *Generalfeldmarschall* Keitel sentenced him to seven days' imprisonment and he was later dismissed from the Army. He was captured by US forces on 30 June and while in captivity he died in Garmisch-Partenkirchen in Bavaria on 17 March 1947.

Max August FREMEREY

Generalleutnant

* 5 May 1889, Cologne
+ 20 September 1968, Krün, Upper Bavaria

Knight's Cross: Awarded on 28 July 1942 as *Generalmajor* and Commander of the 29th Motorised Infantry Division, part of the XXXX. Army Corps, for actions on the Russian Front. Under order of his divisional commander, he launched a bold thrust on 14 July to penetrate into the city of Morosovskaja, where he ejected the enemy forces. He showed excellent leadership skills and

Max Fremery entered military service with Dragoon Regiment 7 in March 1910 as an officer candidate and saw action during the First World War. He was seriously wounded in October 1914 and two years later was promoted to *Oberleutnant.* He served as an adjutant and orderly officer throughout the war and was promoted to *Rittmeister* in September 1918. He remained in the Army after the war and served with the Reich Defence Ministry and attended various courses. He was finally given his own command in 1935 when he was appointed commander of Mounted Regiment 17 with the rank of *Oberstleutnant.* He did not see action until the invasion of France and the Low Countries as part of the 12th Army.

his actions pushed the enemy forces away from the Don River area. As a result he was presented with the Knight's Cross by his corps commander. In October he took command of Motorised Division 155, which he completely reorganised and in April 1943 it was redesignated Panzer Division 155 and sent to Rennes in north-western France. Fremerey was promoted to *Generalleutnant* in June 1943 and his command was renamed the 155th Reserve Panzer Division. In May 1944 he took over as Commander of the 233rd Reserve Panzer Division with his headquarters in Horsens, Denmark, where he was responsible for training panzer crews and motorised troops. From March his command was redesignated the 233rd Panzer Division but never saw combat and went into captivity in May 1945.

Friedrich KÖCHLING
General der Infanterie

* 22 June 1893, Ahaus
+ 5 June 1970, Legden, Coesfeld

Knight's Cross: Awarded on 31 July 1942 as *Generalmajor* and Commander of the 254th Infantry Division of the LVI. Army Corps for his bravery and leadership

Friedrich Köchling served with Infantry Regiment 159 from March 1912 and was commissioned as a *Leutnant* a year later and made company leader. He saw action during the First World War and was promoted to *Oberleutnant* in October 1916. He served as a company leader, machine gun officer and regimental adjutant with Infantry Regiment 159 during the war and was awarded both classes of the Iron Cross. He remained in the Army after the war and was by October 1935 serving as Commander of the III. Battalion of Infantry Regiment 58 with the rank of *Oberstleutnant*. From August 1939 he served as Commander of Infantry Regiment 278 with the rank of *Oberst* and saw action during the French Campaign in 1940, where he was awarded both classes of the Bar to the Iron Cross.

for actions on the northern sector of the Eastern Front. He was promoted to *Generalleutnant* on 1 January 1943 and briefly from October to November he served as Acting Commander Crimea. On 1 December he was delegated with the leadership of the XXXXIV. Army Corps as part of the 6th Army in the Dnieper River area in the Soviet Union. From February 1944, now with the rank of *General der Infanterie*, he took command of the XXXXIX. Mountain Corps while part of the 17th Army in the Crimea. He entered the Reserves from March 1944 and in June was appointed Commanding General of the X. Army Corps and saw action as part of the 16th Army in the Soviet Union. On 21 September Köchling was transferred and appointed Commanding General of the LXXXI. Army Corps as part of the 7th Army while located in Aachen, Germany. It took part in the siege of Aachen from October 1944, which ended with the Americans taking the city, and Köchling finally surrendered his forces to US forces on 13 April 1945. He remained in Allied captivity until June 1947.

Eugen KÖNIG

Generalleutnant

* 19 September 1896, Trier
\+ 8 April 1985, Bitburg, Rhineland-Palatinate

Knight's Cross: Awarded on 1 August 1942 as *Major* and leader of Infantry Regiment 352 while attached to the 246th Infantry Division after distinguishing himself on 6 February 1942 during the storming of Turowo in West Pomerania. In July König led a counter-attack, taking many Soviet prisoners, and continued the attack towards Suchowola in north-eastern Poland. His independent decision

Eugen König was a war volunteer from June 1915 attached to Infantry Regiment 69, and was commissioned as a *Leutnant* the following year and served as a platoon leader and then adjutant of II. Battalion. He was a prisoner of the British after the war and was dismissed from the Army in 1920. He worked as a civil servant for a time and entered the Reserves as an *Oberleutnant der Reserve* in December 1936. At the beginning of the war in September 1939 he served as regimental adjutant of Infantry Regiment 352 with the rank of *Hauptmann* but remained in Germany. He then served as Commander of the II. Battalion of his regiment with the rank of *Major* and served in the Saar-Palatinate until September, when he became *Major* and adjutant of the 264th Infantry Division.

to attack and capture Hill 228.4 near Belyj was decisive for the elimination of the Soviet pocket further south as it enabled a link-up with the 1st Panzer Division, which was attacking from the north. From October 1942 his command became Grenadier Regiment 352 and he continued to see action on the Eastern Front as part of the 9th Army. Promoted to *Oberst* in March 1943, the following month König was appointed Acting Commander of the 251st Infantry Division and saw action during the Battle of Kursk.

Knight's Cross with Oakleaves: König became the 318th recipient on 4 November 1943 as *Oberst* and Commander of Grenadier Regiment 451 as part of the 251st Infantry Division after conducting two river crossings and after storming several hills against fierce enemy fire. From August 1943 he was involved in the major defensive fighting south-west of Orel against a strong enemy. König set out with new reserves, launched his own counter-attack against the Soviet forces and smashed the enemy forces with his handful of grenadiers in a bloody engagement. König was presented with the Oakleaves personally by Hitler in December 1943 at *Führer* Headquarters in Rastenburg. In May 1944 he attended the 11th Divisional Leaders Course at Hirschberg and from 7 June he was named Commander of the 91st Air Landing Division, which had already been decimated and its former commander had only just escaped Allied capture. It once again suffered heavy casualties and was reduced to battle group strength; then, following the German retreat to the Siegfried Line, it was disbanded. König had been promoted to *Generalmajor* in September 1944 and from November he took over as Commander of the 344th Infantry Division. From mid-December he took over as Commander of the 272nd *Volksgrenadier* Division, which was virtually destroyed in April 1945. König was promoted to *Generalleutnant* during this time and took over as Commander of the 12th *Volksgrenadier* Division but only briefly as he surrendered to US troops at Wuppertal six days later on 18 April 1945.

Rudolf Karl Peter Georg KONRAD

General der Gebirgstruppe

* 7 March 1891, Kulmbach, Bavaria
+ 10 June 1964, Munich, Bavaria

Knight's Cross: Awarded on 1 August 1942 as *General der Gebirgstruppe* and Commanding General of the XXXXIX. Mountain Corps while attached to the 17th Army for his breakthrough of the strong enemy positions west of Rostov on the Soviet Front. His corps took part in the tough conditions south of Rostov

Rudolf Konrad entered Army service in July 1910 as an officer candidate while attached to Bavarian Field Artillery Regiment 1 and was commissioned as a *Leutnant* the following year. He served with this regiment throughout the First World War and was awarded both classes of the Iron Cross and ended the war as an *Oberleutnant* and adjutant of Bavarian Artillery Commander 1. He remained in the Army after the war and served with various artillery units, being promoted to *Rittmeister* in October 1927. From March 1931 he was attached to the War Ministry and in April 1934 he was made Commander of the III. Battalion of Infantry Regiment 19 with the rank of *Oberstleutnant*. In October 1936 he was appointed Chief of Operations in the General Staff of Group Command 2 and from April 1938 he was Chief of the General Staff of XVIII. Army Corps with the rank of *Oberst*.

and took the city of Bataysk near Rostov, where it created a vital bridgehead south of the Don, where General Konrad put himself at the head of his troops. His command was then deployed near Maykop and then along the Black Sea area, and by the end of the year they had to withdraw and rest. It was not until October 1943 that his corps returned to battle during the fierce fighting near Sevastopol, where it was almost destroyed. From May until December, Konrad was attached to the Reserves and he then served with Army Group South as Commander of the Margarethen Area in the German district of Steinberg in Schleswig-Holstein. From 6 March 1945 he saw action in Western Hungary as part of Operation Spring Awakening, the last major German offensive of the war. The objective was to secure the last of the oil reserves still available to the Axis powers and to prevent the Red Army from advancing towards Vienna. It, of course, failed. Konrad surrendered to the Allies on 8 May 1945 and was not released until mid-1947.

Wilhelm 'Willi' SCHNECKENBURGER

General der Infanterie

* 30 March 1891, Tübingen
+ 14 October 1944, Hospital in Belgrade, Serbia

Knight's Cross: Awarded on 1 August 1942 as *Generalleutnant* and Commander of 125th Infantry Division while attached to the V. Army Corps for his part in the capture of Rostov and for action during the Caucasus campaign. He later took part in the fighting in the Battle of Novorossiysk and in the Kuban

Wilhelm 'Willi' Schneckenburger entered the Army in August 1909 and saw action during the First World War with Infantry Regiments 124 and 246 with the rank of *Leutnant*. He later became company leader and deputy regimental adjutant from December 1915 and was promoted to *Oberleutnant* the following year. He stayed in the Army after the war, serving as ordnance officer and company officer, and later became a battalion adjutant with the rank of *Hauptmann*. He entered the General Staff of the Army in October 1936, now with the rank of *Oberst*, and from August 1939 he was appointed Chief of the General Staff of Commanding General of the Deputy General Command of III. Army Corps and Commander of Military District III, Berlin.

campaign. From 10 January 1943 Schneckenburger served as a General Officer on the Staff of the Romanian 3rd Army. From March he was delegated with the leadership of the XVII. Army Corps and saw action in the Ukraine as part of the 6th Army, and in May 1943 he was promoted to *General der Infanterie* and his command was confirmed. From June 1944 he was Head of the German Mission in Bulgaria and was at the same time attached to the High Command of the Royal Bulgarian Armed Forces. In August 1944 he was appointed Commanding General of Corps *Belgrade* and on 13 October he was seriously wounded and died the following day in a Serbian hospital.

Erich BÄRENFÄNGER

Generalmajor

* 12 January 1915, Meden, Iserlohn in North Rhine-Westphalia
+ 2 May 1945, Berlin

Knight's Cross: Erich Bärenfänger was awarded the Knight's Cross on 7 August 1942 as *Oberleutnant* and leader of the III. Battalion of the 123rd Infantry Regiment, part of the 50th Infantry Division, for the capture of Soviet positions near Sevastopol, conducted at night on his own initiative. This enabled the area to be completely encircled and destroyed the enemy forces in the area with a high number of casualties. This allowed the 50th Infantry Division to advance through to the south-eastern edge of Sevastopol without excessive combat and loss. On 16 November Bärenfänger was wounded for the seventh time when he was hit by shrapnel in the back and lower legs.

Erich Bärenfänger was one of the youngest officers during the Second World War to be promoted to the rank of *General*. After leaving school he joined the RAD, the Reich Labour Service, and joined the SA in 1933. He joined the Army in October 1936 and was attached to the 67th Infantry Regiment in Berlin, with the rank of *Gefreiter*. In November 1938 Bärenfänger was transferred to the 123rd Border Infantry Regiment and in April 1939 he was commissioned as a *Leutnant*. He led a platoon during the invasion of Poland and during the Battle of France. On 6 June 1940 he was wounded by shrapnel in his right forearm and left hand and once he had recovered he was transferred to the 122nd Infantry Replacement Battalion.

Knight's Cross with Oakleaves: *Hauptmann* Bärenfänger was awarded the Oakleaves on 17 May 1943, the 243rd recipient, as Commander of III. Battalion of the 123rd Grenadier Regiment after he distinguished himself in battle during heavy combat along the Terek River and the subsequent withdrawal from the Kuban Bridgehead area. He was personally presented with the Oakleaves by

From June 1941 Bärenfänger served in the Soviet Union, where he fought on the Taman Peninsula and in the Kuban position on the Crimea Peninsula. He was wounded on 12 July when he was shot through the right hand and on 5 August he was seriously wounded by shrapnel when an artillery shell exploded right near him. Then two weeks later his command car hit a mine and he was thrown about 30ft into the air, injuring his knee. On 12 September, Bärenfänger was promoted to *Oberleutnant* and took over as company commander in the 123rd Infantry Regiment. He was hit by a piece of shrapnel on 1 November and the following day both of his knees were hit by shrapnel.

Hitler during a ceremony at the Wolf's Lair in Rastenburg sometime in early May 1943 together with eight other recipients, including *Generalleutnant* Hans-Karl von Scheele, *Oberst* Walter Gorn and *Hauptmann* Waldemar von Gazen. Promoted to the rank of *Major* on 10 June 1943, Bärenfänger was wounded a number of times at the front during heavy action during which his command held important ground during the major offences. He was promoted to *Oberstleutnant* in February 1944, and in June he left the front when he was named General Inspector of the Army Youth Leadership under Hitler Youth Leader *Reichsjugendführer* Artur Axmann.

Knight's Cross with Oakleaves and Swords: Awarded on 23 January 1944 as *Major* and while still Commander of the III. Battalion of the 123rd Grenadier Regiment, becoming the forty-fifth recipient, in recognition of his personal bravery and leadership in the Soviet Union. Between 13 and 17 November and 4 to 6 December Bärenfänger and his men repulsed attack after attack on the Kerch Peninsula. Bärenfänger remained with his men despite having received his sixth and seventh wounds during the attack. On 13 February 1944 he was personally presented with his Swords by Hitler at *Führer* Headquarters in Rastenburg. In November he was appointed Inspector of the Defence Efficiency Camp of the Hitler Youth and was made responsible for the training of the young boys in how to use anti-tank equipment in the defence of Berlin. On 24 April 1945 he was named as the Battle Commandant of Section A and B of the Berlin Defensive District and he became deputy to *General der Artillerie* Helmuth Weidling. Four days later Hitler personally promoted Bärenfänger to the rank of *Generalmajor*, bypassing the rank of *Oberst*, making him one of the youngest generals of the war.

Friedrich Wilhelm Ludwig WETZEL

General der Infanterie

* 15 July 1888, Sarbske
\+ 4 July 1964, Hamburg

Knight's Cross: Awarded on 7 August 1942 as *General der Infanterie* and Commanding General of V. Army Corps as part of Army Group South for his part in the swift seizure of a town in the Soviet Union. He personally led elements of his command across a river following bitter combat and under his leadership they secured a breakthrough past a strongly fortified enemy bunker position in the northernmost part of the town of Rostov. From October 1942

Wilhelm Wetzel entered the Army in February 1907, was appointed a *Leutnant* the following year and from 1912 was a battalion adjutant and court officer. He was promoted to *Oberleutnant* in November 1914 and served as a regimental adjutant during the war. He was later a battalion and then company leader with the rank of *Hauptmann* in April 1916. He remained in the Army after the war and commanded a company and a battalion in Rastenburg, later serving as a trainer at the Engineer School in Munich. From October 1935 Wetzel served as Commander of the War School in Potsdam with the rank of *Oberst*. In August 1939 he was Commander of the 255th Infantry Division and saw action during the invasion of France and the Low Countries, where he was awarded the Bar to the Iron Cross 1st and 2nd Classes.

until June 1943 his command was also known as Group Wetzel and shortly after the Soviet winter offensive began his corps was part of the German withdrawal towards the Kuban Bridgehead area. He spent two months in the Reserves before taking command of the LXXXIV. Army Corps in August 1943, serving as part of the occupation force in Saint-Lô in north-western France. From March 1944 until the end of the war in May 1945 he served as Commanding General of the Deputy X. Army Corps and Commander of Military District X, Hamburg.

Hans von der MOSEL

Generalmajor

* 3 May 1898, Bodenbach
+ 12 April 1969, Nienburg

Knight's Cross: Awarded on 9 August 1942 as *Oberst* and Commander of Infantry Regiment 548 while attached to the 278th Infantry Division for his excellent defence of the area near Rzhev. Mosel personally looked at the plan of attack, analysing the terrain and leading the counter-attack against a strong Soviet assault for more than three hours. It was his bravery and leadership that helped to prevent a Soviet breakthrough south-east of Rzhev, but it came at a price as his command suffered many wounded. By November 1942 Mosel was seeing action in the south of France and from May 1943 he served as Commandant of Brest until August 1944. The following month he was promoted to *Generalmajor*.

Knight's Cross with Oakleaves: He became the 589th recipient on 18 September 1944 as *Generalmajor* and Chief of Staff and Deputy of Fortress Command

Hans von der Mosel entered the Army in November 1916 with Grenadier Regiment 101 and was promoted to *Leutnant* in June 1918. He served with the *Reichswehr* from November 1919 with the 11th Infantry Regiment, rising to the rank of *Hauptmann* in May 1933. From October 1935 he was commander of a machine gun company with Infantry Training Battalion in Döberitz. He was promoted to *Major* in October 1938 and served as Commander of the Army Air Defence School before taking over Command of the I. Battalion of Infantry Regiment 234 in May 1940.

Brest and contributed greatly to the defence of his command. His actions, while under the command of *General der Fallschirmtruppe* Bernhard Ramcke, helped to ensure that Brest could be held for as long as possible and therefore deny its use as a port by the Allies. The staff of Fortress Brest surrendered to US forces on 20 September 1944 and both Mosel and Ramcke went into US captivity until 1948.

Georg-Wilhelm POSTEL
Generalleutnant

* 25 April 1896, Zittau, Saxony
+ 20 September 1953, Hospital Prison in Schachty, Soviet Union

Knight's Cross: Awarded on 9 August 1942 as *Oberst* and Commander of Infantry Regiment 364 of the 161st Infantry Division in recognition of his command and bravery during heavy fighting in the Soviet Union. On 4 February 1942 he was assigned command of all German units located near the area of Rzhev and the following day he launched an attack that managed to close the gap created by the Soviets. On 26 November 1942 he was delegated with the leadership of the 320th Infantry Division and was assigned to the Cotentin Peninsula of Brittany. In January 1943 Postel was promoted to *Generalmajor* and his command was confirmed. He was then sent to the southern sector of the Eastern Front, seeing action near Kharkov from February.

Knight's Cross with Oakleaves: He became the 215th recipient on 28 March 1943 as *Generalmajor* and Commander of 320th Infantry Division while attached to Army Corps *Raus* for his leadership during the defensive battles on the southern sector of the Eastern Front. He led his division during weeks of bitter

Georg Postel entered the Army in August 1914 and from 1916 served as a battalion adjutant with the rank of *Leutnant* and later served as a legal officer. He stayed in the Army after the war and served as a platoon leader and with various regiments in Bautzen and Leipzig. By December 1935 he had been promoted to *Major*. From 1936 until 1939 he served as an instructor at the War School in Munich and then as a battalion commander with the 109th Infantry Regiment, the 433rd Infantry Regiment and the 364th Infantry Regiment. From May 1940 he served as Acting Commander of Infantry Regiment 47 and from July he took over as Commander of Infantry Regiment 364. He saw action in Luxembourg and later in the Soviet Union, where he was awarded both classes of the Iron Cross.

fighting in some of the most difficult weather conditions of the campaign with his troops locked in battle for nine days with the Red Army. By 14 February his troops had pushed back the Soviet forces and had secured the German lines once again. Postel always led from the front, placing himself where the fighting inspired his men to give their best. The following day Postel and his division were mentioned in the Armed Forces Daily Report: 'An Infantry Division pushed forward from its operating base under the leadership of its commander Generalmajor Postel and penetrated the strong enemy forces, destroying them and returning to his own lines in a battle that lasted for nine days.' Postel was decorated with the Oakleaves personally by Hitler on 31 March 1943 at the Berghof. Postel continued to see heavy action on the Eastern Front and was wounded towards the end of May 1943. He returned to the front line in August and was promoted to *Generalleutnant* a month later.

Knight's Cross with Oakleaves and Swords: Awarded on 26 March 1944 to become the fifty-seventh recipient as *Generalleutnant* and Commander of the 320th Infantry Division as part of the XXXXVII. Army Corps for his outstanding leadership during the summer of 1943 in Belgorod and later in Kharkov. On 25 May 1944 Postel was personally presented with the Swords by a grateful Hitler, once again at the Berghof. From 16 July 1944 Postel was appointed Commanding General of the XXX. Army Corps, seeing action in Romania until he was captured on 30 August by Soviet troops. He was sent to various prison camps, including No. 160, 74, 48 and 149, and in June 1949 he was sentenced to twenty-five years' hard labour by a military tribunal near Kharkov. He later contracted tuberculosis and died in the hospital of Prison Camp Schachty on 20 September 1953. He was buried in the camp's cemetery in row 3, grave 14, and his remains have never been transferred to any German war cemetery.

Karl von GRAFFEN

Generalleutnant

* 6 June 1893, Plön, Holstein
+ 1 November 1964, Grödersby, Schleswig-Holstein

Knight's Cross: Awarded on 13 August 1942 as *Generalmajor* and leader of 58th Infantry Division while attached to the XXXVIII. Army Corps for actions on the Russian Front. The Knight's Cross was presented to him by the Commanding General of the L. Army Corps, *General der Kavallerie* Philipp Kleffel. Graffen was promoted to *Generalleutnant* in January 1943 and saw action in the Soviet Union on the northern sector until September, when he was appointed Higher Artillery Commander 316 while attached to the 10th Army in Italy. He saw action against the British on the Italian mainland from early September and then a few days later fought against American troops near Salerno. The Germans managed to prevent an American breakthrough but had to give up Naples on 1 October and began to retreat, with defensive battles following between December 1943 and May 1944. He saw action during the heavy defensive fighting near Ancona, then withdrew to the Adriatic Sea and then towards Rimini, taking part in heavy defensive battles. From April 1945 he saw further defensive battles between the Adriatic Sea and Bologna and was taken prisoner by British troops on 18 July 1945. He remained in Allied captivity until his release on 3 March 1948.

In April 1911 Karl von Graffen entered Army service as a cadet. He was commissioned as a *Leutnant* a year later and served with Field Artillery Regiment 45 at the beginning of the First World War. He transferred into Field Artillery Regiment 65 in December 1914 and was promoted to *Oberleutnant* in December 1917. He remained in the Army after the war and from April 1920 he served with Artillery Regiment 2 until March 1934, and in October 1935 he was adjutant of the Artillery School in Jüterbog. He was promoted to *Oberstleutnant* in January 1937 and was attached to the Army High Command until February 1941.

Karl Julius Reingard Werner MUMMERT

Generalmajor der Reserve

* 31 March 1897, Lüttwitz, Saxony
+ 28 January 1950, prisoner of war camp in Ssuja, Soviet Union

Knight's Cross: Awarded on 17 August 1942 as *Major der Reserve* and Commander of Reconnaissance Battalion 256 while attached to the 265th Infantry Division in recognition of his bravery during the difficult fighting in the area near Polunino, north of Rzhev. He was responsible for an excellent counter-attack that managed to halt an advance by Soviet forces, preventing them from capturing a supply line that was of great importance to the German 9th Army. Mummert was promoted to *Oberstleutnant der Reserve* soon after and appointed Commander of Panzer Reconnaissance Battalion 14 from late 1943.

Knight's Cross with Oakleaves: Awarded on 20 March 1944, to become the 429th recipient as *Oberstleutnant der Reserve* and Commander of *Panzer* Grenadier Regiment 103 while attached to the 14th Panzer Division for actions during defensive battles in the Soviet Union. In February 1944, shortly before being promoted to *Oberst der Reserve*, Mummert led his regiment during the difficult and bloody defensive battles in Kirovograd and in Cherkassy.

Knight's Cross with Oakleaves and Swords: He became the 107th recipient on 23 October 1944 as *Oberst der Reserve* and while still Commander of *Panzer* Grenadier Regiment 103, part of the 14th Panzer Division, for his leadership

Werner Mummert joined the NSDAP in 1932 and the SS seven years later. During the Second World War he took part in campaigns in Poland and on the Western and Eastern Fronts. In 1944 he again served on the Western Front. At the end of the Second World War he served in the final stages of the defence of Berlin, where he became PoW to the Soviets on 3 May 1945. He died as a prisoner on 28 January 1950.

in the northern sector of the Eastern Front. On 5 September he was seriously wounded and flown to a hospital in Germany, where he was operated on and informed that he had been awarded the Oakleaves. On 21 November, now fully recovered, he attended the 16th Divisional Leaders Course in Hirschberg and shortly afterwards he was appointed Commander of the 103rd Panzer Brigade, seeing action in the Saar Region. In early February 1945, Mummert was promoted to *Generalmajor der Reserve* and was delegated with the leadership of Panzer Division Müncheberg, which had been formed from Staff of the 103rd Panzer Brigade. He led this command during the battles in Küstrin, a small village in Brandenburg and later in Berlin where his unit defended its position against a heavy Soviet artillery barrage while trying to attempt a link with Army Group *Wenck*. He very briefly commanded the LVI. Army Corps while *General der Artillerie* Helmuth Widling was on leave in April 1945 and then took over leadership of Panzer Division Müncheberg from 26 April 1945. Mummert was wounded in the right shoulder during the heavy fighting in Berlin, and was taken prisoner by the Soviets on 8 May 1945. He remained in captivity in Prison Camp No: 27 Krasnogorsk and then No: 48 Černcy, Ležnovo. He was finally held in Ssuja prison camp, where he died in 1950.

Alexander von PFUHLSTEIN

Generalmajor

* 17 December 1899, Danzig, Pomerania
+ 20 December 1976, Bad Homburg vor der Höhe, Hesse

Knight's Cross: Awarded on 17 August 1942 as *Oberst* and Commander of Infantry Regiment 154 while attached to the 58th Infantry Division for actions during the Battle of Volkov near Leningrad on the Russian Front. From January 1943 he was attached to the Foreign Office and Defence Department of the High Command of the *Wehrmacht*, and from February he was attached to Special Unit *Brandenburg*. On 1 July Pfuhlstein was promoted to *Generalmajor*. He took command of Division *Brandenburg* at the same time and saw action during the Balkans campaign until March 1944, when he was posted as Task Force Leader for the occupation of Hungary. He attended the 11th Divisional Commanders course from May 1944 and the following month took over the briefly as leader of the 50th Infantry Division in Romania. In late July he was arrested after the failure of the 20 July plot to kill Hitler. He was then taken to a Gestapo prison in Prinz Albrecht Strasse together with *Admiral* Wilhelm Canaris and *Generalmajor* Hans Oster. Pfuhlstein was found guilty of complicity but was spared the death sentence and demoted to the rank of private. He was forced to retire on 14 September 1944, was released from prison in two months later and after the war he rarely spoke about his imprisonment. There was some speculation that he had co-operated with the Gestapo but it is more likely that, being a Knight's Cross and German Cross in Gold holder, and because he had been wounded three times, it was thought that such a hero being attached to the plot to kill Hitler would not look good to the German people and so his involvement was kept quiet.

Erich REUTER

Generalleutnant

* 30 March 1904, Neu-Hückeswagen, Rhine Province
+ 30 October 1989, Lindau, Bavaria

Knight's Cross: Awarded on 17 August 1942 as *Oberstleutnant* and Commander of Infantry Regiment 122 while attached to the 50th Infantry Division for his leadership during the Battle of Sevastopol. His regiment captured an important hill on 25 June 1942, which was vital for the continued successes of his division and which enabled the employment of heavy artillery weapons. In fact, Reuter had already been recommended for the Knight's Cross after his success in the capture of Cornești in Romania on 12 July 1941. He later saw action during the Battles of Kovno, Novgorod and in the Siege of Leningrad. In the spring of 1942 his regiment took part in the Siege of Kholm to successfully rescue Combat Group Scherer, which had been surrounded by enemy forces. From November, Reuter transferred to the Army Personnel Office as Head of department and in April 1943 he served as adjutant of Army Group South, which was later redesignated Army Group Ukraine. Twelve months later he was promoted to *Oberst* and attended the 11th divisional leaders

Erich Reuter entered the I. Battalion of Prussian Infantry Regiment 2 in April 1922 and attended various training schools. He was commissioned as a *Leutnant* in September 1927. He served as a platoon leader from December and the then as an adjutant from June 1932 as an *Oberleutnant*. Promoted to *Hauptmann* in July 1935, he served as company commander still attached to Prussian Infantry Regiment 2. He saw action during the Polish Campaign and was awarded both classes of the Iron Cross in 1940 for his part in the invasion of France.

course in Hirschberg, and from 26 August 1944 he was delegated with the leadership of the 46th Infantry Division. In November he was promoted to *Generalmajor* and his command of the division was confirmed. He had seen heavy fighting in the Ukraine and from late 1944 the division, which was only at regimental strength, was in action on the Slovak–Hungarian frontier.

Knight's Cross with Oakleaves: He became the 710th recipient on 21 January 1945 as *Generalmajor* and Commander of 46th Infantry Division while attached to IV. Panzer Corps for his leadership during the battles between Budapest and Lake Balaton in early 1945. From March his command was redesignated the 46th *Volksgrenadier* Division and continued to see heavy action during the defensive battles in Hungary. Reuter was then promoted to *Generalleutnant* on 20 April 1945. He was captured by Soviet forces on 9 May and taken to Prison Camp No. 476 in Sverdlovsk, later being transferred to Camp No. 48 in Černcy, Ležnovo. On 7 June 1950 he was tried for war crimes by a military tribunal in Moscow and sentenced to twenty-five years' hard labour but he was released on 8 October 1955.

Werner Bernhard Franz von EICHSTEDT

Generalmajor

* 1 January 1896, Saerbeck, Westphalia
+ 26 August 1944, near Mansier, Romania

Knight's Cross: Awarded on 18 August 1942 as *Oberst* and Commander of Infantry Regiment 436 while attached to the 132nd Infantry Division for the part he played on 18 May 1942 in the destruction of enemy forces on the Kertsch Peninsula at the

Werner von Eichstedt entered the Army at the beginning of the war in August 1914 and joined Infantry Regiment 13. In December 1915 he was appointed temporary battalion commander and was wounded and hospitalised in October 1916. He was awarded the Iron Cross 1st and 2nd Class and captured by French soldiers in October 1917, being released in May 1920. He remained in the Army after the war and served with Infantry Regiment 7 until 1934. He became an instructor at the War School in Dresden from October 1936 with the rank of *Major*. He took command of an infantry battalion during the Polish and French campaigns, where he won the Bar to the Iron Cross 1st and 2nd Classes.

eastern end of the Crimea. Eichstedt continued to see action in the region of Leningrad as part of the 18th Army until he entered the Reserves at the end of February 1943. From September he was delegated with the leadership of the 387th Infantry Division and saw action in the areas near Donetsk, Krivoy Rog and Nikopol in Ukraine as part of the 1st Panzer Army. On 24 December he was appointed Commander of the 294th Infantry Division and from January 1944 he fought in Nikopol as part of the 6th Army, being promoted to *Generalmajor* in March. In August his division was encircled by the Soviets and Eichstedt ordered the survivors of the division to form small battle groups to force a breakout. As the battle groups moved into their positions, Eichstedt was observed leading the attack with rifle in his hand, running forward against Soviet machine guns and tank fire. *Generalmajor* Eichstedt was one of many to be killed, near Mansier in Romania, and his body has not yet been moved to a military cemetery.

Kurt VERSOCK

General der Gebirgstruppe

* 14 February 1895, Hütten
+ 17 March 1963, Aachen, North Rhine-Westphalia

Knight's Cross: Awarded on 25 August 1942 as *Oberst* and Commander of Infantry Regiment 31 while attached to the 24th Infantry Division for his part in the fighting during the Siege of Sevastopol and later for his regiment's part in the fighting against the Soviet counteroffensive near Lake Ilmen. In February 1943 he was appointed Commander of the 24th Infantry Division and remained on the Eastern Front for almost eighteen months. He was promoted to *Generalmajor* in May 1943 and to *Generalleutnant* just six months later.

Kurt Versock entered the Royal Saxon Infantry Regiment 13 in October 1914 and was commissioned as a *Leutnant* the following year. He served as liaison officer with Infantry Regiment 9 and later as adjutant and court officer with the III. Battalion of Infantry Regiment 178. He later served as ordnance officer and as regimental adjutant, and remained with the Army after the war. From 1923 until 1934 he served with Infantry Regiment 10 and was promoted to *Major* in 1935. He was appointed as tactics instructor at the Infantry School in Dresden. Promoted to *Oberstleutnant* in January 1938, he later served as battalion commander with Mountain Jäger Regiment 138 until February 1940.

He saw action as part of the 18th Army when the Soviets broke the Siege of Leningrad in mid-January 1944. On 5 September he was delegated with the leadership of the XXXXIII. Army Corps and given the task of organising the coastal defence of the Courland area. On 9 November he was promoted to *General der Gebirgstruppe* and was officially appointed Commanding General of his Army Corps. In March 1945 his command was evacuated over sea from the Courland Pocket and joined the 8th Army in northern Hungary, and on 8 May he surrendered his command to the Americans, being released from captivity in mid-1947.

Friedrich Wilhelm Ernst PAULUS

Generalfeldmarschall

* 23 September 1890, Breitenau-Gershage, Hessen-Nassau
+ 1 February 1957, Dresden

Knight's Cross: Awarded on 26 August 1942 as *General der Panzertruppe* and Commander-in-Chief of the 6th Army while attached to Army Group B for his leadership during the counter-attack east of Kharkov. On 20 May Paulus linked up with the Group *Kleist*, which was west of Kharkov, encircling the main Soviet strike force and by 28 May all Soviet resistance was ended. Under Paulus the 6th Army had killed or taken prisoner 240,000 Soviet soldiers and had destroyed or captured 2,026 tanks and 1,249 guns, all in the Kharkov Pocket. In June 1942 Hitler ordered Paulus to move on Stalingrad and in September the Siege of Stalingrad began, with the Germans making good progress during the early stages. By 20 September the 6th Army had penetrated to the Volga, cutting the Soviet 62nd Army in two, however by the start of October Paulus asked Hitler for reinforcements. During this time the Soviets attacked together as a mass group and by mid-

Friedrich Paulus entered the Army with Baden Infantry Regiment 3 in February 1910 and attended War School. He was later attached to the 7th Company of Infantry Regiment 111. He was commissioned as a *Leutnant* in August 1911 and served as adjutant of the III. Battalion of his regiment from October 1913. He was promoted to *Oberleutnant* in December 1915. He later served as ordnance officer and battalion adjutant and was promoted to *Hauptmann* in September 1918 as a General Staff Officer.

From 15 October 1935 Paulus served as Chief of the General Staff of the Command of Panzer Troops with the rank of *Oberst* and three years later he was Chief of the General Staff of the XVI. Army Corps. Promoted to *Generalmajor* in January 1939, he was shortly after named as Chief of the General Staff of Army Group Command 4 in Leipzig. Paulus served as Chief of the General Staff of the 10th Army during the invasion of Poland, where he was awarded the Bar to the Iron Cross 1st and 2nd Classes.

During the Nuremberg Trials, Paulus was asked about Stalingrad prisoners by a journalist. He told him to tell the wives and mothers that their husbands and sons were well. He failed to tell them that of the 91,000 German prisoners taken at Stalingrad, half had died on the march to the Siberian prison camps, and nearly as many had died in captivity, with only about 6,000 surviving and returning home.

October the reinforcements Paulus had requested finally arrived. By 1 November Paulus and his army controlled 90 per cent of the ruined city of Stalingrad, and nine days later he launched a new counter-attack, which failed. The Red Army began to surround the city and on 22 November two Soviet armies merged together near Kalach and surrounded Paulus and his army. The Germans had insufficient fuel to break out of the city and would have to be supplied by air. On 27 November the generals pressed Paulus to break out but he refused. Three days later Hitler sent him a message that he had been promoted to *Generaloberst* but the Stalingrad airlift had failed.

Knight's Cross with Oakleaves: He became the 178th recipient on 15 January 1943 as *Generaloberst* and while still Commander-in-Chief of the 6th Army, part of Army Group Don, for his bravery and leadership during the fighting in the Stalingrad Pocket. His efforts had tied down six Soviet armies and he was able to prevent, for a time, the complete collapse of the German front in the south. By Christmas 1942, 28,000 men had died at Stalingrad, the 6th Army had fewer than 246,000 men and ammunition and food was low. On 27 December the relief column of the 4th Panzer Army, which was trying to avoid being encircled, was forced to withdraw. Paulus rejected two surrender demands on 8 and 9 January 1943. Two days later the Soviets attacked with seven armies. Paulus had fewer than one hundred tanks but nevertheless he fought on. On 22 January the Red Army broke through the south-western sector of the front and Paulus, who had been told that he now had 12,000 unattended wounded, ordered that they should not be fed any longer. On the 31st Hitler promoted Paulus to *Generalfeldmarschall* and reminded him that no German field marshal had ever been captured: Hitler expected Paulus to commit suicide. That very same day Paulus surrendered to the Red Army. He refused to co-operate with his captors at first but by mid-July 1944, after the attempted assassination of Hitler, he made an anti-Nazi broadcast to the German troops urging them to disobey Hitler. After the war he was a prosecution witness at the Nuremberg Trials and he was released from Soviet captivity in 1953.

Friedrich KARST

Generalleutnant

* 4 September 1893, Deutsch-Eylau, Western Prussia
+ 18 October 1975, Herford, Germany

Knight's Cross: Awarded on 28 August 1942 as *Oberst* and Commander of Infantry Regiment 461, part of the 252nd Infantry Division, for actions near Gzhatsk in the area of Smolensk on the Russian Front. From early September Karst was delegated with the leadership of the 95th Infantry Division and took part in the Rzhev withdrawal. He was promoted to *Generalmajor* on 1 October 1942, his command of the division was confirmed and he continued to direct it as part of the 9th Army during its withdrawal from thc Rzhcv arca against heavy Soviet forces. He was promoted to *Generalleutnant* in April 1943 and his command formed part of the 4th Army at Gomel and west of Smolensk during the summer offensive. In August he was rested and joined the Reserves until November, when he was appointed Senior Field Commandant 672 as well as Commandant of Brussels. From 15 December 1944 he took command of Division 466, also known as Replacement Division *Bielefeld*, and saw brief action on the Western Front near Bad Driburg, a small town in North Rhine-Westphalia. There, on 11 May 1945, Karst surrendered and went into British captivity until October 1947.

Friedrich Kurt Hans 'Fritz' Freiherr von BROICH

Generalleutnant

* 1 January 1896, Strasbourg, Alsace
+ 24 September 1974, Leoni near Starnberg, Bavaria

Knight's Cross: Awarded on 29 August 1942 as *Oberst* and Commander of the 24th Panzer Grenadier Brigade as part of the 24th Panzer Division for his leadership during a fierce thirty-six-hour battle between 20 and 21 August. During the fighting his troops broke through numerous enemy positions and Broich pushed on north on his own initiative, destroying several enemy artillery batteries and capturing various positions. His bold decision-making ensured that the 14th and 24th Panzer Divisions were able to push north and make way for the forces required at the start of the attack on Stalingrad. On 8 September 1942 Broich was given temporary command of the 24th Panzer Division and from November he was given command of Division *von Broich* in North Africa. It had been put together hastily to hold the Bizerte Bridgehead in Tunisia, and was formed of various units, including *Luftwaffe*, engineer and parachute regiments. On 5 February 1943 Broich was ordered to take over command of the 10th Panzer Division following the death of its commander, *Generalleutnant* Wolfgang Fischer, and handed over the command of Division *von Broich* to *Generalmajor* Hasso

Friedrich Broich entered army service in July 1914, being assigned to Ulanen Regiment 9. He was hospitalised three times during the war through illness rather than injury. He was awarded the Iron Cross 1st and 2nd Classes and remained in the Army after the war, now with the rank of *Oberleutnant*. In 1935 he was assigned to the Reich Ministry of Defence with the rank of *Major* and at the beginning of the Second World War. As *Oberstleutnant* he saw action as part of Reconnaissance Battalion 34 during the Polish campaign, where he was awarded the Bar to the Iron Cross 2nd Class.

von Manteuffel. On 15 February Broich was promoted to *Generalmajor* and saw action with the 21st Panzer Division fighting the US 1st Armoured Division at the Battle of Sidi bou Zid. There the Germans savaged the Americans, inflicting 1,600 casualties and destroying almost 100 tanks and twenty-nine artillery guns. Broich later saw action in the Battle of Kasserine Pass and from March the tide began to turn and his command was halted. By May the command was almost destroyed and on the 12th he surrendered to the British at Grombalia, Tunisia, together with the remnants of his unit. He was then held at the Trent Park General Officers' PoW Camp in north London for the duration of the war. Promoted to *Generalleutnant* on 1 June 1943, he was finally repatriated on 7 October 1947.

Ferdinand Karl Theodor HEIM

Generalleutnant

* 27 February 1895, Reutlingen, Württemberg
+ 14 November 1977, Ulm

Knight's Cross: Awarded on 30 August 1942 as *Generalmajor* and Commander of the 14th Panzer Division while attached to the XXXXVII. Panzer Corps for actions during the fighting at Stalingrad. In mid-August, Heim saw heavy action while leading his Panzer Division against a heavily defended Soviet position during uninterrupted heavy combat. Heim was promoted to *Generalleutnant* and delegated with the leadership of the XXXXVIII. Panzer Corps in November

Ferdinand Heim entered Army service as an officer candidate in June 1914 with Field Artillery Regiment 13 and attended various courses before being commissioned as a *Leutnant* in February 1915. He served with Field Artillery Regiment 27 as an adjutant throughout most of the First World War and was awarded the Iron Cross 1st and 2nd Classes and ended the war as an *Oberleutnant*. He remained in the Army after the war and served as an adjutant in various regiments. In 1935 he was an instructor at the War Academy with the rank of *Major*. From March 1937 he served on the General Staff of the XVI. Motorised Army Corps and from August 1939, still attached to the same corps, he was appointed Chief of the General Staff with the rank of *Oberst*. From August 1939 he served as Chief of the General Staff of the 6th Army under *Generalfeldmarschall* Walter von Reichenau.

1942. Together with the 3rd Romanian Army, they were unable to stop the breakthrough made by the Red Army towards Stalingrad. On 26 November 1942 Heim was relieved of his command and placed in the Reserves, and in April the following year he was arrested and placed in solitary confinement in Moabit Prison because of the failure of his corps to relieve the encircled 6th Army at Stalingrad. On 16 August 1943 he was discharged from the Army and allowed to receive a pension until August 1944, when his army service was reactivated. From 5 August he served as Fortress Commandant of Boulogne until he surrendered to the Allies on 23 September 1944, remaining in Allied captivity until 12 May 1948. In 1962 he became a recognised author and wrote the highly acclaimed work, *The Campaign Against Soviet Russia 1941 to 1945: An Operational Overview*, together with *Generalmajor* Alfred Philippi.

Philipp MÜLLER-GEBHARD

Generalleutnant

* 15 October 1889, Heidelberg, Württemberg
+ 2 July 1970, Ludwigsburg, Baden-Württemberg

Knight's Cross: Awarded on 3 September 1942 as *Generalleutnant* and Commander of 72nd Infantry Division while attached to LIV. Army Corps for actions in the Crimea as part of Army Group Centre. Müller-Gebhard also saw action during the Siege of Sevastopol and later during the winter of 1942–43 he saw action in the Rzhev withdrawal, and in the Battle of Kursk. In November 1943 he entered the Reserves and from February 1944 until February 1945 he served as Commandant of Prague, after which he was transferred once again into the Reserves. In May 1945 he was captured by US troops and kept in captivity until his release in mid-1947.

Philipp Müller-Gebhard entered the Army in July 1908 and was commissioned as a *Leutnant* in January 1910 while serving with a training battalion. At the start of the First World War he served as adjutant of I. Battalion of Infantry Regiment 111 and was promoted to *Oberleutnant* the following year. He continued to serve with Infantry Regiment 111 throughout the war and was promoted to *Hauptmann* in April 1917, being wounded soon after. Following the war he joined the Baden State Police. He rejoined the Army in October 1934 as battalion commander in Infantry Regiment 35 with the rank of *Major*, and by the beginning of the Second World War he was Commander of the 165th Division with the rank of *Oberst*.

Erwin SANDER
Generalleutnant

* 5 March 1892, Berlin, Brandenburg
+ 5 December 1962, Bamberg, Bavaria

Knight's Cross: Awarded on 3 September 1942 as *Generalmajor* and Commander of 170th Infantry Division while attached to the XXVI. Army Corps for actions in the northern sector of the Russian Front. As part of von Manstein's 11th Army, his division was tied down in heavy defensive fighting instead of taking part in the attack on Leningrad and later faced the Soviet winter offensive of 1942–43. In January 1943 Sander was promoted to *Generalleutnant* and after four months in the Reserves he was appointed Commander of Division D, which was largely destroyed in southern Russia in August 1943. Sander reformed the division and it was renamed the 245th Infantry Division, stationed in northern France. Although it remained idle during the Normandy campaign, it was heavily engaged against the Allies during the abortive effort to take Arnhem in September 1944. From October to early November Sander led his division during the Battle of Scheldt as part of the 15th Army. It was withdrawn briefly in early April 1945 and Sander was replaced and entered the Reserves, from where he surrendered to the Allies at the end of the war.

Paul SCHULTZ
Generalmajor

* 30 October 1891, Welzheim
+ 15 September 1964, Tübingen

Knight's Cross: Awarded on 3 September 1942 as *Oberst* and Commander of Infantry Regiment 308 while attached to 198th Infantry Division for actions during the attack on the Soviet city of Krasnodar in mid-August 1942. After getting past an anti-tank ditch east of the city, Schultz decided on his own initiative to launch an attack on the heavily defended suburbs despite coming under fire from enemy artillery. His regiment succeeded in penetrating the defences and clearing one block after another of Soviet troops, in doing so opening the way for troops of the division to advance into the city. He continued to see fierce fighting towards the end of the year before seeing action from January until March 1943 at the Kuban Bridgehead.

Paul Schultz joined the Army in July 1912 as an officer candidate and after attending War School he saw action with Infantry Regiment 192 as a platoon and company commander during the First World War. In November 1919 he entered the police in Württemberg and became commander of the Schutzpolizei in Ulm from April 1933 with the rank of *Polizei-Major*. He rejoined the Army from October 1935 as Commander of the III. Battalion of Infantry Regiment 35. From December 1939 he was Commander of Infantry Regiment 308, part of the 198th Infantry Division, and saw action during the invasion of France. He was awarded the Iron Cross 1st and 2nd Classes.

Knight's Cross with Oakleaves: He became the 284th recipient on 26 August 1943 as *Oberst* and Commander of Grenadier Regiment 308, part of 198th Infantry Division, for his leadership and outstanding gallantry during the fierce fighting near Belgorod on 24 July 1943. Shortly after Soviet forces attacked again in a different area, Schultz and his troops managed to push them back in a swift counter-attack. He was presented with the Oakleaves by Hitler on 15 September 1943 at the Wolf's Lair in Rastenburg. Shortly after he briefly commanded the Army Weapons School while attached to the headquarters of the 6th Army and in March 1944 he was promoted to *Generalmajor*. From October he became Commander of the Army Weapons School attached to the 8th Army. Schultz surrendered to US troops on 8 May 1945 and remained in Allied captivity until 11 June 1947.

Hans Bernhard Carl Otto von TETTAU

General der Infanterie

* 30 November 1888, Bautzen, Saxony
+ 30 January 1956, Mönchengladbach, North Rhine-Westphalia

Knight's Cross: Awarded on 3 September 1942 as *Generalleutnant* and Commander of 24th Infantry Division, part of LIV. Army Corps, for his leadership during the Siege of Sevastopol from 7 June 1942. He was particularly recognised for his command of the troops that crossed Severnaya Bay on 29 June and of the storming of the old fort at Malakoff in Sevastopol. He saw further action in July and August 1942 on the southern coast of the Crimea and from early September he led his division during the defensive battles of Lake Ladoga. From February until August 1943 Tettau was attached to the

Hans von Tettau entered the Army in March 1909 and was commissioned as a *Leutnant* the following year, taking over as battalion adjutant at the beginning of the First World War. Promoted to *Oberleutnant* in April 1915, he served as deputy regimental adjutant and as a staff officer with Infantry Division 192. He was promoted to *Hauptmann* in August 1917. He stayed in the Army after the war and was attached to various regiments in Dresden, and from October 1935 he served as *Oberstleutnant* and Commander of Infantry Regiment 101. He later saw action in the area around Flanders in 1940 as part of the 14th Infantry Division and was promoted to *Generalmajor* in March 1940 after being awarded both classes of the Bar to the Iron Cross.

Reserves and from September was made head of Training and Leader of the Training Staff in the Netherlands.

Knight's Cross with Oakleaves: Tettau became the 821st recipient on 5 April 1945 as *Generalleutnant* and leader of Corps Group *von. Tettau* while attached to 3rd Panzer Army for his bravery and leadership. His men soon found themselves encircled by Soviet troops and under Tettau's determined leadership his corps, which totalled 10,700 men, managed to fight their way out over the course of eight tough days. With 10,000 civilians in tow, they reached the German lines on 13 March 1945. From early November 1944 he was Commander of the 604th Division and at the same time was Commandant of Coastal Defence in Holland. Tettau was promoted to *General der Infanterie* in April and was attached to the Reserves until the end of the war. At the end of the war he was kept in Allied captivity until mid-1948.

Hans HÜTTNER

Generalmajor

* 19 November 1885, Hirschberglein, Bavaria
\+ 11 September 1956, Hof-Saale, Bavaria

Knight's Cross: Awarded on 4 September 1942 as *Oberst* and Commander of Infantry Regiment 520 while attached to the 296th Infantry Division for actions during the defensive battles around Orel on the central sector of the Russian Front. From August 1943, Hüttner commanded the East Troops Special Purpose 709 and a few months later he took command of a similar unit, seeing action in the Soviet Union. On 1 January 1944 he was appointed

Hans Hüttner entered Army service in October 1905 as a volunteer with Bavarian Infantry Regiment 19, and from 1914 he saw action during the First World War. He was wounded at the start of the war and then served with the same unit. Shortly after being commissioned as a *Leutnant* in May 1918 he was captured by British troops. He stayed in the Army after the war and was promoted to the rank of *Major* in April 1934. At the beginning of the Second World War he was Commander of the I. Battalion of Infantry Regiment 480 with the rank of *Oberstleutnant.*

Battle Commandant of Kirovograd, just nine days later he took over the leadership of the 167th Infantry Division. The division had been totally shattered north-west of Belgorod during fighting with the Soviet 6th Guards Army. From February his command was downgraded and he was leader of Division Group 167. On 17 June he was named as Commandant of Fortress Kristiansand in Norway and in January 1945 he was promoted to *Generalmajor*. On 20 January Hüttner was named as Commandant of Fortress Iymuiden in Holland, and from March it formed the 703rd Infantry Division while attached to the 25th Army. Hüttner surrendered his command to the British at the end of the war, being released from captivity in 1947.

Botho KOLLBERG

Generalmajor

* 11 July 1898, Neuhäuser, East Prussia
+ 24 January 1944 near Great Ruslova, south of Leningrad

Knight's Cross: Awarded on 6 September 1942 as *Oberstleutnant* and Commander Infantry Regiment 23, part of the 11th Infantry Division, for his outstanding performance while defending the Volkhov Bridgehead at Kirischi in the Soviet Union for four weeks. On 1 November Kollberg was promoted to *Oberst* and from mid-1943 took part in the opening phase of the Mga Offensive, near Lake Ladoga, to break the Siege of Leningrad. The attack began on 15 September 1943 with the Soviets pushing forward but the Germans pushed back with three divisions and quickly sealed off the Soviet advance. In the days that followed the Red Army tried again to push forward but all their attempts were unsuccessful, the attack from the Soviet 8th Army barely gained ground and by 24 September the Germans had stabilised the area.

Botho Kollberg entered the Army as an officer candidate with Infantry Regiment 150 in July 1915 and was commissioned as a *Leutnant* the following year. He saw action with his regiment and served as platoon and company leader, and later as battalion adjutant. He retired from the Army in December 1920 and joined the Reichsbank in Leipzig and then in Königsberg. In July 1934 he rejoined the Army as a *Hauptmann*. He was appointed as company commander with Infantry Regiment 2 and saw action in Belgium from May 1940 and later on occupation duty in France on the Atlantic coast as part of the 7th Army.

Knight's Cross with Oakleaves: He was awarded the Oakleaves posthumously on 8 February 1944 to become the 384th recipient as *Oberst* and Commander of Grenadier Regiment 23 while still attached to the 11th Infantry Division for his continued actions on the Russian Front. On 17 January *Oberst* Kollberg and his men found themselves at the heart of the fierce defensive battles south of Leningrad but they offered an aggressive defence, constantly denying the Soviets a breakthrough. In just one day of fighting the Soviets lost fifty-nine tanks but it was a success that Kollberg would give his life for just south of Leningrad. His family were sent the Oakleaves and he was posthumously promoted to the rank of *Generalmajor*.

Heinrich Lorenz Paul Alfons SCHEUERPFLUG

Generalleutnant

* 3 July 1896, Niedernetphen, Westphalia
+ 8 August 1945 PoW Camp at Auschwitz, Poland

Knight's Cross: Awarded on 6 September 1942 as *Oberst* and Commander of Infantry Regiment 116 while attached to the 9th Infantry Division for the decisive role he and his command played in the capture of Krasnodar in the Soviet Union. All of this was as a direct result of Scheuerpflug's independent decisions when he launched an attack on the city of Nowotitarowska. From December 1942 he served as Adjutant on the General Staff of Army Group A, serving under *Generalfeldmarschall* Ewald von Kleist. From September 1943 he attended the 7th Divisional Leaders Course in Döberitz and from late October he was delegated with the leadership of the 68th Infantry Division, seeing action in Kiev as part of the VII. Army Corps. On 1 January 1944 Scheuerpflug was promoted to *Generalmajor* and officially took over as Commander of the 68th Infantry Division, seeing further action in northern Ukraine, and in August that year he was promoted to *Generalleutnant*.

Knight's Cross with Oakleaves: He became the 791st recipient on 16 March 1945 as *Generalleutnant* and Commander of 68th Infantry Division while attached to the XXXXVIII. Panzer Corps in recognition of his leadership during heavy fighting from July 1944 on the Eastern Front. Between 11 and 19 September his command destroyed more than 100 enemy tanks and he personally led a counter-attack that was pushed back by Soviet forces, so more German troops were moved up to the front; clearly a greater effort was required. Following a breakthrough, he was able to stabilise the situation by building a strong defensive line, causing the Soviets to lose seventy tanks and 3,500 troops. Scheuerpflug had led his division successfully during the attacks and had played a vital role in the success of the XXXXVIII. Panzer Corps during the battle for Warthegau, Poland, and the struggle for the industrial area around Upper Silesia. On 8 May 1945, after being seriously wounded near Jägerndorf, Czechoslovakia, he was captured by Soviet troops and later died of his wounds in the hospital at the former Auschwitz-Birkenau concentration camp in Poland.

Heinrich-Anton DEBOI

Generalleutnant

* 6 April 1893, Landshut, Bavaria
+ 20 January 1955, Cherntsy, Soviet Union

Knight's Cross: Awarded on 10 September 1942 as *Generalmajor* as Commander of the 44th Infantry Division while attached to the XI. Army Corps for actions on the Russian Front. On 22 June 1942 his command was ordered to open a path through the Soviet defences towards Kupiansk on the Oskil River in support of Group von *Mackensen*, named after its commander *General*

Heinrich-Anton Deboi entered Army service in July 1912 as an officer candidate with Bavarian Infantry Regiment 2, and after attending the War School in Munich he was commissioned as a *Leutnant*. He saw action during the First World War as company leader and was promoted to *Oberleutnant* in December 1917 and was awarded both classes of the Iron Cross. He stayed in the Army after the war and served as tactics instructor at the War School in Munich from October 1935 with the rank of *Major*. He saw action during the Polish campaign as commander of Infantry Regiment 191 and was awarded both classes of the Bar to the Iron Cross in October 1939.

der Kavallerie Eberhard von Mackensen. Deboi succeeded in breaking through the Soviet positions within just four hours of his attack, and by doing so he opened a way forward for the Panzer Corps to commence a relentless pursuit all the way to the Don River. From November 1942 his division fought on the Don flank north-west of Kalach and withstood the attacks of the Soviet 65th Army, and the following month he was promoted to *Generalleutnant*. By January 1943 the German 6th Army was surrounded and Deboi's command was cut off from all supplies accept via air. Towards the end of January, Deboi faced his final battles for the Pitomnik airfield near Stalingrad, and during the fighting the bulk of his command was annihilated. He was taken prisoner by the Soviets on 29 January 1943 and died in captivity in Camp Voikovo.

Karl GÖBEL

Generalmajor

* 20 October 1900, Adelschlag, Eichstätt
+ 27 February 1945, Esslingen am Necker, Baden-Württemberg

Knight's Cross: Awarded on 10 September 1942 as *Major* and Commander of the III. Battalion of Infantry Regiment 420 while attached to the 125th Infantry Division for his part in the successful defence of Rostov. On 22 July 1942 his battalion attacked the Soviet defensive ring north of Rostov, which was heavily defended, and at one point the attack began to stall but Göbel was able to inspire his men and push them forward. He used his battalion to dig anti-tank ditches and through his leadership played an important part in the city's defences. He continued to see heavy fighting on the Eastern Front and was appointed Commander of Infantry Regiment 420 from December 1942. He was promoted to *Oberst* on 1 June 1943.

Karl Göbel entered the Army as a recruit on 28 June 1918 with Bavarian Infantry Regiment 13 and saw very little action. He left the Army in December 1918 but returned in March 1919 and served with Infantry Regiment 20 until September 1930 with the rank of *Oberfeldwebel*. He re-entered the Army once again in March 1935 and from October 1936 he was company commander with Infantry Regiment 119 and now with the rank of *Hauptmann*. Promoted to *Major* in December 1940, he saw very little action until June 1941 during the invasion of the Soviet Union.

Knight's Cross with Oakleaves: He became the 252nd recipient on 8 June 1943 as *Oberstleutnant* and Commander of Grenadier Regiment 420 while attached to the 125th Infantry Division, awarded for his outstanding leadership of his regiment during the defensive battle near Krymsk in the Kuban Bridgehead area. The Oakleaves were presented to Göbel by Hitler during a ceremony at *Führer* Headquarters in Rastenburg. From May until July 1944 Göbel commanded Grenadier Regiment *Böhmen* 1, which later became Grenadier Regiment 305 while attached to the 198th Infantry Division. From August his command faced the Allied invasion of southern France and in August suffered heavy casualties before withdrawing to the Vosges Mountains. In late September Göbel transferred to the Reserves and from October attended the 15th Divisional Leaders Course. From December he was delegated with the leadership of the 299th Infantry Division and saw action on the Eastern Front once again. He was severely wounded on 16 February 1945 near Schalmey on the Courland Front and was hospitalised, where he died from his wounds. He was posthumously promoted on 1 March 1945, to the rank of *Generalmajor*.

Otto HERFURTH

Generalmajor

* 22 January 1893, Hasserode, Wernigerode
+ 29 September 1944, Berlin-Plötzensee Prison

Knight's Cross: Awarded on 14 September 1942 as *Oberst* and Commander of Infantry Regiment 117 for actions on the Russian Front. His regiment saw action in the early campaigns of Army Group South as part of the 111th Infantry Division, seeing action in Zhitomir, Kiev and the Donets and taking part in the early stages of the Caucasus campaign. In March 1943 he was appointed Chief of the General Staff of the Replacement V. Army Corps in Military District V, Stuttgart. He was promoted to *Generalmajor* in October 1943 and from June 1944 he was Chief of the General Staff of the Replacement III. Army Corps in the Military District of Berlin. On 14 August 1944 he was arrested in connection with the 20 July bomb plot to kill Hitler. He had been initially supportive of the coup but later he changed his mind. Nevertheless, his name was mentioned and he was arrested, held for trial in front of the People's Court and sentenced to death. He was hanged in Berlin-Plötzensee Prison on 29 September 1944 together with *Oberst* Joachim Meichssner, *Oberstleutnant der Reserve* Fritz von der Lancken and *Oberstleutnant* Joachim Sadrozinski.

Otto Herfurth entered the Army as a Fahnenjunker in Infantry Regiment 50 from August 1914 and served as a Platoon Leader and then as an adjutant with Infantry Regiment 403. He was commissioned as a Leutnant in September 1915 and remained in the army after the war, serving in the Reichswehr with Infantry Regiment 9 and in February 1925 he was promoted to Oberleutnant and served on the Staff of the Command Office of the Troop Exercise Grounds Hammerstein. In October 1929 he was promoted to Hauptmann and attended Subsidiary Leadership Training to the Staff of 1st Division and two years later he was transferred to Mounted Regiment 2. He later served as Company Chief in Infantry Regiment 15 and was promoted to Hauptmann in September 1935 and took over as Adjutant of the Army Weapons Office, Reich Defence Ministry. In June 1938 he was promoted to Oberstleutnant and served as battalion commander with Infantry Regiment 17 and at the beginning of the Second World War he was serving as head of a department in the Army High Command and from November he took command of Infantry Regiment 117 and was promoted to Oberst in June 1941.

Otto Hellmuth BOEHLKE

Generalleutnant

* 7 February 1893, Lubahn, Berent, West Prussia
+ 8 April 1956, Bad Mergentheim, Baden-Württemberg

Hellmuth Boehlke was a war volunteer and joined Replacement Jäger Battalion 2 in August 1914. A few months later he was taken ill with typhus. He returned to duty in April 1915 and was appointed *Leutnant der Reserve* in September 1915. He was awarded the Iron Cross 2nd Class the following month and the Iron Cross 1st Class in July 1916. He joined the police after the war, rising to the rank of *Polizei-Major* in September 1935, before rejoining the Army the following month. From May 1937 he commanded a battalion with Infantry Regiment 21 and was promoted to *Oberstleutnant* in June 1938.

Knight's Cross: Awarded on 24 September 1942 as *Oberst* and Commander of Infantry Regiment 430, part of the 72nd Infantry Division, for his bravery and determination in personally leading the counter-attack to prevent a major enemy breakthrough attempt in the Rzhev area of the Russian Front. His Knight's Cross was personally presented to him by the Commanding General of the XXVII. Army Corps, *General der Infanterie* Walter Weiss. In February 1943 Boehlke was appointed commander of the *Reichs* Grenadier Regiment *Hoch und Deutschmeister,* part of the 44th Reichs Grenadier Division, and was deployed to Italy in August of that year to bolster the German defences following the downfall of Mussolini. Promoted to *Generalmajor* in January 1944, he attended divisional leaders before taking command of the 334th Infantry Division the following month.

Knight's Cross with Oakleaves: He became the 716th recipient on 25 January 1945 as *Generalleutnant* and Commander of the 334th Infantry Division while attached to the LXXVI. Panzer Corps when he prevented a major breakthrough of strong British forces near Cossignano, Italy, in December 1944. He did so through personally led counter-attacks in which heavy losses were inflicted on the enemy. Boehlke was transferred to the Reserves in April 1945 and on the 26th he was captured by Allied forces. He remained in captivity until 12 May 1948.

Heinz FURBACH

Generalmajor

* 27 September 1895, Karlshof, near Förstenau, Pomerania
\+ 23 October 1968, Munich, Bavaria

Knight's Cross: Awarded on 4 October 1942 as *Oberst* and Commander of Infantry Regiment 58 of the 6th Infantry Division for actions on the Russian Front. On 31 July 1942 his regiment was transferred and took part in the attack north of Rzhev; in fact, Furbach's division was the first to arrive. He was wounded during the first attack and held its positions while fighting much superior enemy forces, and as a result his regiment was mentioned in the Armed Forces Communiqué for its particular defensive

Heinz Furbach entered the Army in August 1914 as a *Leutnant* and platoon leader with Grenadier Regiment 5 and was wounded in September 1914. He later transferred to Grenadier Regiment 5 and was once again wounded. From January 1916 served as battalion adjutant and ended the war as regimental adjutant. He remained in the Army after the war and was promoted to *Oberleutnant* in November 1924. By October 1935, when the *Wehrmacht* was formed, he served as tactics instructor at the War School in Munich with the rank of *Major*. He was promoted to *Oberstleutnant* in April 1938 and did not see action during the Second World War until 1940, when he was named as Commander of Machine Gun Battalion 7 and saw action in France.

combat near Rzhev. *Oberst* Furbach remained with his men even after receiving a further wound, one that saw him receive about fifteen shell splinters to the face after an artillery round struck a truck loaded with mines. From June he was delegated with the leadership of the 97th *Jäger* Division and saw heavy action during the Battle of Kursk from July 1943. In November he was transferred to the 331st Infantry Division as temporary commander while the division was resting and retraining in Germany after being mauled on the Eastern Front for two years. Furbach was promoted to *Generalmajor* in March 1944 and took over as the official Commander of the 331st Infantry Division in Germany, where it had incorporated members of Infantry Shadow Division *Wahn*. Later his division was transferred to Calais and saw action in Normandy until July 1944, when Furbach was transferred to the Reserves due to ill health. From February 1945 he participated as an assessor with the Reich War Court and surrendered to American troops on 30 April.

Paul Moritz Maximilian WENGLER

Generalmajor der Reserve

* 14 January 1890, Rosswein-Döbeln, Saxony
+ 25 April 1945, Pillau-Neutief, East Prussia

Knight's Cross: Awarded on 6 October 1942 as *Oberstleutnant der Reserve* and Commander of Infantry Regiment 366 while attached to 227th Infantry Division for actions in the German Corridor to Lake Ladoga in mid-1942 and in the fighting near Leningrad, where his units repelled numerous attacks. The troops under his command held firm even when the situation deteriorated when the Soviets achieved a breakthrough and cut off his regiment from the rest of the division.

Maximilian Wengler joined the 9th Royal Saxony Infantry Regiment No. 33 in Zwickau in November 1909 as an officer candidate. He saw action during the First World War as a platoon leader with the 9th Royal Saxony Infantry Regiment No. 33 August 1914 with the rank of *Leutnant*. He left the Army after the war but rejoined just before the beginning of the Second World War, joining Infantry Regiment 40, part of the 27th Infantry Division, as a *Hauptmann der Reserve*. He saw action during the invasion of Poland and from May 1940 during the invasion of Luxembourg and France, where he was awarded the Iron Cross 1st and 2nd Classes.

For eight days his regiment fought off all attacks, only being able to reopen their supply route for short periods using small attack groups. The supply of food and ammunition could only be maintained by air and was necessary on more than one occasion but eventually Wengler and his troops were able to link up with a German relief force and secure their position. He was promoted to *Oberst der Reserve* in December 1942 and from early January 1943 the division was encircled and took part in the Battle of Lake Ladoga, with elements of the division managing to break out of the pocket.

Knight's Cross with Oakleaves: He became the 404th recipient on 22 February 1944 as *Oberst der Reserve* and Commander of Infantry Regiment 366 while still attached to the 227th Infantry Division in recognition of his leadership during the heavy fighting near Narva in early 1944. His troops destroyed seventy-three of the 105 attacking Soviet tanks during a two-day period during continued defence in Narva. The Oakleaves were presented to Wengler by Hitler on 27 April 1944 at the Berghof on the Obersalzburg during a special ceremony together with fourteen others, including *General der Infanterie* Hans Jordan, *General der Panzertruppe* Hermann Breith and *Oberstleutnant der Reserve* Dr Franz Bäke. In May Wengler attended the 11th Divisional Leaders Course in Hirschberg and from 11 May he was appointed Commander of the 227th Infantry Division. He later took part in the Leningrad withdrawal and saw heavy combat in the Courland Pocket in October 1944. In early January 1945 he was promoted to *Generalmajor der Reserve*.

Knight's Cross with Oakleaves and Swords: Awarded on 21 January 1945 to become the 123rd recipient as *Generalmajor der Reserve* and Commander of 227th Infantry Division while attached to XVI. Army Corps for distinguished leadership during the summer of 1944, specifically during the fighting around the town of Liepna in Latvia. He later saw battles in West Prussia and in February 1945 he led his division during the Battle for Tuchola in Poland, where his command suffered heavy casualties and as a consequence of losing so many men it was disbanded. On 28 March Wengler took command of the 83rd Infantry Division, seeing action near Gdynia in Poland and then being pushed towards Schleswig-Holstein, where he and his troops were to be evacuated by sea. On 25 April, during an aerial attack by Soviet bombers in Pillau-Neutief, East Prussia, Wengler and members of his staff were killed.

Heinrich Eberhard Alexander von HARTMANN

General der Infanterie

* 11 December 1890, Berlin
\+ 26 January 1943, near Trebnitz, Stalingrad

Alexander Hartmann wrote forty-eight hours before his death: I won't shoot myself, but I'll let the Russians shoot me. I'll stand alone on the railway embankment, firing at the enemy, and they'll kill me. My wife is a competent woman, she'll surely get on as best she can without me; my son has been killed and my daughter is married. We won't win this war and the man who is in Supreme Command is not the man we took him for.'

Knight's Cross: Awarded on 8 October 1942 as *Generalmajor* and Commander of the 71st Infantry Division while attached to the LI. Army Corps for actions while fighting as part of the 6th Army at Stalingrad. The Knight's Cross was personally presented by *Generaloberst* Friedrich Paulus and *General der Artillerie* Walter von Seydlitz-Kurzbach. Promoted to *Generalleutnant* in December 1942, Hartmann continued to see heavy action while trapped in the pocket at Stalingrad. On 26 January 1943 he led a small group of troops consisting of three officers, seven non-commissioned officers and 183 enlisted men to the southern sector of Stalingrad and began engaging Soviet troops advancing across the snow. He knew the fate of his division and was convinced the 6th Army would be lost, so he said to his men, 'An officer has to die in combat. I am not going to shoot myself but will sell my skin as expensively as possible.' He gave the order to fire and then he took a machine pistol and fired at the enemy near the railroad embankment of Stalingrad South. At 8 a.m. Hartmann was shot in the head and killed instantly. He was posthumously promoted to *General der Infanterie* on 15 February 1943 and his obituary stated that '... the Army had lost one of its most outstanding officers. Already proving himself as an excellent regimental commander during the Western Campaign ... Hartmann fought in the battle for Kharkov in May 1942 and at Stalingrad where he set an example and inspired his troops ... he died with his men.' Hartmann is buried today in an unknown grave at the German War Cemetery Rossoshki in the Soviet Union together with 1,639 soldiers and officers.

Carl RODENBURG

Generalleutnant

* 17 May 1894, Geestemünde, Bremen
+ 5 November 1992, Lübeck, Schleswig-Holstein

Carl Rodenburg entered the Infantry Regiment 113 in Freiburg am Breisgau in October 1913 as a volunteer and form 1915 he served as a platoon and company leader with the rank of *Leutnant*. He remained in the Army after the war and served as an adjutant. From 1928 he served as Chief of the 5th Company of Baden Infantry Regiment 14 with the rank of *Hauptmann*.

Knight's Cross: Awarded on 8 October 1942 as *Generalmajor* and Commander of 76th Infantry Division while attached to the VIII. Army Corps for his leadership during the battles between the Don and the Volga during August 1942. As part of Army Group South his command held critical positions on the high ground south of Kotluban, a rural area, where his troops were able to repel all attacks from the Soviets. He led his division with great skill during the fierce fighting, destroying 227 enemy tanks, with Rodenburg proving to be an excellent commander. In November his division was pushed back by a strong Soviet force, suffering heavy losses at Stalingrad, which is where, on 1 December, he was promoted to *Generalleutnant*.

Knight's Cross with Oakleaves: He became the 189th recipient on 31 January 1943 as *Generalleutnant* and Commander of 76th Infantry Division while still

From October 1935, now with the rank of *Major*, Rodenburg served as Commander of the II. Battalion of Infantry Regiment 12 and from November 1938 he served on the training staff of the Infantry School in Döberitz. From August 1939 he was Commander of the School for Officer Candidates.

attached to the VIII. Army Corps for his bravery and leadership in the Stalingrad area. He continued to distinguish himself in battle from 18 January, during which his men managed to storm Soviet positions near Rossoschka, a village near Volgograd. His command was hit hard by the Soviets and the remnants of his division saw action near to the tractor factory at Stalingrad, where his command was completely surrounded by the Red Army on 31 January 1943. That same day he was informed by radio he had been awarded the Oakleaves to his Knight's Cross and shortly after he surrendered his command. Rodenburg was imprisoned in the NKVD prison No. 160 at Suzadal and then moved to various prisons in Selenodolsk and Minsk. He was tried as a war criminal by a military tribunal in Minsk on 15 November 1949 and sentenced to twenty-five years' imprisonment with hard labour. He was finally released after a general amnesty on 10 October 1955 and returned to Germany.

Erwin JAENECKE

Generaloberst

* 22 April 1890, Freren-Lingen, Hannover
+ 3 July 1960, Cologne

It seems that there are two versions of Erwin Jaenecke's escape from Stalingrad. One is that he was struck by Soviet shrapnel and was evacuated with sixteen holes in his body! The other version is less heroic, in that the building Jaenecke was in was hit by Soviet artillery, causing a piece of plaster to fall. It struck him on the head and drew blood. After that he acted like lightning and had himself medically evacuated and remained in hospital until he recovered.

Knight's Cross: Awarded on 9 October 1942 as *Generalleutnant* and Commander of the 389th Infantry Division, part of the VIII. Army Corps, for actions on the southern sector of the Russian front at Kharkov during the drive across the Don and the Volga. He was presented with the Knight's Cross in late October by his friend *Generaloberst* Friedrich Paulus near Stalingrad. Jaenecke was promoted to *General der Pioniere* on 1 November and appointed Commanding General of the IV. Army Corps while part of the 4th Panzer Army at Stalingrad. On 17 January 1943 he was wounded and hospitalised, and on 23 January he was airlifted out of Stalingrad just days before it fell. Once recovered he was appointed

Commanding General of the LXXXVI. Army Corps in France in April 1943 and just two months later he took over as leader of the 17th Army. He saw action while defending the Kuban Bridgehead until mid-September, when he was involved in the retreat to the Crimea. He was promoted to *Generaloberst* on 30 January 1944 and appointed Commander-in-Chief of the 17th Army. During the summer offensive Hitler demanded that Sevastopol be held at all costs. Jaenecke, together with Generals Ferdinand Schörner, Kurt Zeitzler and Karl Allmendinger, tried in vain to sway Hitler from his halt order. Jaenecke sent a telex to Hitler demanding that he had reinforcements and wanted some 'freedom of action' as he was the commander on the spot. On 29 April he was ordered to fly to Berchtesgaden and meet Hitler, in which he did not hold back on his criticism of the *Führer*. As a result he was arrested and placed before a court martial, with General Guderian tasked by Hitler to examine the case. Hitler wanted Jaenecke to take sole responsibility in the loss of the Crimea but Guderian managed to save Jaenecke and obtained an acquittal, although he was dismissed from the Army on 31 January 1945 on Hitler's orders. Jaenecke was captured by the Soviets in June and was later tried by a court in Sevastopol for war crimes and sentenced to death. However, the term was commuted to twenty-five years' imprisonment. He served time in Camp 7048 Ivanovo-Vorkuta-Sverdlovsk until he was released in a general amnesty on 13 October 1955.

Alexander Edmund CONRADY

Generalmajor

* 16 July 1903, Neu-Ulm, Swabia in Bavaria
+ 21 December 1983, Augsburg, Bavaria

Knight's Cross: Awarded on 17 October 1942 as *Oberstleutnant* and Commander of I. Battalion of Motorised Infantry Regiment 118, attached to the 36th Infantry Division, after repeatedly distinguishing himself throughout the Eastern campaign through his personal devotion to duty and his leadership. During the heavy, decisive battles east of Rzhev he led the regiment when its commander was on leave and achieved great success during the period 11 to 21 August 1942. The attacks from the Soviet forces were strong, with more than sixty launched against his command, but his battalion was able to push these back, and even after a few tanks broke through his command managed to hold their ground. Even though the enemy's co-ordinated mortar attacks inflicted great losses on the regiment all their attacks failed and the Soviets lost more than a thousand troops.

Alexander Conrady entered Army service with Infantry Regiment 19 in April 1923, and became an officer candidate in October 1925. Commissioned as a *Leutnant* in December 1926, he was promoted to *Oberleutnant* in April 1929, and attended the War Academy from October 1934. He was appointed company commander with Infantry Regiment 40 in October 1936 and from 1938 he was assistant adjutant with the Staff of the 27th Infantry Division. He was awarded the Iron Cross 2nd Class in October 1939 and in July 1940 he was awarded the Iron Cross 1st Class and promoted to the rank of *Major*.

Knight's Cross with Oakleaves: Conrady became the 279th recipient on 22 August 1943 as *Oberst* and Commander of Grenadier Regiment 118 while still attached to the 36th Infantry Division. Conrady once again pushed back Soviet assaults from 14 July, when 180 tanks and infantry attacked his position. His command held their ground despite Conrady being wounded and he remained at the front of his troops. He was an inspiration to his troops and as a result of his leadership and strong resistance by his men the Soviet assault collapsed in early August. Conrady was presented with the Oakleaves by Hitler at the Wolf's Lair in Rastenburg in September 1943. He was promoted to *Generalmajor* in April 1944 and given command of the 36th Infantry Division, which he led until his capture by Soviet troops in July. He remained in captivity until October 1955.

<u>Carl</u> Hans Wilhelm Ludwig BECKER

Generalleutnant

* 16 January 1895 in Varel, Oldenburg
+ 24 March 1966, Heidelberg, Germany

Knight's Cross: Carl Becker was awarded the Knight's Cross on 29 October 1942 as an *Oberst* and Commander of the 18th Infantry Regiment in recognition of his bravery and leadership during the fighting north-east of Rzhev's city edge. Strong enemy fire brought heavy losses and Becker ordered a counter-attack that prevented the Soviets from taking the Volga River Bridge. This enabled the German 6th Infantry Division to advance. It was reported that Becker was the soul of the resistance during the bitter fighting for the city. On the first day of 1943 Becker was appointed temporary commander of the 2nd *Luftwaffe* Field Division, and took part in the fighting in Smolensk as part of the 9th Army. On 18 January he was appointed Commander of the 253rd Infantry Division and

In October 1919 Carl Becker left the Army and entered the Security Police in Mecklenburg-Schwerin, where he stayed for fifteen years, rising to the rank of *Polizei-Hauptmann*. In October 1934 he rejoined the army as a *Hauptmann* and was attached to the I. Battalion of Infantry Regiment Osnabrück. The regiment was renamed in October 1935, becoming Infantry Regiment 37. Becker served as a company commander and was promoted to *Major* in November. On 1 February 1937 he was appointed commander of the III. Battalion, and was promoted to *Oberstleutnant* in August 1938. As part of the 6th Infantry Division, his battalion was posted to the Saar sector of the Western Front at the beginning of the Second World War.

saw action in Bobruisk in eastern Belorussia as part of the 1st Panzer Army. Promoted to *Generalmajor* in April, his command went on to see action during the fierce fighting in the area of Orel and during the retreat of Bryansk. He was promoted to *Generalleutnant* in October and from April 1944 he led his division during the recapture of Kovel in the Volyn Oblast in north-western Ukraine and then moved to Kholm.

Knight's Cross with Oakleaves: On 14 April 1945, *Generalleutnant* Becker became the 829th recipient of the Oakleaves as Commander of the 253rd Infantry Division. He led this division during the major assault by Soviet forces on 10 March 1945 that consisted of thirteen rifle divisions, three rifle brigades and two tank brigades. Becker, who knew the attack was coming, pulled back his forces and when the Soviet artillery barrage opened it struck an empty trench line and Becker's division was able to hold off the assault. On 9 May 1945, the war ended for Becker just east of Prague when he was taken prisoner by Soviet forces. He remained a prisoner in the Soviet Union for ten years, finally being released on 12 October 1955.

Siegfried Paul Leonhard Wilhelm von THOMASCHKI

General der Artillerie

* 20 March 1894, Miswalde, East Prussia
+ 31sMay 1967, Bad Neuenahr, Rhineland-Palatinate

Knight's Cross: Awarded on 1 November 1942 as *Generalmajor* and Commander of 11th Infantry Division while attached to the XXVIII. Army Corps for the success in his division's defence of the Kirishi Bridgehead near Volkhov in the Soviet Union. Between 5 June and 5 September 1942 the Soviets tried to

Siegfried Thomaschki served as an officer candidate from March 1913 and was wounded in December 1914 while serving with the I. Battalion of Field Artillery Regiment 52 with the rank of *Leutnant*. He continued to serve with this regiment throughout the war and was promoted to *Oberleutnant* in September 1917. He ended the war as company leader and was awarded both classes of the Iron Cross. He stayed in the Army after the war and by October 1936 was an *Oberstleutnant* and battalion commander with Artillery Regiment 11. In November 1938 he served as Commander of Artillery Regiment 3, and was promoted to *Oberst* in March 1939. He and saw action in Poland, where he was awarded the Bar to the Iron Cross 1st and 2nd Classes, and from May 1940 saw further action during the French Campaign.

eliminate the bridgehead but failed, despite a total of 154 attacks! After taking command of the 11th Infantry Division in March 1942 he took part in the fighting near Leningrad and Volkhov, where he distinguished himself as a skilful commander. Thomaschki continued to see continued action in the Soviet Union of the following year and was promoted to *Generalleutnant* in January 1943.

Knight's Cross with Oakleaves: Thomaschki became the 299th recipient on 11 September 1943 as *Generalleutnant* and Commander of 11th Infantry Division while attached to XXVI. Army Corps for his outstanding bravery during the heavy fighting near Ladoga in the Soviet Union. He once again showed his skill as a commander and took part in the heavy fighting in the northern sector of the Soviet front line between Volkhov and Lake Ladoga as part of Army Group North. The Oakleaves were presented personally by Hitler in late September 1943 at his headquarters in Rastenburg. At this time he was serving as Higher Artillery Commander 303 while attached to the 18th Army, seeing action on the Eastern Front. From the end of December 1944 he was delegated with the leadership of the X. Army Corps in the Courland area. Thomaschki was promoted to *General der Infanterie* in March 1945, his command was confirmed and he continued to serve in the Courland area until 9 May, when he surrendered to the Soviets. He was sentenced to twenty-five years in a labour camp by a military tribunal but was released as part of a general amnesty on 10 October 1955.

Kurt Hermann Freiherr von MÜHLEN

Generalleutnant

* 22 January 1905, Ulm, Württemberg
+ 15 January 1971, Kressbronn on Lake Constance, Baden-Württemberg

Karl-Hermann von Mühlen joined Pioneer Battalion 5 in Ulm in March 1923 and four years later he was serving as a *Leutnant* with the 9th Company of Infantry Regiment 13. By October 1935 he was Commander of the 14th Company of Infantry Regiment 55 and he was promoted to *Hauptmann* in October 1936. From June 1940 he served as adjutant on the Staff of the 5th Infantry Division, seeing action in France and then from June 1941 in the Soviet Union.

Knight's Cross: Awarded on 6 November 1942 as *Oberstleutnant* and leader of *Jäger* Regiment 75, part of the 5th *Jäger* Division, for his leadership and bravery during actions at the Demyansk Salient between 27 September and 9 October 1942. During the attack Mühlen, using his own initiative, seized the crossing over the Lovat River and his men captured Cherenchitsy near Demyansk, where they were able to surprise the Soviet units in the town and force them out. Later, during the second half of 1942 and throughout 1943, he saw action in the battles around Staraya Russa, and was promoted to *Oberst* in March of that year. From mid-April 1944 he served as an instructor at the Infantry School in Döberitz and from mid-July he was made temporary commander of the newly formed 559th *Volksgrenadier* Division. In November he was promoted to *Generalmajor* and his command was confirmed.

Knight's Cross with Oakleaves: He became the 690th recipient on 9 January 1945 as *Generalmajor* and Commander of 559th *Volksgrenadier* Division while attached to the XIII. SS-Army Corps and distinguished himself during the defensive battles north of Morhange in northern France from 15 November 1944 and later in the Saarland area. In late March 1945 his division was holding part of the southern sector of the German line on the Western Front, during which time it was cut off and almost destroyed on the western bank of the Rhine. On 20 April he was promoted to *Generalleutnant* and shortly after remnants of his division, including Mühlen, surrendered to American forces near Muensingen in May 1945.

Richard SCHMIDT

Generalmajor

* 29 April 1899, Butschkowa, Posen
\+ 7 November 1977, Bad Ems, Rhineland-Palatinate

Knight's Cross: Awarded on 6 November 1942 as *Oberstleutnant* and Commander of Infantry Regiment 473, attached to 253rd Infantry Division, while taking part in the defeat of Soviet forces that were attempting to breakthrough near Rzhev in September 1942. Schmidt was promoted to Oberst on 21 January 1943 and at the end of March he was transferred from the Soviet Union and took command of the Training Staff 4 of the Infantry School. In February 1944 he was appointed Commander of Grenadier Regiment 290 and took part in the retreat to the Sevastopol Fortress, where he was wounded on 25 April and hospitalised. From July he took command of Grenadier Regiment 1037 and in October he attended the 15th Divisional Leaders Course before being appointed to the leadership of the 254th Infantry Division in December 1944. Schmidt took part in the defence near Kaschau, Slovakia, from November and in March 1945 he was promoted to *Generalmajor* and his command was confirmed. Later he took part in the retreat into Silesia and ended the war in Czechoslovakia, where he and his division surrendered to Soviet forces. In 1951 he was sentenced to death by hanging for the destruction of the Slovak village of Beniky but this was commuted to life imprisonment on 14 October 1953. He was released from prison on 20 December 1961, one of the last to be freed.

Erich Gottfried ABRAHAM

General der Infanterie

* 27 March 1895,Marienburg, West Prussia
+ 7 March 1971, Wiesbaden, Germany

Erich Abraham was commissioned as a *Leutnant der Reserve* in July 1915, serving on the Western Front during the First World War as an adjutant with Infantry Regiment 341. He later served as an ordnance officer and was awarded both classes of the Iron Cross. Abraham left the Army in May 1920, joining the police in Stettin, where he served as adjutant to the Police President of Berlin and rose to the rank of *Polizei-Major* in April 1934.

Knight's Cross: Awarded on 13 November 1942 as *Oberst* and Commander of Infantry Regiment 230, part of the 76th Infantry Division, for his bravery and leadership during the fierce fighting around the area of Stalingrad. Abraham distinguished himself during the Soviet attacks on 18 and 23 September 1942, during which time his forces had been weakened severely by previous combat. On both of these days the Soviet army was able to wipe out the garrison in two locations, and tank and infantry forces managed to advance all the way to Abraham's command post. He fought in the front line with his men, and with a gun in his hand he led the attacks against far numerically superior enemy formations. *Oberst* Abraham's personal devotion to duty was enough to inspire his men to risk going on to the offensive. In the resultant combat the enemy was torn apart, the hostile tanks destroyed and the front line totally restored by the evening. Abraham later led his regiment against the Soviet advance near Stalingrad, where he distinguished himself before being transferred out of the city before it fell in February 1943. In May he was promoted to *Generalmajor* and took over as Commander of the

Abraham rejoined the Army in October 1935, serving as company commander with the 18th Infantry Regiment. He was promoted to *Oberstleutnant* in September 1938 and appointed battalion commander with the 105th Infantry Regiment, part of the 76th Infantry Division.

76th Infantry Division, which had been rebuilt in France after being destroyed at Stalingrad. Abraham went on to command the division in Italy before moving to the Eastern Front. There he was promoted to *Generalleutnant* in March 1944 and led the division during the heavy fighting of the Dnieper withdrawal.

Knight's Cross with Oakleaves: While *Generalleutnant* and Commander of the 76th Infantry Division of the XXIX. Army Corps he was awarded the Oakleaves on 26 June 1944 for his part in the success of establishing a bridgehead over the eastern bank of the Latka River north-west of Odessa at the beginning of April 1944. The Oakleaves were personally presented to Abraham by Hitler sometime in early July 1944 during a ceremony at his Berghof mountain retreat. From February 1945 he took part in the fighting around the area of Alsace and finally led his troops as part of Army Group B during the fighting in the Ruhr Pocket. On 8 May 1945 he surrendered to US troops and spent the next two years in Allied captivity, being released in August 1947.

Friedrich-Wilhelm OTTE

Generalmajor

* 22 September 1898, Neurode
+ 8 May 1944, Sevastopol, Soviet Union

Knight's Cross: Awarded on 13 November 1942 as *Oberst* and Commander of *Jäger* Regiment 207 while attached to the 97th *Jäger* Division for actions during the Soviet winter offensive. He took part in the Battle of Isyum in the Ukraine and in the fighting in the Caucasus campaign, where he proved himself to be an excellent commander. From 30 May until 3 June 1943 he was acting commander of the 97th Jäger Division and saw action on the Russian Front until he was transferred to the Reserves on 4 June 1943. In April 1944 he was appointed Commander of Grenadier Regiment 213, which had by mid-April come into close contact with Soviet forces. One of his battalion commanders had been killed and on 8 May during a counter-attack near Sevastopol Otte was killed. He was posthumously promoted to the rank of *Generalmajor*.

Hans Ludwig Rudolf WULF

Generalmajor

* 12 December 1905, Elmshorn, Schleswig-Holstein
+ 14 November 1972, Breitbrunn, Bavaria

Rudolf Wulf entered the Army in April 1924 with the 14th Company of Infantry Regiment 6 and was commissioned as a *Leutnant* in March 1928. He served with Infantry Regiment 2 for the next five years and was appointed adjutant of the III. Battalion of Infantry Regiment 23 in October 1934. He was promoted to *Hauptmann* in September 1935 and a month later was made Commander of the 10th Company. Two years later he served as a training officer at the War School in Munich. In August 1939 he served as an ordnance officer on the Staff of the 46th Infantry Division and saw action during the invasion of Poland, where he was awarded the Iron Cross 2nd Class. Then, from January 1940 until May 1941, he served as an army trainer and later saw action as a battalion commander with Infantry Regiment 89, with the rank of *Major*.

Knight's Cross: Awarded on 13 November 1942 as *Major* and leader of Infantry Regiment 422 of the 126th Infantry Division for actions during the harsh winter conditions near Demyansk on the Soviet Front from October 1942 and was promoted to *Oberstleutnant*. He took part in the defensive battles of Army Group North and in the spring of 1943 his regiment played a vital role in the successful evacuation and relief of the Demyansk Salient. Shortly after he was promoted to *Oberst*. In February 1944 his regiment absorbed part of the 9th *Luftwaffe* Field Division and was later pushed back to the coast of Latvia.

Knight's Cross with Oakleaves: He became the 556th recipient on 19 August 1944 as *Oberst* and Commander of Grenadier Regiment 422 while still attached to the 126th Infantry Division for actions on the Eastern Front. His Oakleaves were awarded for his contributions to the defensive battles near Staraya Russa at the Sinyavino Heights, for his regiment's contribution to the Battle of Leningrad and in the fighting from March to July 1944 at Pskov. He was severely wounded during the fighting in the Courland on 19 October 1944 and did not return to duty until 13 February 1945, when he attended the 19th Divisional Leaders Course in Neustadt. Two weeks later he was confirmed as Commander of the 319th Infantry Division and was appointed Commandant of the British Channel Island of Guernsey. He was promoted to *Generalmajor* on 1 March and remained in Guernsey until the surrender to British troops on 9 May, remaining in British captivity until 12 May 1948.

Otto Karl Gerd Lorenz Adolf BÜSING
Generalmajor

* 22 August 1896, Kiel, Schleswig-Holstein
+ 8 March 1944, near Rownoje-Kirovograd, Soviet Union

Otto Büsing entered military service in January 1915 as an officer candidate, served in Horse Regiment 1 and was awarded the Iron Cross 1st and 2nd Classes. He left the Army after the war, and did not return to active service until September 1937 with Mounted Regiment 10. From November 1938 until January 1940 he served as adjutant of the 5th Panzer Division with the rank of *Major*. In April he was appointed Commander of Panzer Reconnaissance Battalion 8 and was awarded both classes of the Bar to the Iron Cross. On 16 October 1942 he was awarded the Honour Roll Clasp of the Army.

Knight's Cross: Awarded on 21 November 1942 as *Oberstleutnant* and Commander of Panzer Regiment 39 as part of the 17th Panzer Division for actions at the edge of a forest on the far side of the Zhizdra River north of Orel. Büsing managed to cross the river with his panzer at night in very difficult conditions; the roads were very marshy and there was a lot of enemy traffic. Nevertheless, his panzers managed to destroy four enemy tanks and encountered strong artillery fire. With Büsing in the lead tank, they searched for the enemy. He even left his vehicle and went on foot, locating the enemy batteries, which were then attacked and destroyed. Later that day thirty-five Soviet tanks drove towards his convoy in order to prevent his regiment from advancing. During the attack his troops destroyed a total of sixteen Soviet tanks and pushed them back across the river. Büsing was promoted to *Oberst* in December 1942 and continued to command Panzer Regiment 39 until February 1944. He was then delegated with the leadership of Panzer Division *Grossdeutschland*. On 8 March 1944, Büsing was fatally injured by enemy artillery fire near Lozuvatka. He died the same day from his injuries in the medical clearing station at Rovnoye, Soviet Union, and was posthumously promoted to the rank of *Generalmajor*.

Hans Gustav Wilhelm GOLLNICK

Generalleutnant

* 22 May 1892, Gut Gursen, Pomerania
+ 15 February 1970, Hamburg, Lower Saxony

Knight's Cross: Awarded on 21 November 1942 as *Generalmajor* and Commander of the 36th Motorised Infantry Division, part of the XXXXVI. Panzer Corps, for his distinguished service during the Division's defensive battle north-east of Sychyovka in the Soviet Union, between 4 and 8 August 1942. In January 1943 Gollnick was promoted to *Generalleutnant* and from May 1943 his division was declared de-motorised and became the 36th Infantry Division, although it did retain more motorised vehicles than the average infantry division. In July Gollnick led his division during the bitter fighting at Kursk, and on 5 August he was transferred as leader of the XXXXVI. Panzer Corps and saw action in Orel as part of the 9th Army.

Knight's Cross with Oakleaves: He became the 282nd recipient on 24 August 1943 as *Generalleutnant* and Commander of the 36th Panzer Grenadier Division, part of the XXXV. Army Corps, for proving himself an able commander during the defensive fighting east of Orel. On 1 October 1943 Gollnick was promoted to *General der Infanterie* and was confirmed as Commanding General of the XXXXVI. Panzer Corps, seeing further action on the Russian Front. He was personally presented with the Oakleaves on 13 February 1944 by Hitler at *Führer* Headquarters in Rastenburg together with *General der Infanterie* Kurt von der Chevallerie, *General der Infanterie* Friedrich Wiese and *Generalleutnant* Hans

Hans Gollnick entered the Army in March 1912 and saw action during the First World War as a *Leutnant* with Infantry Regiment 21. He served as adjutant of the II. Battalion of his regiment for the remainder of the war and was promoted to *Oberleutnant* in October 1916. He was awarded the Iron Cross 1st and 2nd Classes. He stayed in the Army after the war, serving with Infantry Regiment 129. In 1920 to 1934 he served in various positions with Infantry Regiment 4, and had been promoted to *Major*. From October 1935 until May 1939 he was Commander of the I. Battalion of Infantry Regiment 25 and from May 1939, now with the rank of *Oberst*, he served as Commander of Motorised Infantry Regiment 76 during the Polish Campaign, where was awarded the Bar to the Iron Cross 1st and 2nd Classes.

Schlemmer. He continued to see action with his Panzer Corps on the Eastern Front until March 1944, when he was rested and placed in the Reserves. From March 1944 he was Commanding General of the XXVIII. Army Corps and saw heavy action during the defensive battles around Pskov in north-eastern Russia. In mid-July the Soviets recaptured Pskov and broke through German defences south of Ostrów, and by 31 July his corps was fighting a defensive front and was under heavy Soviet artillery. By early September his corps had been pushed back and after the encirclement of Army Group North in the Baltic States he moved his corps into a new line of defence south-west of Riga. In January 1945 his corps was withdrawn and used to support the defensive action near Königsberg, and in February his command was transferred to East Prussia. From mid-May 1945 he was appointed Wehrmacht Commander of Flensburg, where Hitler's successor, Reich President *Grossadmiral* Karl Dönitz, had set up his headquarters. He finally went into Allied captivity with the British on 20 January 1946 but was released the following month.

Vollrath Friedrich Bogislav Maximilian von HELLERMANN

Generalmajor

* 18 May 1900, Ratzeburg, Schleswig-Holstein
\+ 25 August 1971, Munich, Bavaria

Knight's Cross: Awarded on 21 November 1942 as *Oberstleutnant* and Commander of Panzer Grenadier Regiment 21 while attached to the 24th Panzer Division for leading his regiment with great skill and bravery during an attack by Soviet forces north of Stalingrad. At the time of his award he was Department Head in the Army Personnel Office, Department 1 for 'Aspiring Officers'. Promoted to *Oberst* in February 1943, he was appointed Office Head with the High Command of the Army (OKH) from April. On 1 October 1944 he was promoted to *Generalmajor* and appointed General Inspector for Officer Candidates within the High Command of the Army.

Louis TRONNIER

Generalmajor

* 21 November 1897, Braunschweig
+ 27 January 1952, Voikovo Prison Camp, Soviet Union

Knight's Cross: Awarded on 28 November 1942 as *Oberst* and Commander of Grenadier Regiment 70 while attached to LII. Army Corps for the major role he and his command played in the capture of the city of Malgobek in the Soviet Union. He later took part in the latter stages of the Caucasus campaign and in the battles for Rostov in late 1943. From 15 January 1944 Tronnier was delegated with the leadership of the 123rd Infantry Division. This saw action on the southern sector of the Eastern Front, where it suffered heavy losses towards the end of February 1944 and was downgraded and renamed Corps Battalion F. Tronnier took command of the new battalion and was promoted to *Generalmajor* in April that year, and from July he took command of the 62nd Infantry Division. However, he was captured on 27 August and spent time in various Soviet prison camps, being sentenced to twenty-five years' imprisonment by a Moscow military court in June 1950. He died in the Černcy Prison in the Soviet Union on 27 January 1952, with a report stating that the cause was a cerebral haemorrhage caused by hypertension.

Günther Ernst Albrecht WÜSTENHAGEN

Generalleutnant

* 19 October 1892, Klostermansfeld, Saxony
+ 26 April 1944, south-west of Vitebsk, Soviet Union

Knight's Cross: Awarded on 2 December 1942 as *Oberst* and Commander of Artillery Regiment 129 while attached to XXVII. Army Corps for his initiative, bravery and leadership during various attacks by Soviet troops in the Soviet Union. Following a three-hour artillery barrage by Soviet troops that included five rifle divisions and two tank brigades he personally intervened on his own initiative and deployed five batteries against the enemy in close combat. Here he rallied stragglers and other infantry elements and by his skilful leadership and the boldness of his troops he brought the Soviet attack to a halt. By the evening of the attack hundreds of Soviet troops lay dead on the battlefield and ten enemy tanks had been destroyed. It was later written in a report of the attack that *Oberst* Wüstenhagen had prevented a strong Soviet breakthrough aimed at the flank and rear of the Germans near Rzhev as well as the railway line nearby that was vital for the German XXVII. and VI. Army Corps. He remained in command of the 129th Infantry Division until September 1943, when he was delegated with the leadership of the 110th Infantry Division between September and November. On 1 December he took command of the 256th Infantry Division and seven days later he was promoted to *Generalmajor* and saw action as part of the 3rd Panzer Army at Vitebsk. On 1 June 1944 Wüstenhagen was promoted to *Generalleutnant* but he was killed on 28 June while attempting to break out of the encirclement of Army Group Centre. As his command vehicle moved across the country to avoid Soviet forces it received a direct hit from a tank shell and Wüstenhagen died instantly.

Willy LANGKEIT

Generalmajor

* 2 June 1907, Schuchten, East Prussia
+ 27 October 1969, Bad Bramstedt, Schleswig-Holstein

Knight's Cross: Awarded on 9 December 1942 as *Major* and Commander of the II. Battalion of Panzer Regiment 36 while attached to the 14th Panzer Division for his leadership and courage during the pursuit battles towards the Lower Don in mid-1942. He particularly distinguished himself on 23 July 1942 in the area west of Novocherkassk and a week later his battalion destroyed a tank nearby while patrolling on the Russian Front. The Knight's Cross was presented to Langkeit by *Oberst* Martin Lattmann, the Commander of the 14th Panzer Division, during a special ceremony on Christmas Eve 1942, and by that time he had been promoted to the rank of *Oberstleutnant*. He saw action during the Battle of Stalingrad, where he was seriously wounded and was one of the last officers to be flown out of the pocket on 19 January 1943.

Willy Langkeit entered Army service as a volunteer in October 1924 and was assigned to Motor Transport Battalion 1. He was commissioned as a *Leutnant* in 1934 and served as a company leader. From October 1935 he served with Panzerjäger Battalion 1 and was promoted to the rank of *Hauptmann* in January 1938. He was appointed Commander of the 8th Company of Panzer Regiment 36 in November and served as battalion commander from November 1941.

Knight's Cross with Oakleaves: Langkeit became the 348th recipient on 7 December 1943 as *Oberstleutnant* and Commander of Panzer Regiment 36 while still part of the 14th Panzer Division for his part in the fierce tank battle on 20 November 1943. His men destroyed twenty-two enemy tanks near Novoivanovka. He was promoted to *Oberst* on 1 December and was presented with the Oakleaves personally by Hitler at the Wolf's Lair in Rastenburg later that month. In March 1944 he was appointed Commander of Panzer Regiment *Grossdeutschland* and served as a rearguard in Romania, where his troops protected the important oilfields that were vital to the German war effort. On 26 April almost twenty Soviet infantry divisions with tanks struck at the German lines and Lankeit's forces were drawn into a four-day battle that slowed the Soviet advance. During one of the engagements Langkeit and General Manteuffel launched an offence that destroyed fifty-six Soviet tanks. Later Langkeit took his troops into East Prussia and he was put in command of an all-new Replacement Brigade from October. However this was not an elite unit but rather a mix of old and fresh troops who had never fought before. He later led a breakthrough and for three days his men fought a battle to escape the Soviet encirclement, taking a stream of military and civilian vehicles towards the Oder River. On 20 April 1945 Langkeit was promoted to *Generalmajor* and ordered to hold enemy forces from crossing the Oder, being credited with stalling the Soviet advance. However, by the last few days of the war he was fighting with a decimated panzer force and on 7 May he surrendered to US forces. He was handed over to the British and remained in their captivity until 8 July 1947. During the post-war years he rejoined the German Army and by January 1955 had risen to the rank of *Brigadegeneral.*

Paul Gustav VÖLCKERS

General der Infanterie

* 15 March 1891, Kiel, Schleswig-Holstein
+ 25 January 1946, Prison Camp 7048 in Ivanovo, Soviet Union

Knight's Cross: Awarded on 11 December 1942 as *Generalleutnant* and Commander of 78th Infantry Division while attached to the XXXIX. Army Corps for his bravery and leadership during the heavy combat in the area south-west of Kaliningrad Oblast in the Soviet Union, where his troops destroyed 127 tanks. In June 1943 he was took command of the XXVII. Army Corps as part of the 4th Army at Smolensk, where during the beginning of the summer offensive his troops repelled the Soviet attacks. In September Völckers was promoted to

General der Infanterie and soon after had to withdraw his troops from Smolensk to Orsha. The position remained unchanged until the summer of 1944 at the beginning of the Soviet offensive, when his command was deployed in the area east of Orsha. By the end of June his corps had been pushed back across the Dnieper River and was surrounded by Soviet units in the forests east of Minsk and almost destroyed. Völckers surrendered his command on 9 July 1944 and was taken prisoner. He died in January 1946 in Prison Camp 7048 in Ivanovo.

Richard LEPPER

Generalmajor

* 15 July 1897, Potsdam
+ 31 March 1943, Camp Frolov, Stalingrad (Soviet captivity)

Knight's Cross: Awarded on 17 December 1942 as *Oberst* and Artillery Commander 6 and leader of Battle Group *Lepper* in the XI. Army Corps in Kessel near Stalingrad for his part in preventing an enemy penetration along the Don Front. A few weeks after being presented with his Knight's Cross he was captured at Stalingrad by the Soviets and imprisoned at Camp Frolov near Stalingrad, where he died on 30 March 1943, probably of cold and malnutrition. He was posthumously promoted to the rank of *Generalmajor* and later it is thought that his body was moved to the Rossoschka German War Cemetery, north-west of Volgograd.

Karl Robert Rudolf Albert Arnold LORENZ

Generalmajor

* 24 January 1904, Hanau am Main, Hesse-Nassau
+ 3 October 1964. Bad Godesberg-Mehlem, North Rhine-Westphalia

Knight's Cross: Awarded on 17 December 1942 as *Major* and Commander of Engineer Battalion *Grossdeutschland*, part of Infantry Division *Grossdeutschland*, for actions on the Russian Front. On 2 December 1942, after days of heavy defensive fighting and despite being wounded, Lorenz led his battalion as the main line of resistance against overwhelming numbers of enemy forces. On his own initiative he carried out a successful counter-attack with assault guns and averted a serious threat to the German supply route. He was promoted to *Oberstleutnant* in February 1943, and the following month his command was

Karl Lorenz entered the Army as an officer candidate in Pioneer Battalion 3 in April 1924, and was commissioned as a *Leutnant* four years later. From 1935 he served as an adjutant with Higher Pioneer Officer 2 with the rank of *Hauptmann* and three years later he served as company commander in Pioneer Battalion 18. He was awarded the Iron Cross 2nd Class during the Polish Campaign, and in June 1940 he was awarded the Iron Cross 1st Class during the French Campaign.

renamed Panzer Grenadier Regiment *GD*. He saw further action near Kharkov and continued to prove himself as a brave and responsible commander.

Knight's Cross with Oakleaves: Lorenz became the 395th recipient on 12 February 1944 as *Oberst* and Commander of Grenadier Regiment *Grossdeutschland*, part of Panzer Grenadier Division *Grossdeutschland*, in recognition of his outstanding leadership and bravery during Operation Citadel. He took part in the defensive battles around Kharkov, the counter-attack near Okhtyrka and the retreat to the Dnieper, displaying very calm and superior leadership. Hitler presented him with the Oakleaves at *Führer* Headquarters in Rastenburg towards the end of February 1944. After the withdrawal from the Ukraine during the spring of 1944 he saw further action in Romania, still part of the Grenadier Regiment *Grossdeutschland*. From 7 August until 2 September 1944 he attended the 13th Divisional Leaders Course at Hirschberg and was then appointed Commander of Panzer Grenadier Division *Grossdeutschland*. Promoted to *Generalmajor* in November, Lorenz took part in the heavy fighting in East Prussia towards the end of the war and his division was almost destroyed at the Heiligenbeil Pocket. The remnants of his division managed to escape to the Western lines and in May 1945 he surrendered to British forces near Schleswig-Holstein. He remained in captivity until 19 March 1948.

Alexander Reinhard Maximilian Ludwig Moritz Edler von DANIELS

Generalleutnant

* 17 March 1891, Trier, Rhine Province
\+ 6 January 1960, Bielefeld, North Rhine-Westphalia

Knight's Cross: Awarded on 18 December 1942 as *Generalmajor* and Commander of the 376th Infantry Division, part of the XIV. Army Corps, for his actions

Alexander von Daniels entered Army service in March 1910 as a *Leutnant* with Infantry Regiment 143, and from October 1913 served as adjutant of the I. Battalion. He was appointed legal officer with his regiment from October 1915, and two months later was promoted to *Oberleutnant*. After the war he joined the *Freikorps* and from September 1919 he was part of the *Reichswehr* and was promoted to *Hauptmann* in February 1922. At the beginning of the Second World War, now with the rank of *Oberst*, he was Commander of Infantry Regiment 18 and saw action in Poland and France, where he was awarded both classes of the Bar to the Iron Cross.

in November 1942 in the area around Stalingrad. As enemy forces penetrated towards the German division he created a new defensive front and thereafter led the defensive battle successfully against the Soviets. His division was the most exposed to Soviet attack and had been reduced to just 4,200 men, becoming trapped on the west bank of the Don. In late December the Sixth Army had been encircled at Stalingrad and Daniels had been promoted to *Generalleutnant* as the Soviet forces advanced ever closer. He surrendered himself and his division to *Colonel* Ivan Konstantinovich Morozov, the commander of the 422nd Rifle Division, and was marched into captivity on 31 January 1943. He was not released until 12 October 1955.

Hans Eberhard KINZEL

General der Infanterie

* 18 October 1897, Berlin
\+ 23 May 1945, Idstedt, Flensburg

Knight's Cross: Awarded on 21 December 1942 as *Oberst im Generalstab* as Chief of the Central Department of the General Staff of the Army and until November 1942 as Chief of the General Staff of the XXIX. Army Corps. While attached to the 8th Italian Army, he fought with bravery by holding a forward strongpoint along the Don River. Kinzel was promoted to *Generalmajor* in January 1943 and was appointed Chief of the General Staff of Army Group North while under the command of *Generalfeldmarschall* Georg von Küchler, and later under *Generaloberst* Walter Model, whom he found to be extremely difficult to satisfy. He was promoted a year later to *Generalleutnant* in September 1943, and received his own command when he was appointed Commander of the

Eberhard Kinzel entered the Army as a war volunteer with Infantry Regiment 20 in October 1914, and was commissioned as a *Leutnant* in May 1915. He was wounded shortly but soon rejoined his regiment and was awarded both classes of the Iron Cross and the Wound Badge in Black. When the war finished Kinzel joined the *Freikorps* and then transferred back into the Army and was appointed an orderly officer with the III. Battalion of Reichswehr Infantry Regiment 6. He was promoted to *Oberleutnant* in July 1925 and served with various units, including signals and transport. In 1929 he transferred into the Reich Defence Ministry and from October 1933, now with the rank of *Hauptmann*, he served as an assistant of the Military Attaché in Warsaw, Poland. At the beginning of the Second World War he was a department head with the Army General Staff, where he stayed until the end of April 1942.

570th *Volksgrenadier* Division. Within two weeks this command was reformed into the 337th *Volksgrenadier* Division. The division had been reformed in East Prussia and Kinzel saw action there and in Poland near Warsaw and on the Vistula. The unit was virtually destroyed near Danzig in February 1945 and was dissolved in West Prussia. From early March, Kinzel took over as Chief of the General Staff of Army Group Vistula, serving under *Generaloberst* Gotthard Heinrici. On 20 April Kinzel was promoted to *General der Infanterie* and two days later he was appointed Chief of the General Staff of the Operations Staff North under *Grossadmiral* Karl Dönitz. From 3 May he was a member of the German Surrender Delegation, which was led by *Generaladmiral* Hans-Georg von Friedeburg. He was ordered by *Grossadmiral* Dönitz, Hitler's successor, to negotiate a truce with the Western Allied forces. When the delegation arrived at the headquarters of Field Marshal Montgomery in Lüneburg they were informed that the Allies would only accept an unconditional surrender. He was present on 4 May when Admiral Friedeburg signed the surrender of all German armed forces in Holland, north-west Germany and Denmark. On 23 May 1945 Kinzel and his girlfriend, Erika von Aschoff, committed suicide.

Walther Ernst Theodor von HÜNERSDORFF

Generalleutnant

* 28 November 1898, Cairo, Egypt
+ 17 July 1943, Kharkov hospital, Soviet Union

Knight's Cross: Awarded on 22 December 1942 as *Oberst* and Commander of Panzer Regiment 11 while attached to the 6th Panzer Division for his outstanding leadership during the German Offensive known as Operation Winter Storm. As part of the 4th Panzer Army he led his regiment during the attempted seizure of the bridgehead over the Volga River near Myshkin, just 30 miles from Stalingrad.

Knight's Cross with Oakleaves: Awarded on 14 July 1943 as *Generalmajor* and the 259th recipient as Commander of the 6th Panzer Division, part of the III. Panzer Corps, for his command during Operation Citadel between 5 and 9 July 1943. His division had succeeded in breaking through the heavily defended anti-tank ditches north-east of Belgorod, and they destroyed twenty Soviet tanks and thirty heavy anti-tank guns. However, on 14 July Hünersdorff was shot in the head by a sniper near Belgorod and a fragment of his steel helmet penetrated his brain. He was flown by aircraft to hospital in Kharkov. A specialist neurosurgeon, *Oberstarzt der Reserve* Prof. Wilhelm Tönnis, was flown

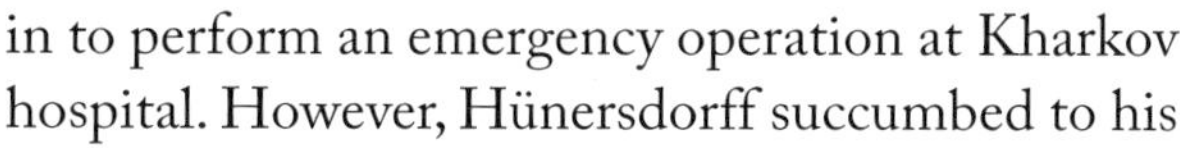

in to perform an emergency operation at Kharkov hospital. However, Hünersdorff succumbed to his

Walther von Hünersdorff entered Army service in August 1915 as an officer candidate with Hussar Regiment 4 and served as an orderly officer and adjutant with the rank of *Leutnant*. He remained in the Army after the war and by April 1936 had been promoted to *Major* and was serving on the staff of the Command of Panzer Troops. From February 1938 he served as Chief of Operations in the Staff of the 1st Panzer Division and was promoted to *Oberstleutnant* in June 1938. He served as Chief of Operations on the General Staff of the II. Army Corps from October 1939 and was awarded the Bar to the Iron Cross 1st and 2nd Classes during the French Campaign.

wound three days later, and was buried at the Soldiers Cemetery in Kharkov with full military honours. Present were *General der Panzertruppe* Erhard Raus, *Generaloberst* Hermann Hoth and *Generalfeldmarschall* Erich von Manstein, who read the eulogy. Hünersdorff was posthumously promoted to *Generalleutnant* on 10 August 1943.

Arno Friedrich Adam JAHR

Generalleutnant

* 3 December 1890, Prittitz, Weissenfels
+ 21 January 1943 near Podgornoje, near Orel, Soviet Union

Knight's Cross: Awarded on 22 December 1942 as *Generalleutnant* and Commander of the 387th Infantry Division while attached to the XXIV. Army Corps for his successful defence along the Don, where he pushed back Soviet forces that had penetrated friendly lines. Jahr took part in the fighting near Kursk during the Battle of Voronezh and the drive to the Volga, when he later saw action in the Don Bend battles and his command suffered heavy casualties. On 20 January 1943 Jahr was delegated with the leadership of the XXIV. Panzer Corps and within just one day was trapped during the Battle of Stalingrad. The following day, with the enemy approaching, he shot himself. He is buried today in an unmarked grave at the German War Cemetery at Kursk-Besedino.

Eugen OTT

General der Infanterie

* 20 May 1890, Sinzig
+ 11 August 1966, Schäftlarn

Knight's Cross: Awarded on 25 December 1942 as *General der Infanterie* and Commanding General of the LII. Army Corps while attached to the 1st Panzer Army. Ott's forces pushed back Soviet forces across the Terek River in the Northern Caucasus before the establishment of a bridgehead across the river. By the end of December the LII. Army Corps had withdrawn from the area around Stalingrad and began to retreat as far as the Protoka River in the Ukraine. By July his corps had retreated as far as Kharkov and later had moved to the area north of Belgorod, where the Soviet offensive soon began. On 1 October 1943 Ott was transferred and became Inspector of Army Infantry, and from

February 1944 he was appointed Inspector of Italian Troops. From mid-January 1945 he took over as Inspector of Italian Troops with the Commander-in-Chief Southeast under *Luftwaffe Generaloberst* Alexander Löhr.

Herbert Karl MICHAELIS

Generalmajor

* 5 February 1897, Neuruppin, Brandenburg
+ 20 August 1969, Bonn, North Rhine-Westphalia

Knight's Cross: Awarded on 27 December 1942 as *Oberst* and Commander of Grenadier Regiment 525 while attached to the 298th Infantry Division for his leadership during the fighting on the southern sector of the Soviet Front. He saw action during the drive to Kiev, in the Battle of Kharkov and in the campaigns on the southern sector of the Eastern Front. On 27 December 1942 Michaelis was delegated with the leadership of the 298th Infantry Division while the commander was on leave, then from January 1943 he was Commander of Group *Michaelis* while attached to the 8th Italian Army. He entered the Reserves from March 1943 and in July was attached to the Chief of the General Staff of the Army. From 15 January 1944 he was appointed as head of the 306th Infantry Division, seeing action at Nikopol. He was then delegated with the leadership of the 254th Infantry Division from March 1944 and saw action in the Ukraine, taking part in the retreat on the southern sector of the front. He was promoted to *Generalmajor* on 1 April 1944 and his command of the division was confirmed, however in May he was transferred and appointed Commander of the 95th Infantry Division. At the beginning of the Soviet summer offensive

Herbert Michaelis entered the Fusilier Regiment 'Generalfeldmarschall Graf Blumenthal' No: 36 in August 1914 and was commissioned as a *Leutnant* the following year. He served the rest of the war as a platoon and company leader and a battalion adjutant with the 225th Infantry Brigade. When the war was over he joined the *Schutzpolizei* and then the *Landespolizei*, rising to the rank of *Major*. From March 1936 he entered the Army once again as a *Major* and was Chief of the 9th Company of Infantry Regiment 78 in Bonn from October 1936. From February 1940 he served as *Oberstleutnant* and Commander of the II. Battalion of Infantry Regiment 523, and from December 1940 he was Battalion commander with Infantry Regiment 442.

Michaelis's division was virtually destroyed near Vitebsk and he was taken prisoner. In October 1948 he was sentenced to twenty-five years' hard labour by a military tribunal in Vitebsk. However, he was released on 8 October 1955 and returned to Germany.

Wilhelm August Theodor LORENZ

Generalmajor

* 25 April 1894, Hamburg
+ 2 January 1943, Demyansk, Soviet Union

Knight's Cross: Awarded on 28 December 1942 as *Oberst* and Commander of Infantry Regiment 376 while attached to the 225th Infantry Division for his leadership in the Soviet Union during the heavy defensive fighting from 23 to 27 December. On 26 December elements of his regiment recaptured the village of Vyazovka, something the Soviet forces thought would not happen. During the fighting Lorenz was seriously wounded and was taken to the field hospital in Demyansk, where he died of his wounds on 2 January 1943. He was posthumously awarded the Knight's Cross and posthumously promoted to the rank of *Generalmajor* on 8 February 1943.

Walther WENCK

General der Panzertruppe

* 18 September 1900, Wittenberg
+ 1 May 1982, Ried, Austria

Knight's Cross: Awarded on 28 December 1942 as *Oberst im Generalstab* and Chief of the General Staff of 3rd Romanian Army as part of Army Group B for his advice to the Romanian General Petre Dumitrescu. Wenck was invaluable to the general and following the commencement of the Soviet Operation Uranus, the code name of the strategic operation on the Eastern Front between 19 and 23 November 1942, which prevented the total disintegration of the army. Although the Soviet forces pushed back the Romanian army, *Generalfeldmarschall* Erich von Manstein was full of praise for the contribution Wenck made and totally supported the award of the Knight's Cross. From 26 December 1942 Wenck was Chief of the General Staff of Army Group Hollidt and on 1 February 1943 he was promoted to *Generalmajor*. From March 1943 he was named as Chief of

Walther Wenck joined the *Freikorps Reinhard* in February 1919 and a year later he joined the *Reichswehr* with Infantry Regiment 5 with the rank of *Gefreiter*. He later joined the 12th Machine Gun Company of Infantry Regiment 9 and was commissioned as a *Leutnant*. He was later assigned to the War Academy in Berlin. From October 1936 he served as a General Staff Officer to the Commander of Panzer Troops in Berlin, now with the rank of *Hauptmann*. In March 1939 he was promoted to *Major* and a month later he was appointed Chief of Operations of the 1st Panzer Division. He took part in the invasion of Poland, where he was awarded both classes of the Iron Cross, and from May 1940 he took part in the invasion of Luxembourg and France.

the General Staff of the 6th Army, which had been reformed after Stalingrad and was commanded by *Generaloberst* Karl-Adolf Hollidt. He was promoted to *Generalleutnant* in April 1944 and on 21 July was appointed Chief of the Operations Department of the Army High Command. At the same time he was made Deputy Chief of the General Staff of the Army. Wenck was promoted to *General der Panzertruppe* on 7 April 1945 and three days later was appointed the Commander-in-Chief of the 12th Army. However, his new command was formed of mainly new recruits, who were young and had seen very little action. He was given the task of liberating Berlin from the Soviets and so he decided to establish a bridgehead across the Elbe River and link up with the Americans. On 7 May 1945 he signed an armistice with the US forces and so went into captivity, from which he was released two years later.

Hermann Leopold August von OPPELN-BRONIKOWSKI

Generalmajor

* 2 January 1899, Berlin
+ 19 September 1966, Gaissbach, Bavaria

Knight's Cross: Awarded on 1 January 1943 as *Oberst* and Commander of Panzer Regiment 204 while attached to the 22nd Panzer Division for his leadership during the desperate fighting on the Russian Front in the winter of 1942–43. From May 1942 until January 1943 Oppeln-Bronikowski's regiment had destroyed more than 450 Soviet tanks and 209 assault guns, and had destroyed or captured just over 750 heavy infantry weapons. This was an outstanding achievement, especially when in November 1942, although he in theory had more

Hermann von Oppeln-Bronikowski entered the Army in March 1917 as a *Leutnant*, seeing action with Lancer Regiment 10 during the First World War and attending Artillery School from January 1922. He was promoted to *Oberleutnant* in July 1925 and joined Infantry Regiment 10, serving as an adjutant from February 1928. He was promoted to *Rittmeister* in June 1933 and then served as adjutant of the Riders School in Hannover from October 1934. He was attached to the Cavalry School from October 1935 and took part in the Berlin Olympic Games as part of the dressage team, winning a gold medal. He joined the Cavalry in 1938 and later served as a Cavalry consultant during the early stages of the Second World War with the rank of *Oberstleutnant*.

than 100 tanks at his disposal, only thirty-nine were operational because vermin had chewed cables inside and they had to be repaired. From 18 February 1943 he took command of the 11th Panzer Regiment and took part in the Manstein offensive that led to the encirclement of Kharkov in March. Later, Oppeln-Bronikowski saw action at Kursk, Belgorod and at Kharkov once again, and later in the Dnieper battles. In November 1943 he took over as Commander of Panzer Regiment 100, part of the newly reformed 21st Panzer Division, which had been destroyed in Tunisia in May 1943.

Knight's Cross with Oakleaves: He became the 536th recipient on 28 July 1944 as *Oberst* and Commander of Panzer Regiment 22 of the 21st Panzer Division for his accomplishments during the battle of Normandy, where his Panzer Regiment held its position for thirty-two days in the area around Caen against overwhelming Allied superiority. He was personally decorated with the Oakleaves by Hitler at *Führer* Headquarters in Rastenburg in September 1944. From October Oppeln-Bronikowski attended the 15th Divisional Leaders Course before on 7 November taking over command of the 20th Panzer Division, seeing action in East Prussia. On 30 January 1945 he was promoted to *Generalmajor* and led the division into Hungary.

Knight's Cross with Oakleaves and Swords: Awarded on 17 April 1945 as the 142nd recipient as *Generalmajor* and Commander of 20th Panzer Division while attached to XXXX. Panzer Corps for his part in the success of his division during the heavy battles in Upper Silesia. By the end of March he had seen action through Lower Silesia and into Dresden, where he led his division during the bloody counter-attack against the Soviets in Spremberg, Brandenburg. He was captured by US forces in May 1945 and in June, together with other staff officers, he was transferred to a British holding camp near Paderborn. The British wanted to charge him with a war crime in connection with the Caen trial of SS-Brigadeführer Kurt Meyer for the shooting of Allied prisoners of war. However, early interrogations proved that Oppeln-Bronikowski was innocent of all charges. In 1946 he was transferred to another camp near Paderborn and was eventually released from Allied captivity on 14 July 1947.

Paul Johannes Nikolaus KLATT

Generalleutnant

* 6 December 1896, Kroppen-Hoyerswalda, Silesia
+ 3 July 1973, Olching, Bavaria

Knight's Cross: Awarded on 4 January 1943 as *Oberst* and Commander of Mountain Jäger Regiment 138 while attached to the 3rd Mountain Division for his bravery and leadership during the defensive fighting and heavy attacks near Tschernosem in the Soviet Union. From 27 November until 5 December 1942 Klatt launched counter-thrusts on his own initiative against enemy forces, which succeeded in pushing through enemy lines. His outstanding leadership and his devotion to duty inspired his men during heavy fighting in ice and snow. His units destroyed sixty-eight enemy tanks, captured 565 prisoners, twenty heavy machine guns, twenty-nine light machine guns, seven anti-tank rifles, eleven mortars, four truck and two field kitchens. Klatt himself was seriously wounded during the heavy fighting on 24 December 1942 and was presented with his Knight's Cross while recovering at home. He was promoted to *Generalmajor* in February 1944 and remained in the Reserves until June while still recovering

Paul Klatt entered Army service as a war volunteer with Field Artillery Regiment 57 in August 1914 and trained as an officer. In June 1915 he was commissioned as a *Leutnant* while recovering in hospital after being wounded and was shortly after transferred into Infantry Regiment 51. He was captured by British forces in April 1917 and attempted to escape three times. He was finally released and returned home in October 1919. He stayed in the Army and served in the *Reichswehr* in various different regiments and in the early 1930s he attended various different training courses and was promoted to *Major* in January 1936. From November 1938 he was Commander of Mountain Pioneer Battalion 83, part of the 3rd Mountain Division, and saw action in Poland in September 1939, in the Eifel area of Germany and later in Narvik.

from his wounds. He briefly took command of the 44th Reichs-Grenadier Division *Hoch-und Deutschmeister* from 15 June but went back into the Reserves just over a week later.

Knight's Cross with Oakleaves: Klatt became the 686th recipient on 26 December 1944 as *Generalleutnant* and Commander of the 3rd Mountain Division part of the XXIX. Army Corps for his part in the successful destruction of three Soviet mobile corps north-west of Debrecen, Hungary. Promoted to *Generalleutnant* on 15 January 1945, he later prevented a Soviet breakthrough by showing great inspiration to his men, although he was hindered by the seriousness of his wounds. At the end of the war he was taken prisoner in Slovakia by Soviet troops and spent the next ten years in a Soviet prison camp.

Konrad Theodor BARDE

Generalmajor

* 13 November 1897, Alt-Rosenburg, Prussia
\+ 4 May 1945, Traunstein, Bavaria

Knight's Cross: Awarded on 5 January 1943 as *Oberst* and Commander of Artillery Regiment 104 while attached to the 102nd Infantry Division for his leadership and bravery during the heavy battles on the Eastern Front. He later led his regiment during the heavy fighting during the Battle of Kursk in July and August 1943, and near Gomel and later during the withdrawal at Rzhev. From February until June 1944 he was in the Reserves and then served briefly as leader of Artillery Commander 186 before returning to the Reserves in September. In October he attended the 15th Divisional Leaders Course at Hirschberg and was briefly attached to *Reichsführer-SS* Heinrich Himmler's staff in December. He took command of the 338th Infantry Division from 29 December, which had been largely destroyed during its retreat from southern France, and Barde now led a refitted and reorganised division through southern Germany, taking part in the Battle of the Linnich Bridgehead in North Rhine-Westphalia. He was made Commander of the 198th Infantry Division on 18 January 1945, taking over the division after the disaster of Operation Northwind, with the division down to only the strength of 6,800 men. Parts of his division were crushed in the Colmar Pocket in Alsace but Barde did manage to escape with some of his command across the Rhine to Germany, where they took part in the defensive battles near Traunstein, Bavaria. It was there that he committed suicide.

Eduard METZ

Generalleutnant

* 28 November 1891, Munich, Bavaria
+ 9 June 1969, Bad Tölz, Bavaria

Knight's Cross: Awarded on 5 January 1943 as *Generalmajor* and Commander of 5th Panzer Division while attached to the XXXIX. Panzer Corps for his distinguished service during the heavy defensive combat south-west of Kalinin as a result of his determined leadership of his Panzer Division. Soon after he was awarded with the Knight's Cross, Metz was seriously ill and away from the front line until September 1943. From 25 September he served as Higher Artillery Commander 302 while attached to the 4th Army on the Eastern Front as part of Army Group Centre. He was promoted to *Generalleutnant* in January 1944 and from November 1944 was once again seriously ill and hospitalised until April 1945. He was captured by US forces in May and remained in US captivity until his release on 17 October 1947.

Arthur SCHMIDT

Generalleutnant

* 25 October 1895, Hamburg
+ 5 November 1987, Karlsruhe

Knight's Cross: Awarded on 6 January 1943 as *Generalmajor* and Chief of the General Staff of the 6th Army for his command and personal bravery during the fighting between the Volga and Don Rivers near Stalingrad. On 22 November 1942, together with *Generaloberst* Friedrich Paulus, he met with *Generaloberst* Hermann Hoth and *Generalmajor* Wolfgang Pickert, the commander of the 9th Anti-aircraft Division. They told Schmidt to get out of Stalingrad, but he believed there was nothing to panic about and Paulus agreed. However, by January 1943 the German 6th Army became trapped in the city. Schmidt was promoted to *Generalleutnant* on 17 January, and just five days later the Soviets offered the Germans chance to surrender. On the 31st, the 6th Army finally surrendered and the Soviets took 91,000 prisoners, which included twenty-two generals. Schmidt, however, refused to cooperate with his captors in any way and maintained the same attitude throughout his imprisonment, even through torture. He was finally sentenced to twenty-five years' imprisonment but was released under a general amnesty in October 1955 and returned to Germany.

Franz Fritz August BÄKE

Generalmajor

* 28 February 1898, Schwarzenfels in Main-Kinzig- Kreis, Hesse
+ 12 November 1978, Bochum in North Rhine-Westphalia

Franz Bäke joined the Army in May 1915, after putting his career in medicine on hold. He was posted to the 3rd Infantry Regiment based in Cologne and saw action on the Western Front, where he won the Iron Cross 2nd Class. He served briefly with the artillery in early 1918 and was wounded twice but soon returned to the front as an *Unteroffizier*. When the war ended, Bäke left the Army and returned to his medical studies at university and was later involved with the *Freikorps* movement.

Knight's Cross: Awarded the Knight's Cross on 11 January 1943 as *Major der Reserve* and as Commander of II. Battalion of the 11th Panzer Regiment for actions in the Soviet Union. On 1 January he and his men took part in bitter fighting against two Soviet battalions and thirty tanks near Nowo Marjewka. During the fighting twenty-seven tanks were destroyed by Bäke's men and using his own initiative he launched a counter-attack in which thirty-two more were put out of action and the Soviet advance across the railway line west of Morosowskaja was prevented. In June Bäke took part in the fighting at Kursk and was again wounded, and on 14 July he took temporary command of the 11th Panzer Regiment. During this time Bäke destroyed three of the Soviet tanks and was awarded the tank destruction sleeve in silver.

Knight's Cross with Oakleaves: On 1 August 1943 Bäke became the 262nd recipient of the Knight's Cross with Oakleaves as *Major der Reserve* while still Commander of II. Battalion with the 11th Panzer Regiment. On 11 July his regiment reached the village of Kasatschja near Belgorod on the Soviet front, and that night his command thrust its way past enemy anti-tank gun positions and found itself next to a column of Soviet T-34 tanks. Bäke persuaded his regimental commander, *Oberst* Hermann von Oppeln-Bronikowski, to go against orders and allow him to recapture the village of Rschawez by night, creating a bridgehead over the Sswernyi Donez. During the following night, Bäke and *Leutnant* Zobel left the command Panzer and tried to eliminate four T-34 tanks with magnetic anti-tank grenades but the charges did not explode. So Bäke then clambered on to a panzer and directed it to destroy the enemy tanks, which it did and partially destroyed a bridge. On 15 September Bäke, together with *Oberst* Paul Schultz, *Oberst* Walter Lange, *Major* Theodor Tolsdorff

From September 1939 Bäke saw action during the Polish Campaign while attached to Anti-tank Battalion 6 and was awarded the Iron Cross 2nd Class. He showed real promise as a panzer leader during the campaign and was made a company leader in January 1940, with a promotion to *Oberleutnant der Reserve* at the same time. On 10 May he took part in the invasion of France and was wounded twice but stayed with his unit. He later received the Wound Badge in Gold and the Iron Cross 1st Class for his actions in securing the bridges over the Meuse at Arques.

and *Oberst* Günther Pape, were presented with the Oakleaves by Hitler at the Wolf's Lair in Rastenburg. In November he was promoted to *Oberstleutnant der Reserve* and the following month he was tasked with putting together a special tank formation named the Heavy Panzer Regiment *Bäke*, consisting of Panther and Tiger tanks. It was to be used in special duties in the southern sector of the Eastern Front. At the beginning of 1944 Bäke led his regiment during the battles of the Balabonowka Pocket in the Ukraine, and during a five-day battle his regiment destroyed 267 Soviet tanks with the loss of only four panzers.

Knight's Cross with Oakleaves and Swords: Awarded on 21 February 1944, the 49th recipient as *Oberstleutnant der Reserve* as Commander of the 11th Panzer Regiment for his success during special operations by his regiment in the Soviet Union. Bäke had thirty-four Tiger tanks and forty-seven Panther tanks at his disposal and during the raid near Shaskow from 23 January to 1 February his command destroyed 268 Soviet tanks and assault guns. Bäke was presented with Swords personally by Hitler on 27 April at the Berghof, and at the same time he was also presented with the Tank Combat Badge in Silver for '100' kills. On 1 January 1945, Bäke was transferred from the reserve to active service and in

March took command of the 13th Panzer Division in Hungary and then into Czechoslovakia. On 20 April he was promoted to *Generalmajor* and led the remnants of his division in a successful breakout towards the western lines. On 8 May he surrendered his command to US forces and spent two years as a prisoner.

Dr Georg PFEIFFER

General der Artillerie

* 5 May 1890, Wendessen, Braunschweig
+ 28 June 1944, near Mogilev an der Beresina, Soviet Union

Knight's Cross: Awarded on 15 January 1943 as *Generalleutnant* and Commander of 94th Infantry Division while attached to the XI. Army Corps for his role in the encirclement and destruction of an enemy battle group near Stalingrad on the Russian Front. From March 1943 he took command of a second 94th Infantry Division as the first had been lost at Stalingrad after Pfeiffer had been evacuated. A new division had been formed in France and was sent to Italy in mid-1943 after the collapse of Mussolini's government. In August his command occupied the Mount Cenis Pass and was on coastal defence duty in the Genoa area, while from November it saw combat on the Bernhardt Line. From early January 1944 Pfeiffer attended the 1st Training Course for Commanding Generals and from February he was given the leadership of the XII. Army Corps as part of the 4th Army, seeing action in Minsk. From 20 March 1944 he was delegated with the leadership of the VI. Army Corps and in May he was promoted to *General der Artillerie* and took over as Commanding General. As part of the 3rd Panzer Army, Pfeiffer saw action in Vitebsk, in north-east Belarus on the Eastern Front, but on 28 June he was killed in a Soviet air strike near Mogilev.

Helmuth Otto Ludwig WEIDLING

General der Artillerie

* 2 November 1891, Halberstadt, Saxony Anhalt
+ 17 November 1955, Moscow Prison Camp, Soviet Union

Knight's Cross: Awarded on 15 January 1943 as *Generalmajor* and Commander of 86th Infantry Division while attached to the XXIII. Army Corps for his actions, especially in the repulse of a strong Soviet attack. In late 1942 he led

Helmuth Weidling entered the Army in March 1911 as an officer candidate with the Airship Battalion and saw action during the First World War as Commander of airship LZ97, which bombed London three times. He remained in the Army after the war and was attached to Artillery Regiments 4 and 6 until June 1922, now with the rank of *Hauptmann*. From October 1935 he was Commander of Panzer Artillery Regiment 75 with the rank of *Oberstleutnant*, and three years later he took command of Artillery Regiment 56, part of the 20th Infantry Division. Weiding was now an *Oberst* and saw action during the invasion of Poland, where he was awarded both classes of the Iron Cross. He then he took part in the attack on France from May 1940.

his division west of Rzhev, where it took part in some very tough defensive battles and with his award came the promotion on 1 February 1943 to the rank of *Generalleutnant*. Weidling went on to lead his division with distinction during the Battle of Kursk. From October 1943 he was appointed deputy leader of the XXXXI. Panzer Corps and saw action in Babruysk, Belarus, as part of the 9th Army. Weidling was promoted to *General der Artillerie* in January 1944 and the same day he was officially appointed Commanding General of the XXXXI. Panzer Corps.

Knight's Cross with Oakleaves: Awarded on 22 February 1944, to become the 408th recipient as *General der Artillerie* and Commanding General of the XXXXI. Panzer Corps while attached to the 9th Army for his outstanding leadership in the Soviet Union. Weidling distinguished himself in the tough defensive battles near Krichev in Belarus and near the Berezina River in early 1944, and was presented with the Oakleaves personally by Hitler at the Berghof in early March 1944. In late June he was appointed Commanding General of the VI. Army Corps and saw action in East Prussia as part of the 4th Army.

Knight's Cross with Oakleaves and Swords: Weidling became the 115th recipient on 28 November 1944 while *General der Artillerie* and Commanding General of the XXXXI. Panzer Corps while attached to the 2nd Army for his successful leadership during the defensive fighting in East Prussia. Weidling built up the defences on the Vistula Front, which held back the Soviets for some time and gained valuable time for the Germans to regroup. Weidling was presented with the Swords by Hitler at the Reich Chancellery in Berlin in late 1944 and he continued to command his panzer corps in East Prussia. On 23 April 1945 Weidling was appointed Commandant of Berlin by Hitler but that same day the *Führer* had ordered him to be executed by firing squad after he received a report that he had ordered a retreat in the face of advancing Soviet forces. However, it soon became apparent that Weidling had not ordered a retreat and he was summoned to the Bunker to see Hitler and to clear up the misunderstanding. During the meeting Weidling asked Hitler if he could break out of Berlin, and after a few hours Hitler finally agreed. On 2 May, with Hitler dead, Weidling, together with his Chief of Staff *Oberst* Theodor von Dufving, arranged a meeting with Soviet General Chuikov and told him of the *Führer*'s death. After the meeting Weidling and his staff were taken into custody by the Soviets and on 27 February 1952 Weidling was sentenced to twenty-five years' imprisonment by a military court. He died in prison on 17 November 1955 of an apparent heart attack and is buried in an unmarked grave in Wladimir at the former prison cemetery.

Fritz ROSKE

Generalmajor

* 20 January 1897, Gera, Thuringia
+ 25 December 1956, Düsseldorf, North Rhine-Westphalia

Knight's Cross: Awarded on 20 January 1943 as *Oberst* and Commander of Infantry Regiment 194, part of the 71st Infantry Division, for actions on the Russian Front. He was assigned to southern Russia in the spring of 1942 as part of the 6th Army and saw action at Kharkov and in the Battle of the Izyum Pocket in May. On 27 January 1943 he was appointed commander of the 71st Infantry Division and was promoted to *Generalmajor*, but only four days later he was captured at Stalingrad by Soviet forces. Roske was kept in various NKVD prisons throughout his time in captivity, and was eventually tried by a military tribunal near Stalingrad on 29 December 1948. He was found guilty of war crimes and sentenced to twenty-five years' forced labour. He was released early after a general amnesty and repatriated to Germany on 28 September 1953.

Dr rer.pol. Otto KORFES

Generalmajor

* 23 November 1889, Wenzen-Gandershein, Braunschweig
+ 24 August 1964, Potsdam, Brandenburg

Otto Korfes was the joint founder of the Federation of German Officers and was later selected as a member of the National Committee for Free Germany. He was dismissed from the *Wehrmacht* in November 1944. He was released from Soviet captivity in October 1948. He became a member of the NDPD (National Democratic Party of Germany) and was Director of the Central Archives in Potsdam until August 1949. He became Deputy Director of the Staff of the Operations Department of the *Volkspolizei* of the DDR (German Democratic Republic) in East Germany. From January 1952 he was Director of the Historical Department of the Ministry of the Interior, and was appointed 1st Chairman of District Committee Potsdam of the National Front of the DDR in 1957.

Knight's Cross: Awarded on 22 January 1943 as *Generalmajor* and Commander of the 295th Infantry Division while attached to the LI. Army Corps for actions during the Soviet winter offensive during the fighting on the Volga and during thc Battle of Stalingrad. He never received his Knight's Cross as he was captured together with 91,000 prisoners, which included at least twenty-two generals and the Commander of the 6th Army, *Generalfeldmarschall* Friedrich Paulus, who had been promoted that same day.

Richard-Heinrich Ernst von REUSS

Generalmajor

* 23 November 1896, Bromberg, Posen
+ 22 December 1942, Nowo-Astaschoff, Soviet Union

Knight's Cross: Awarded posthumously on 24 January 1943 as *Generalmajor* and Commander of 62nd Infantry Division while attached to the XVII. Army Corps. He destroyed a tank single-handedly using a hand-held weapon on the Russian Front. He had taken over the command of the 62nd Infantry Division from September 1942 and on the afternoon of 22 December 1942 a Soviet tank broke through the German defences near Nowo-Astaschoff, where he was struck by a bullet and killed.

Gerhard Heinrich LINDEMANN

Generalmajor

* 8 March 1896, Verden an der Aller
+ 25 September 1963, Bremen

Gerhard Lindemann entered Army service as a war volunteer in August 1914 with Field Artillery Regiment 7 and was commissioned as a *Leutnant* a year later. He later served as platoon leader and company leader and was awarded the Iron Cross 1st and 2nd Classes. He left the Army in March 1930. He rejoined the Army in July 1934 and was Company Chief in Infantry Regiment 65. From the start of the Second World War in September 1939 he served as *Major* and battalion commander with Infantry Regiment 489.

Knight's Cross: Awarded on 25 January 1943 as *Oberst* and Commander of Infantry Regiment 216 while attached to the 86th Infantry Division and saw action during Operation Mars, the code name for an offensive launched by Soviet forces near Moscow towards the end of 1942. Lindemann's infantry regiment was deployed to the Lutchessa Valley area, where he was given operational control of the area's defence. On 28 November the Soviets renewed their attack with about 200 tanks and under Lindemann this was contained successfully. The situation was later resolved completely by German forces making a successful counter-attack. Lindemann showed great leadership and courage during these defensive battles and despite heavy snow won a decisive victory. He continued to lead his regiment until November 1943, when he attended the 8th Divisional Leaders' Course at Döberitz-Elsgrund and was promoted in July to the rank of *Generalmajor.*

Knight's Cross with Oakleaves: He became the 580th recipient on 10 September 1944 as *Generalmajor* and Commander of the 361st Infantry Division, part of the XIII. Infantry Corps, in recognition of his command during the heavy fighting in the Brody Pocket in the Ukraine. However, in July 1944 he was captured by Soviet troops near Brody and remained in captivity unaware that he had been awarded the Oakleaves until his release on 7 October 1955.

Walther LUCHT

General der Artillerie

* 26 February 1882, Berlin
+ 18 March 1949, Heilbronn, Baden-Württemberg

Knight's Cross: Awarded on 30 January 1943 as *Generalleutnant* and Commander of 336th Infantry Division while attached to the XXIV. Army Corps, attached to the 19th Army, and saw action near during the desperate battles on the Chir River near Rostov in the Soviet Union from December 1942. On 7 December 1942 he led his division during successful counter-attacks and the following day held his ground against overwhelming Soviet forces with the support of the 11th Panzer Division. He was personally presented with the Knight's Cross by *Generalleutnant* Friedrich Mieth in February 1943. From July 1943 he commanded the area of Kerch in the Crimea and was promoted to *General der Artillerie* in October that year. The following month Lucht took command of the LXVI. Reserve Corps in south-western France, where he saw action during the Allied invasion of Europe in June 1944.

Knight's Cross with Oakleaves: Awarded on 9 January 1945, to become the 691st recipient, as *General der Artillerie* and Commanding General of the LXVI. Army Corps in recognition of his successful command during the defensive battles of the Battle of the Bulge. From early September 1944 his corps, as part of the 19th Army, linked up with the 1st Army and prevented an impending Allied advance. During the Battle of the Bulge it was his corps that surrounded the bulk of the US 106th Infantry Divison and captured just over 8,000 US soldiers. In fact, it was the second largest mass capitulation of US forces in the Second World War. In April 1945 he took command of the 11th Army in central Germany, and from the 24th he was the Commanding General of the XIII. Army Corps in North Württemberg. He was captured in Augsburg in May 1945 and spent three

Walther Lucht entered the Army as an officer candidate in June 1901 and after service in various schools and academies was appointed adjutant of the I. Battalion of Foot Artillery Regiment 1 in October 1907. Promoted to *Oberleutnant* four years later, he went on to serve during the First World War as battery leader with the same regiment with the rank of *Hauptmann*. He was awarded both classes of the Iron Cross during the war and remained in the Army after the war, rising to the rank of *Major* in December 1925.

years in Allied captivity. On 18 March 1949, while travelling near Heilbronn in Baden-Württemberg, he was killed during a car accident.

Josef SCHMIDT

Generalmajor

* 18 August 1893, Breslau, Silesia
+ 28 January 1943, near Voronezh Oblast, Soviet Union

Knight's Cross: Awarded on 31 January 1943, posthumously, as *Oberst* and Commander of Grenadier Regiment 199 'List' while attached to the 57th Infantry Division for his part in preventing a breakout of Soviet forces along the Don River while leading at the head of his regiment. As part of the 57th Infantry Division, Schmidt saw action on the southern sector of the Russian Front, taking part in the Battle of Voronezh in June and July 1942. He later saw action during the Second Battle of Voronezh from January 1943, during which time he was killed, being posthumously promoted to *Generalleutnant*.

Ernst-Eberhard HELL

General der Artillerie

* 19 September 1887, Stade, Lower Saxony
+ 15 September 1973, Wiesbaden, Hesse

Knight's Cross: Awarded on 1 February 1943 as *General der Artillerie* and Commanding General of the VII. Army Corps, part of the 2nd Army, for his part

Ernst-Eberhard Hell entered Army service as an officer candidate in March 1906 and saw action during the First World War, serving in Turkey at the Military Mission from June 1915. He then spent the remainder of the war as a Staff Officer and ended the war with the rank of *Hauptmann*. He was awarded both classes of the Iron Cross. He remained in the Army after the war and served as a General Staff Officer at the Naval Station of the North Sea in Wilhelmshaven until April 1922. He attended various military courses and from October 1935, now with the rank of *Oberst*, he was Commander of Artillery Regiment 32. He served as Artillery Commander 22 from October 1937 and two years later he saw action in France and the Soviet Union as Commander of the 15th Infantry Division.

in the fierce fighting near Voronezh from the summer of 1942, when almost a thousand Soviet tanks were destroyed. In February 1943 he led his men further east, where they twice broke through Soviet encirclements, and it was through his leadership and commitment that the VII. Army Corps escaped destruction. He saw action during the Battle of Kursk during the summer of 1943 and had to withdraw via Belgorod to Kiev. He was granted leave from early October until the end of November. He then saw action near Zhitomir and from the spring of 1944 he took part in retreats towards the Romanian border as part of the 4th Panzer Army.

Knight's Cross with Oakleaves: He became the 487th recipient on 4 June 1944 as *General der Artillerie* and Commanding General of the VII. Army Corps of Army Group *Wöhler* for his leadership during the contribution his command made to the relief of the Cherkassy Pocket. On 20 June 1944 he was personally presented with the Oakleaves by Hitler at the Berghof. From August he saw further fighting in the Jassy-Kishinev Offensive and was captured by the Soviets. He spent the next eleven years in a Soviet prison camp, finally being released during a general amnesty on 8 October 1955.

Bibliography

Angolia, John R., *On the Field of Honor: A History of the Knight's Cross Bearers*, Volume 1, San Jose, California, Roger James Bender, 1979.

Angolia, John R., *On the Field of Honor: A History of the Knight's Cross Bearers*, Volume 2, San Jose, California, Roger James Bender, 1980.

Barnett, Correlli (ed.), *Hitler's Generals*, Weidenfeld & Nicholson, 1989.

Beevor, Antony, *Ardennes 1944: Hitler's Last Gamble*, Viking Press, 2015.

Beevor, Antony, *Arnhem. The Battle for the Bridges, 1944*, Viking, 2018.

Beevor, Antony, *Stalingrad*, Viking Press, 1998.

Binns, Stewart, *Barbarossa and the Bloodiest War in History*, Wildfire, 2021.

Bouysse, Grégory & Mark Spencer, *Encyclopaedia of the New Order. Knight's Cross of the Iron Cross Holders Part 1 September 1939 – May 1940*, Author Publisher, 2021.

Bradley, Dermot, Karl-Friedrich Hildebrand & Markus Rövekamp, *Die Generale des Heeres 1921–1945 Band: 1–7*, Osnabrück, Bibili-Verlg, 1993–2004.

Brett-Smith, Richard, *Hitler's Generals*, Osprey, 1976.

Buttar, Prit, *Retribution. The Soviet Reconquest of Central Ukraine, 1943*, Osprey, 2019.

Buttar, Prit, *The Reckoning. The Defeat of Army Group South, 1944*, Osprey, 2020.

Caddick-Adams, Peter, *Monte Cassino. Ten Armies in Hell*, Arrow, 2013.

Chales De Beaulieu, W., *General Erich Hoepner. A Military Biography*, Casemate, 2021.

Clark, Alan, *Barbarossa. The Russian-German Conflict 1941–45*, Hutchinson, 1965.

Cooper, Matthew, *The German Army 1933–1945. Its Political and Military Failure*, Macdonald & Janes, 1978.

Dimbleby, Jonathan, *Barbarossa. How Hitler Lost the War*, Viking, 2021.

Dixon, Jeremy, *The Knight's Cross with Oakleaves 1940–1945. Biographies and Images of the 889 Recipients Vols 1+2*, Schiffer Ltd, 2012.

Ellis, Frank, *The Stalingrad Cauldron. Inside the Encirclement and Destruction of the 6th Army*, University Press of Kansas, 2013.

Erickson, John, *The Road to Berlin*, Weidenfeld & Nicolson, 1983.

Erickson, John, *The Road to Stalingrad*, Weidenfeld & Nicolson, 1977.

Forczyk, Robert, *Case Red: The Collapse of France*, Osprey Publishing, 2017.

Forczyk, Robert, *Case White: The Invasion of Poland 1939*, Osprey Publishing, 2019.

Forczyk, Robert, *Where the Iron Crosses Grow. The Crimea 1941–44*, Osprey, 2014

Fraser, David, *Knight's Cross. A Life of Field Marshal Erwin Rommel*, Harper Collins, 1993.

Gerbet, Klaus Editor, *Generalfeldmarschall Fedor von Bock. The War Diary 1939–1945*, Schiffer, 1996.

Giziowski, Richard, *The Enigma of General Blaskowitz*, Leo Cooper, 1997.

Glantz, David M., *To the Gates of Stalingrad. Soviet–German Combat Operations, April–August 1942. The Stalingrad Trilogy, Volume 1*, University Press of Kansas, 2009.

Glantz, David M., *Armageddon in Stalingrad September–November 1942. The Stalingrad Trilogy, Volume 2*, University Press of Kansas, 2009

Glantz, David M., *Endgame at Stalingrad Book One: November 1942. The Stalingrad Trilogy, Volume 3*, University Press of Kansas, 2014.
Glantz, David M., *Endgame at Stalingrad Book Two: December 1942–February 1943. The Stalingrad Trilogy, Volume 3*, University Press of Kansas, 2014.
Glantz, David M., *The Battle for Leningrad 1941–1944*, University Press of Kansas, 2002.
Glantz, David M. & Jonathan M. House, *The Battle of Kursk*, Ian Allan, 1999.
Goeritz, Walter, *Paulus and Stalingrad*, Methuen & Co Ltd, 1963.
Hébert, Valerie G., *Hitler's Generals on Trial. The Last War Crimes Tribunal at Nuremberg*, University Press of Kansas, 2010.
Holland, James, *Normandy '44. D-Day and the Battle for France*, Bantam Press, 2019.
Holland, James, *Sicily '43. The First Assault on Fortress Europe*, Bantam Press, 2020.
Holland, James, *The War in the West. A New History Germany Ascendant 1939–1941*, Bantam Press, 2015.
Isaev, Alexey, *Hitler's Fortresses in the East. The Sieges if Ternopol, Kovel, Poznan & Breslau 1944–1945*. Pen & Sword, 2021.
Jacobsen, Hans-Adolf. *Dunkirk. German Operations in France 1940*, Casemate Publishers, 2019.
Kursietis, Andris J., *The Fallen Generals: The Destruction of the German Officer Corps in World War II and its aftermath.* Netherlands, Andris J. Kursietis, 2015.
Lucas, James, *Hitler's Commanders. German Bravery in the Field 1939–1945*, Cassell & Co., 2000.
Luther, Craig W.H. and David Stahel, *Soldiers of Barbarossa. Combat, Genocide, and Everyday Experiences on the Eastern Front, June–December 1941*, Stackpole Books, 2020.
MacLean, French L., *Quiet Flows the Rhine. German General Officer Casualties in World War II*, J.J. Fedorowicz Publishing, 1996.
Manstein, Erich von, *Lost Victories*, Henry Regnery Company, 1958.
May, Ernest R., *Strange Victory. Hitler's Conquest of France*, I.B. Tauris, 2000.
McCroden, William T. & Thomas E. Nutter, *German Ground Forces of World War II. Complete Orders of Battle for Army Groups, Armies, Army Corps & other Commands of the Wehrmacht*, Savas Beatie, 2019.
Melvin, Mungo, *Manstein. Hitler's Greatest General*, Weidenfeld & Nicholson, 2010.
Messenger, Charles, *The Last Prussian. A Biography of Field Marshal Gerd von Rundstedt 1875–1953*, Brasseys, 1991.
Mitcham, Samuel W., *Blitzkrieg No Longer. The German Wehrmacht in Battle, 1943*, Pen & Sword, 2010.
Mitcham, Samuel W., *Defenders of Fortress Europe. The Untold Story of the German Officers during the Allied Invasion*, Washington DC: Potomac Books, Inc., 2009.
Mitcham, Samuel W, *The German Defeat in the East* 1944–45, Stackpole, 2007.
Mitcham, Samuel W., *German Order of Battle. Volume One: 1st–290th Infantry Divisions in WWII*, Stackpole Books, 2007.
Mitcham, Samuel W., *German Order of Battle. Volume Two: 291st–999th Infantry Divisions, Named Infantry Divisions, and Special Divisions WWII*, Stackpole Books, 2007.
Mitcham, Samuel W., *German Order of Battle. Volume Three: Panzer, Panzer Grenadier, and Waffen-SS Divisions in WWII*, Stackpole Books, 2007.
Mitcham, Samuel W., *Hitler's Field Marshals and their Battles*, Guild Publishing, 1988.
Mitcham, Samuel W., *The Men of Barbarossa. Commanders of the German Invasion of Russia, 1941*, Casemate Publishers, 2009.
Mitcham, Samuel W., *Panzer Commanders of the Western Front. German Tank Generals in WWII*, Stackpole, 2008.

Mitcham, Samuel W., *Panzers in Winter. Hitler's Army and the Battle of the Bulge*, Praeger Security International, 2006.

Mitcham, Samuel W., *Rommel's Lieutenants. The Men who Served the Desert Fox, France, 1940*, Stackpole, 2007.

Mitcham, Samuel W. & Gene Mueller, *Hitler's Commanders*, Leo Cooper, 1992.

Möbus, Ingo, *Die Sächsischen Ritterkreuzträger 1939–1945 Band 1: Ahnert-Haude*, Westermann Druck Zwickau GmbH, 2021.

Moorhouse, Roger, *Poland 1939. The Outbreak of World War II*, Basic Books, 2020.

Müller, Rolf-Dieter, *Enemy in the East. Hitler's Secret Plans to Invade the Soviet Union*, I.B. Tauris, 2015.

Nafziger, George F., *The German Order of Battle. Infantry in World War II*, London: Greenhill Books, 2000.

Nafziger, George F., *The German Order of Battle. Panzers and Artillery in World War II.* London: Greenhill Books, 1999.

Newton, Steven H., *Hitler's Commander. Field Marshal Walther Model – Hitler's Favorite General*, Da Capo Press, 2006.

Parker, Danny S. (ed.), *The Battle of the Bulge. The German View*, Greenhill Books, 1999.

Sadarananda, Dana v., *Beyond Stalingrad. Manstein and the Operations of Army Group Don*, Stackpole Books, 1990.

Scherzer, Veit, *Deustche Truppen im Zweiten Weltkrieg: Die Divisionen*, Band 2–7. Scherzers Militaer Verlag, 2007–2011.

Scherzer, Veit, *Ritterkreuzträger 1939–1945*, Scherzers Militaer-Verlag Ranis, 2007.

Seaton, Albert, *The German Army 1933–1945*, Weidenfeld & Nicholson, 1982.

Stockert, Peter, *Die Eichenlaubträger 1940–1945 Band: 1–4*, Verlag Friedrichshaller Rundblick, 1997.

Taylor, Brian, *Barbarossa to Berlin: A Chronology of the Campaigns on the Eastern Front 1941 to 1945*, Two Volumes, Spellmount, 2003 & 2004.

Thomas, Franz & Günter Wegmann, *Die Ritterkreuzträger der Deutschen Wehrmacht 1939–1945 Band: 1–7*, Osnabrück, Biblio-Verlag, 1987–2010.

Thomas, Franz & Günter Wegmann, *Die Ritterkreuzträger der Gebirgstruppe Band: 1–2*, Osnabrück, Biblio-Verlag 1993–1994.

Trig, Jonathan, *Barbarossa Through German Eyes. The biggest invasion in history*, Amberley, 2021.

Tucker-Jones, Anthony, *Hitler's Panzers. The Complete History 1933–1945*, Pen & Sword, 2020.

Turney, Alfred, *Disaster at Moscow. Von Bock's Campaigns 1941–42*, Cassell, 1970.

Wegmann, Günter, *Die Ritterkreuzträger der Panzertruppe Band: 1–2* Bissendorf, Biblio-Verlag, 2004–2009.

Williamson, Gordon, *Knight's Cross and Oakleaves Recipients 1939–40*, Osprey, 2004.

Williamson, Gordon, *Knight's Cross and Oakleaves Recipients 1941–45*, Osprey, 2005.

Williamson, Gordon, *Knight's Cross, Oakleaves and Swords Recipients 1941–45*, Osprey, 2005.

Williamson, Gordon, *Knight's Cross with Diamonds Recipients*, Osprey, 2006.

Yerger, Mark C. & Leslie K. Fiorenza, *Honoring Those They Led. Decorated Field Commanders of the Third Reich: Command Authorities, Award Parameters, and Ranks*, Helion & Co., 2016.

Zetterling, Niklas & Anders Frankson, *The Korsun Pocket. The Encirclement and Breakout of a Germany Army in the East, 1944*, Casemate Publishers, 2008.

Ziemke, Earl F., *Stalingrad to Berlin. The German Defeat in the East*, US Army Center of Military History, 1968.

Ziemke, Earl F. and Magna E. Bauer, *Moscow to Stalingrad. Decision in the East*, Military Heritage Press, 1988.